THE REFERENCE SHELF

Vol. 16   No. 6

REPRESENTATIVE AMERICAN SPEECHES: 1942-1943

Selected by

A. CRAIG BAIRD

Department of Speech, State University of Iowa

THE H. W. WILSON COMPANY

NEW YORK   1943

PS
668
.R4
v.16 No6

3307

319p.

PREFATORY NOTE

REPRESENTATIVE AMERICAN SPEECHES: 1942-1943 is the sixth of an annual series. The power of the spoken word, despite the alleged decline of the golden age of oratory of Webster, Clay, and Wendell Phillips, continues undiminished. Indeed, in this World War II, with the voices of national leaders broadcasting continuously over the globe, the influence of public speaking was probably never so potent. This annual collection aims to furnish a record, year by year, of significant speech-making as it has expressed itself in the United States.

The six volumes that have appeared in this series include some 164 addresses by about a hundred different speakers. All have given repeated demonstration of their speaking ability before certain types of listeners: collegiate, industrial, congressional, judicial, or ecclesiastical. Almost all of these speeches and speakers have stirred more than local or regional attention; they have presumably affected, at least in slight degree, the national current. The Cumulative Author Index accompanying this volume enables the reader to survey these various representatives in their formal addresses, academic lectures, legislative debates, or radio broadcasts. High school, college and other students of public speaking, then, will analyze these addresses as examples of the art of speaking.

These six volumes, furthermore, reveal characteristic American ideas and attitudes. The Tables of Contents, accompanying the various editions, have classified the addresses with respect to war, peace, industry, education, religion, and other topics, so as to facilitate this examination of "ideas." The introductory note to each speech and the Index to each volume are further aids to such approach.

Perhaps only a scant four or five of these hundred orators will be long remembered. Each, however, has contributed to the thinking and feeling of his hour, or has been an interpreter of

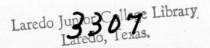

American thought. These voices, ephemeral though they are, combine to explain clearly the America of 1937-1943.

The present volume, edited in the midst of World War II, is, like its predecessor, a book of "War Speeches." It thus should be serviceable both to civilians and to members of the armed forces.

A. C. B.

July, 1943

CONTENTS

CONTENTS

RELIGION AND THE WAR

REPRESENTATIVE AMERICAN SPEECHES

INTRODUCTION

This volume of speeches reflects American thinking and speaking during the immediate months before July 1943. The collection also offers examples for analysis by those interested in the art of effective speaking.

Speech-making, perhaps more than literature, registers the immediate mental and emotional temper of the people. Because speeches are literally born in public forums or on platforms, audiences are more than bystanders; they share in the creation. The oral spokesman of political-social ideas counts himself to have scored best when he articulates with the listeners. The larger the group and the more responsive are they, the more successful is he, or so he thinks. He is more concerned with immediate effect than he is with compositional qualities of permanency.

The creative speaker's product is thus a fusion of factors—an audience; an occasion or impelling situation; an orator, sensitive to these influences; and a discourse, the outcome of these historical, psychological, and rhetorical elements.

The speaker, no matter how well he fulfills Carlyle's concept of the Great Man in History, comes by his personality partly because he moves in this social medium, and to an extent yields to it. He is both leader and follower. The sentiments and perplexities of the citizens become articulate through him. His orations, then, become an index of his time, a key to current attitudes and actions. To speech-making, then, we turn, as an important source for understanding our contemporary life.

EVALUATION OF SPEECHES

How are we to evaluate a speech?

First, *it should be placed in its general and specific setting*. With facts concerning the scene and some historical imagination we can recreate the original situation. We can join the audience.

The addresses here included took on the character of the global storm in which they were born. Note the events that lay behind the words of these twelve months prior to July 1, 1943: General Rommel at El Alamein 75 miles from Alexandria, Egypt, only to fade back into long retreat; the Anglo-American invasion of Morocco and Algeria and the final destruction of the Axis divisions in Tunisia; the fall of Sevastopol after a historic defense of at least 225 days; the Axis sweep into the Ukraine and the Caucasus foothills; the amazing Russian victory at Stalingrad and the recession of the Nazi tide; the self-destruction of the French fleet at Toulon; the Atlantic battle against Vice Admiral Donitz' German U-boat "wolf packs"; the "block buster" devastation by the R.A.F. and the precision bombing by the U.S. Army flying fortresses; the seizure of Guadalcanal, and the naval, air, and land triumphs over the Japanese elsewhere in the Pacific; the resurgence of the Republican Party in the 1942 election; the battle over the 'teen age draft bill; the argument concerning ration policies; the problem of "black markets"; the controversy concerning ways and means of rubber production; the dispute concerning the solution of Eastern fuel shortages; the sharply drawn battle over inflation; the struggle of the nation against John L. Lewis and his striking miners, and the consequent quick passage of a Federal anti-strike law; the recurrent conflict between the Farm Bloc and their Congressional opponents; the debates over the Ruml plan and other programs for dealing with Federal taxes; the long wrangling over the details of the Federal budget; the attack upon alleged administration inefficiency and bureaucracy, with O.W.I., O.P.A., and other agencies under heavy fire; and the growing differences between Roosevelt and Congress. The speeches that follow mirror these events and conflicts.

Second, *the speech should be weighed according to its ideas.* Is the address freighted with thought? Does it reveal important social and political principles? Is its impact upon the problems of the moment decisive? Does the speaker reveal somewhat the character of our national thinking? He need not be erudite nor profound; but he should be an interpreter of the American mind. [1]

[1] For further discussion of American ideas in speeches see *Representative American Speeches: 1940-41*, Introduction, p. 11.

Aside from the specific controversial topics listed above and found in these speeches, one theme increasingly cropped out: "What principles or programs shall America turn to at the end of World War II?" The postwar world concerned most of these speech-makers of 1942-1943, whatever their subject or occasion. Probably they discovered that any discussion of war aims or problems moved on logically to an analysis of the consequences of these aims or war programs. Whatever the explanation, it is significant that an increasing amount of hard thinking and speaking should channel in the direction of the endless economic, political, and military problems to be faced by the American people after the armistice.

Third, *the motives of the speaker should be considered.* It is not enough for us to understand what was said. The aim governing the selection and shaping of materials is important. Even though the talker is apparently oblivious to all except his "message," he does design his talk to secure certain audience reactions. Accordingly, he stresses certain theses, incorporates certain illustrations, plays up certain slogans, suppresses other ideas or appeals. Whether the obvious aims are the real ones or whether the speaker is employing rare diplomacy in his rhetorical emphasis, the students of speeches must determine.

But much more is included in a speech than is found in the text itself. This speech-behind-the-speech, the emotional and motivative elements accompanying the more tangible "ideas," is also to be reckoned with. For the addresses of seasoned speakers have a certain subtlety, an adroitness of appeal, that may go far to explain the motives behind the obvious purpose to inform or convince.

Fourth, in addition to such essential factors of speaking as organization, language, and delivery, *the immediate and ultimate effectiveness of the discourse should be gauged.* What is the total effect of a given speech? Most difficult is it to measure results. Shall we judge audience reaction by the amount of applause? By audience votes? By the ballots cast in November? By the opinion of qualified observers in the audience? By the decision of a courtroom jury? By the size of the radio mail? By the length and prominence of the report in next morning's paper? By the information given to a Gallup poll investigator? By the number of converts after the sermon? These and various other criteria of response to a speaker are pertinent. They are, however, largely uncontrolled measures. Whatever the weaknesses of these standards of judging, we must, like any good historian, do the best we can with whatever evidence we can assemble. Our conclusions are tentative and are based pretty much on the immediate audience behavior. Then, like the historian, we note carefully the widening circles of impression made by the speaker and his speech. Time, as in the case of literary judgments, will help us to describe the effectiveness of a given oration. On such basis have we rightly placed Lincoln's speaking at Gettysburg among the notable orations.

Use of This Book in High School and College

This book is arranged partly for students in secondary schools and in colleges, especially debaters, extempore speakers, orators, discussion participants, and oral readers of speeches; for students of contemporary history and of American issues; for members of courses in composition, oral and written; and for student members of the Army Specialized Training Program and of the Navy V-12 Program.

Topical Arrangement of Speeches

To facilitate the use of this book for study, the selections are arranged under such representative topics as The Progress of the War, America's War Aims, Inside Warring Europe, America and the Postwar World, The American Democratic Tradition, The Home Front, Education and the War, Religion and the War. These categories, I agree, are only tentative. For the purpose outlined above, the topical grouping has been more serviceable than the chronological plan, or that according to speech types. This last-mentioned classification the student can arrange for himself by placing the speeches under the proper headings of deliberative or motivative, demonstrative, occasional, or expositional addresses, radio talks, sermons, and similar types.

AMERICAN SPEECHES

In general, only speeches delivered by Americans have been included. Exceptions are the addresses recently given in the United States by Madame Chiang Kai-shek, President Eduard Beneš, Anthony Eden, and Winston Churchill.

ACKNOWLEDGMENT

The author is grateful to the numerous colleagues in speech and in other fields who in conference or by mail have given valuable suggestions concerning the selections for this book and to Elizabeth Martin McCollister, who assisted with the preparation of the volume. To the speakers who have generously permitted the reprinting and, in most cases, provided the texts, and to publishers who have cooperated by allowing the use of copyright materials, the author is also much indebted. Specific acknowledgment is made in the introductory Note accompanying each selection.

A. CRAIG BAIRD

July 10, 1943

PROGRESS OF THE WAR

MESSAGE TO CONGRESS [1]

FRANKLIN DELANO ROOSEVELT [2]

President Roosevelt delivered this state-of-the-nation speech before a joint session of the Seventy-eighth Congress, gathered in the House of Representatives, on January 7, 1943.

Lawmakers, joined by Cabinet members, high-ranking diplomats, and gallery visitors (some five or six hundred persons) made up the audience. It was the President's fifteenth appearance before a joint session, "one of the greatest ceremonies of state which a democracy can offer."

The Representatives were first seated; then in filed the Senators, two by two, to occupy the front rows. Vice President Wallace was seated on the rostrum with Speaker Rayburn.

Then entered the diplomats, including Ambassadors from Brazil and Chile. Lord Halifax, Ambassador of the United Kingdom, and Maxim Litvinov were also there, as well as representatives of practically all the other United Nations.

Finally came the members of the Cabinet.

The President's gallery included wives of Cabinet members and Mrs. Roosevelt.

At 12:31 the President was escorted into the Chamber. The audience arose and applauded for two minutes.

The President gave his address with restrained delivery. It was more of a report than an oration. Here and there were the typical Rooseveltian humorous allusions and the persuasive climaxes. At such points the President's voice took on more intensity and flexibility. The listeners applauded some forty-five times.

Strong applause followed the statement, "Our enemies did not win this war in 1942." Even stronger acclaim came when the speaker referred to the fact that in the attacks on Japan, America would be "joined by the heroic people of China."

The President paid tribute to Winston Churchill, Joseph Stalin, and Chiang Kai-shek. Applause for the Chinese leader was the most prolonged of all.

---

[1] Reprinted from the *Congressional Record*, v. 89, no. 2, p. 4549, January 7, 1943 (daily edition), proceedings and debates of the 78th Congress, first session.

[2] For biographical note see Appendix.

The speaker again secured maximum audience response as he ironically suggested the impossibility of revealing the plans for our next military move. His castigation of Hitler and Mussolini likewise evoked prolonged cheers. He drew much laughter when he poked fun at the government questionnaires.

His reference to the "prayer" that the "sons and grandsons" would not have to repeat the present "horror" stirred deep response. His final phrases were delivered with high emotion—a suitable peroration.

The audience continued its ovation until the President left the Chamber. "One woman seemed to sum up the general feeling: 'I don't care whether you're for him or against him. To see him standing there delivering his speech before our elected representatives is a thrilling thing.'" [3]

The President's report dwelt mainly on the military situation. His review of the war of 1942 stressed the significant upsurge of the United Nations cause by reason of (1) the heroic Russian victory at Stalingrad, (2) the passing of air superiority from the Axis to the United Nations, (3) the victory off Midway Island, (4) the strong development of our naval and military power in the Pacific, and (5) the remarkable results in our military production.

The President prophesied that in 1943 our side would "strike hard" at Europe and at Japan. In our review of 1943 it is interesting to note to what extent the President's optimism and prophecies of January 1943 were justified.

With notable scorn did the speaker admonish the isolationists: "Undoubtedly a few Americans, even now, think that this nation can end this war comfortably and then climb back into an American hole and pull the hole in after them."

The message was quite conciliatory. It was directed to the entire world. Moreover, the character of the new Congress, in which only a slender Democratic majority remained, and the sharp divisions existing there concerning domestic policy, made it advisable for the speaker to add no concrete issues to those already promising to create an anti-New Deal, anti-Roosevelt Congress.

The President thus avoided concrete references to issues that later stirred Congress to sharp debate: (1) subsidies for food to stabilize prices, (2) reciprocal trade agreements, (3) extensive social security plans, (4) strikes in essential industries, (5) anti-inflation measures, (6) operations of O.P.A., O.W.I., O.C.D., and other agencies that later were under fire.

Hearty support of the President's aims and endorsement of the speech were voiced by the press, by leaders of both political parties, by the American people generally, and by the spokesmen of Great Britain, China, and the other United Nations. Said the New York *Herald Tribune*, "The President's annual message rises, with great force and

[3] Sidney M. Phalett in *The New York Times*, p. 13, January 8, 1943.

dignity, to the solemnity of the hour in which it is delivered." The Kansas City *Star* observed, "It was a masterful statement of America's position in the war and of the entire United Nations cause." The London *Daily Mail* said, "Mr. Roosevelt has given us one of the most encouraging, stimulating, and statesmanlike addresses of recent years."

Mr. Vice President, Mr. Speaker, Members of the Seventy-eighth Congress:

The Seventy-eighth Congress assembles in one of the great moments in the history of this nation. The past year was perhaps the most crucial for modern civilization; the coming year will be filled with violent conflict—yet with high promise of better things.

We must appraise the events of 1942 according to their relative importance; we must exercise a sense of proportion.

First in importance in the American scene has been the inspiring proof of the great qualities of our fighting men. They have demonstrated these qualities in adversity as well as in victory. As long as our flag flies over this Capitol, Americans will honor the soldiers, sailors and marines who fought our first battles of this war against overwhelming odds—the heroes, living and dead, of Wake and Bataan and Guadalcanal, of the Java Sea and Midway and the North Atlantic convoys. Their unconquerable spirit will live forever.

By far the largest and most important developments in the world-wide strategic picture of 1942 were the events on the long fronts in Russia: first, the implacable defense of Stalingrad, and, second, the offensives by the Russian armies at various points that started in the latter part of November and which still roll on with great force and effectiveness.

The other major events of the year were, the series of Japanese advances in the Philippines, the East Indies, Malaya and Burma; the stopping of that Japanese advance in the Mid-Pacific, the South Pacific and the Indian Oceans; the successful defense of the Near East by the British counter-attack through Egypt and Libya; the American-British occupation of North Africa. Of continuing importance in the year 1942 were the unending, bitterly contested battles of the convoy routes, and the gradual passing of air superiority from the Axis to the United Nations.

The Axis powers knew that they must win the war in 1942—or eventually lose everything. I do not need to tell you that our enemies did not win this war in 1942.

In the Pacific area our most important victory in 1942 was the air and naval battle off Midway Island. That action is historically important because it secured for us for our use communication lines stretching thousands of miles in every direction.

In placing this emphasis on the Battle of Midway, I am not unmindful of other successful actions in the Pacific, in the air and on land and afloat—especially those in the Coral Sea and New Guinea and in the Solomon Islands. But these actions were essentially defensive. They were part of the delaying strategy that characterized this phase of the war.

During this period we inflicted steady losses upon the enemy—great losses of Japanese planes, naval vessels, transports and cargo ships. As early as one year ago, we set as a primary task in the war of the Pacific a day-by-day, and week-by-week, and month-by-month destruction of more Japanese war material than Japanese industry could replace. Most certainly that task has been and is being performed by our fighting ships and planes. A large part of the task has been accomplished by the gallant crews of our American submarines who strike on the other side of the Pacific at Japanese ships—right at the very mouth of the harbor of Yokohama.

We know that as each day goes by, Japanese strength in ships and planes is going down and down, and American strength in ships and planes is going up and up. The eventual outcome can be put on a mathematical basis. That will become evident to the Japanese people themselves when we strike at their own home islands, and bomb them constantly from the air.

In the attacks against Japan, we shall be joined with the heroic people of China, whose ideals of peace are so closely akin to our own. Even today we are flying as much lend-lease material into China as ever traversed the Burma Road, flying it over mountains 17,000 feet high, flying blind through sleet and snow. We shall overcome all the formidable obstacles, and get the battle equipment into China to shatter the power of our common enemy. From this war China will realize the security, the prosperity and the dignity, which Japan has sought so ruthlessly to destroy.

The period of our defensive attrition in the Pacific is passing. Now our aim is to force the Japanese to fight. Last year, we stopped them. This year, we intend to advance.

In the European theater of war during this past year it was clear that our first task was to lessen the concentrated pressure on the Russian front by compelling Germany to divert part of her manpower and equipment to another theater of war.

After months of secret planning and preparation in the utmost detail, an enormous amphibious expedition was embarked for French North Africa from the United States and the United Kingdom in hundreds of ships. It reached its objectives with very small losses, and has already produced an important effect upon the whole situation of the war. It has opened to attack what Mr. Churchill well described as "the under-belly of the Axis," and it has removed the always dangerous threat of an Axis attack through West Africa against the South Atlantic Ocean and the continent of South America itself.

The well-timed and splendidly executed offensive from Egypt by the British Eighth Army was a part of the same major strategy of the United Nations.

Great rains and appalling mud and very limited communications have delayed the final battles of Tunisia. The Axis is reinforcing its strong positions. But I am confident that though the fighting will be tough, when the final Allied assault is made, the last vestige of Axis power will be driven from the south shores of the Mediterranean.

Any review of the year 1942 must emphasize the magnitude and diversity of the military activities in which this nation has become engaged. As I speak to you, approximately one and a half million of our soldiers, sailors, marines, and fliers are in service outside our continental limits, all through the world. Our merchant seamen are carrying supplies to them and to our allies over every sea lane.

Few Americans realize the amazing growth of our air strength, though I am sure our enemy does. Day in and day out our forces are bombing the enemy and meeting him in combat on many different fronts over the world. And for those who question the quality of our aircraft and ability of our fliers, I point to the fact that in Africa we are shooting down two enemy planes to every one we lose, and in the Pacific and in the southwest Pacific we are shooting them down four to one.

We pay the tribute of the United States of America to the fighting men of Russia and China and Britain and the various members of the British Commonwealth—the millions of men who through the years of this war have fought our common enemies and have denied to them the world conquest which they sought.

We pay tribute to the soldiers and fliers and seamen of others of the United Nations whose countries have been overrun by Axis hordes.

As a result of the Allied occupation of North Africa, powerful units of the French Army and Navy are going into action with the United Nations forces. We welcome them as allies and as friends. They join with those Frenchmen who since the dark days of June 1940 have been fighting valiantly for the liberation of their stricken country.

We pay tribute to the fighting leaders of our allies, to Winston Churchill, to Joseph Stalin, and to the Generalissimo Chiang Kai-shek. There is a very real unanimity between the leaders of the United Nations. This unity is effective in planning and carrying out the major strategy of this war and in building up and maintaining the lines of supplies.

I cannot prophesy. I cannot tell you when or where the United Nations are going to strike next in Europe. But we are going to strike—and strike hard. I cannot tell you whether we are going to hit them in Norway, or through the Low Countries, or in France, or through Sardinia or Sicily, or through the Balkans, or through Poland—or at several points simultaneously. But I can tell you that no matter where and when we strike by land, we and the British and the Russians will hit them from the air heavily and relentlessly. Day in and day out we shall heap tons upon tons of explosives on their war factories and utilities and seaports.

Hitler and Mussolini will understand the enormity of their miscalculations—that the Nazis would always have the advantage of superior air power as they did when they bombed Warsaw, Rotterdam, London, and Coventry. That superiority has gone—forever.

Yes—the Nazis and the Fascists have asked for it—and they are going to get it.

Our forward progress in this war has depended upon our progress on the production front.

There has been criticism of the management and conduct of our war production. Much of this self-criticism has had a healthy effect. It has spurred us on. It has reflected a normal American impatience to get on with the job. We are the kind of people who are never quite satisfied with anything short of miracles.

But there has been some criticism based on guesswork and even on malicious falsification of fact. Such criticism creates doubts and fears, and weakens our total effort.

I do not wish to suggest that we should be completely satisfied with our production progress—today, or next month, or ever. But I can report to you with genuine pride on what has been accomplished during 1942.

A year ago we set certain production goals for 1942 and 1943. Some people, including some experts, thought that we had pulled some big figures out of a hat just to frighten the Axis. But we had confidence in the ability of our people to establish new records. That confidence has been justified.

Of course, we realized that some production objectives would have to be changed—some adjusted upward and others downward; some items would be taken out of the program completely, and others added. This was inevitable as we gained battle experience and as technological improvements were made.

Our 1942 airplane production and tank production fell short, numerically, of the goals set a year ago. Nevertheless, we have plenty of reason to be proud of our record for 1942. We produced about 48,000 military planes—more than the airplane production of Germany, Italy, and Japan put together. Last month, December, we produced 5,500 military planes, and the rate is rapidly rising. Furthermore, as each month passes by, the averages of our types weigh more, take more man-hours to make, and have more striking power.

In tank production, we revised our schedule—and for good and sufficient reasons. As a result of hard experience in battle, we have diverted a portion of our tank-producing capacity to a stepped-up production of new, deadly field weapons, especially self-propelled artillery.

Here are some other production figures:

In 1942 we produced 56,000 combat vehicles, such as tanks and self-propelled artillery.

In 1942, we produced 670,000 machine guns, six times greater than our production in 1941 and three times greater than our total production during the year and a half of our participation in the First World War.

We produced 21,000 antitank guns, six times greater than our 1941 production.

We produced ten and a quarter billion rounds of small arms ammunition, five times greater than our 1941 production and three times greater than our total production in the First World War.

We produced 181,000,000 rounds of artillery ammunition, twelve times greater than our 1941 production, and ten times greater than our total production in the First World War.

The arsenal of democracy is making good.

These facts and figures will give no aid and comfort to the enemy. On the contrary, I can imagine they will give him considerable discomfort. I suspect Hitler and Tojo will find it difficult to explain to the German and Japanese people just why it is that "decadent, inefficient democracy" can produce such phenomenal quantities of weapons and munitions—and fighting men.

We have given the lie to certain misconceptions—especially the one which holds that the various blocs or groups within a free country cannot forego their political and economic differences in time of crisis and work together toward a common goal.

While we have been achieving this miracle of production, during the past year our armed forces have grown from a little over 2,000,000 to 7,000,000. In other words, we have withdrawn from the labor force and the farms some 5,000,000 of our younger workers. And in spite of this, our farmers have contributed their share to the common effort by producing the greatest quantity of food ever made available during a single year in all our history.

Is there any person among us so simple as to believe that all this could have been done without creating some dislocations in our normal national life, some inconveniences, and even some hardships?

Who could have hoped to have done this without burdensome government regulations which are a nuisance to everyone —including those who have the thankless task of administering them?

We all know that there have been mistakes—mistakes due to the inevitable process of trial and error inherent in doing big things for the first time. We all know that there have been too many complicated forms and questionnaires. I know about that. I have had to fill some of them out myself.

But we are determined to see to it that our supplies of food and other essential civilian goods are distributed on a fair and just basis—to rich and poor, management and labor, farmer and city dweller alike. And we are determined to keep the cost of living at a stable level. All this has required much information. The forms and questionnaires represent an honest and sincere attempt by honest and sincere officials to obtain this information.

We have learned by the mistakes that have been made.

Our experience will enable us during the coming year to improve the necessary mechanisms of wartime economic controls and to simplify administrative procedures. But we do not intend to leave things so lax that loopholes will be left for cheaters, for chiselers, or for the manipulators of the black market.

Of course, there have been inconveniences and disturbances —and even hardships. And there will be many, many more before we finally win. Yes, 1943 will not be an easy year for us on the home front. We shall feel in many ways in our daily lives the sharp pinch of total war.

Fortunately, there are only a few Americans who place appetite above patriotism. The overwhelming majority realize that the food we send abroad is for essential military purposes, for our own and Allied fighting forces, and for necessary help in areas that we occupy.

We Americans intend to do this great job together. In our common labors we must build and fortify the very foundation of national unity—confidence in one another.

It is often amusing, and it is sometimes politically profitable, to picture the city of Washington as a madhouse, with the Congress and the administration disrupted with confusion and indecision and general incompetence.

However, what matters most in war is results. And the one pertinent fact is that after only a few years of preparation and only one year of warfare, we are able to engage, spiritually as well as physically, in the total waging of total war.

Washington may be a madhouse—but only in the sense that it is the capital city of a nation which is fighting mad. And I think that Berlin and Rome and Tokyo, which had such contempt for the obsolete methods of democracy, would now gladly use all they could get of that same brand of madness.

We must not forget that our achievements in production have been relatively no greater than those of the Russians and British and Chinese who have developed their war industries under the incredible difficulties of battle conditions. They have had to continue work through bombings and blackouts. They have never quit.

We Americans are in good, brave company in this war, and we are playing our own, honorable part in the vast common effort.

As spokesmen for the United States Government, you and I take off our hats to those responsible for our American production—to the owners, managers, and supervisors, to the draftsmen and engineers, to the workers—men and women—in factories and arsenals and shipyards and mines and mills and forests and railroads and highways.

We take off our hats to the farmers who have faced an unprecedented task of feeding not only a great nation but a great part of the world.

We take off our hats to all the loyal, anonymous, untiring men and women who have worked in private employment and in government and who have endured rationing and other stringencies with good humor and good will.

We take off our hats to all Americans who have contributed magnificently to our common cause.

I have sought to emphasize a sense of proportion in this review of the events of the war and the needs of the war.

We should never forget the things we are fighting for. But, at this critical period of the war, we should confine ourselves to the larger objectives and not get bogged down in argument over methods and details.

We, and all the United Nations, want a decent peace and a durable peace. In the years between the end of the First World War and the beginning of the Second World War, we were not living under a decent or a durable peace.

I have reason to know that our boys at the front are concerned with two broad aims beyond the winning of the war; and their thinking and their opinion coincide with what most Americans here back home are mulling over. They know, and we know, that it would be inconceivable—it would, indeed, be sacrilegious—if this nation and the world did not attain some real, lasting good out of all these efforts and sufferings and bloodshed and death.

The men in our armed forces want a lasting peace, and, equally, they want permanent employment for themselves, their families and their neighbors when they are mustered out at the end of the war.

Two years ago I spoke in my annual message of four freedoms. The blessings of two of them, freedom of speech and freedom of religion, are an essential part of the very life of this nation; and we hope that these blessings will be granted to all men everywhere.

The people at home, and the people at the front—men and women—are wondering about the third freedom—freedom from

want. To them it means that when they are mustered out, when war production is converted to the economy of peace, they will have the right to expect full employment—for themselves and for all able-bodied men and women in America who want to work.

They expect the opportunity to work, to run their farms, their stores, to earn decent wages. They are eager to face the risks inherent in our system of free enterprise.

They do not want a postwar America which suffers from undernourishment or slums—or the dole. They want no get-rich-quick era of bogus "prosperity," which will end for them in selling apples on a street corner, as happened after the bursting of the boom in 1929.

When you talk with our young men and women you will find they want to work for themselves and their families; they consider they have the right to work; and they know that after the last war their fathers did not gain that right.

When you talk with our young men and women you will find that with the opportunity for employment they want assurance against the evils of all major economic hazards—assurance that will extend from the cradle to the grave. This great government can and must provide this assurance.

I have been told that this is no time to speak of a better America after the war. I am told it is a grave error on my part. I dissent.

If the security of the individual citizen, or the family, should become a subject of national debate, the country knows where I stand.

I say this now to this Seventy-eighth Congress, because it is wholly possible that freedom from want—the right of employment and the right of assurance against life's hazards—will loom very large as a task of America during the coming two years.

I trust it will not be regarded as an issue—but rather as a task for all of us to study sympathetically, to work out with a constant regard for the attainment of the objective, with fairness to all and with injustice to none.

In this war of survival we must keep before our minds not only the evil things we fight against but the good things we are fighting for. We fight to retain a great past—and we fight to gain a greater future.

Let us remember, too, that economic safety for the America of the future is threatened unless a greater economic stability comes to the rest of the world. We cannot make America an island in either a military or an economic sense. Hitlerism, like any other form of crime or disease, can grow from the evil seeds of economics as well as military feudalism.

Victory in this war is the first and greatest goal before us. Victory in the peace is the next. That means striving toward the enlargement of the security of man here and throughout the world—and, finally, striving for the fourth freedom—freedom from fear.

It is of little account for any of us to talk of essential human needs, of attaining security, if we run the risk of another world war in ten or twenty or fifty years. That is just plain common sense. Wars grow in size, in death and destruction, and in the inevitability of engulfing all nations, in inverse ratio to the shrinking size of the world as a result of the conquest of the air. I shudder to think of what will happen to humanity, including ourselves, if this war ends in an inconclusive peace and another war breaks out when the babies of today have grown to fighting age.

Every normal American prays that neither he nor his sons nor his grandsons will be compelled to go through this horror again.

Undoubtedly a few Americans, even now, think that this nation can end this war comfortably and then climb back into an American hole and pull the hole in after them.

But we have learned that we can never dig a hole deep enough to be safe against predatory animals. We have also learned that if we do not pull the fangs of the predatory animals of this world they will multiply and grow in strength—and they will be at our throats once more in a short generation.

Most Americans realize more clearly than ever before that modern war equipment in the hands of the aggressor nations can bring danger overnight to our own national existence or to that of any other nation—or island—or continent.

It is clear to us that if Germany and Italy and Japan—or any one of them—remain armed at the end of this war, or are permitted to rearm, they will again, and inevitably, embark upon an ambitious career of world conquest. They must be disarmed and kept disarmed, and they must abandon the philosophy, and the teaching of that philosophy, which has brought so much suffering to the world.

After the First World War we tried to achieve a formula—a formula for permanent peace, based on a magnificent idealism. We failed, but, by our failure, we have learned that we cannot maintain peace at this stage of human development by good intentions alone.

Today the United Nations are the mightiest military coalition in all history. They represent an overwhelming majority of the population of the world. Bound together in a solemn agreement that they themselves will not commit acts of aggression or conquest against any of their neighbors, the United Nations can and must remain united for the maintenance of peace by preventing any attempt to rearm in Germany, in Japan, in Italy, or in any other nation which seeks to violate the Tenth Commandment—"Thou shalt not covet."

There are cynics, there are skeptics who say it cannot be done. The American people and all the freedom-loving peoples of this earth are now demanding that it must be done. And the will of these people shall prevail.

The very philosophy of the Axis powers is based on a profound contempt for the human race. If, in the formation of our future policy, we are guided by the same cynical contempt, then we should be surrendering to the philosophy of our enemies and our victory would turn to defeat.

The issue of this war is the basic issue between those who believe in mankind and those who do not—the ancient issue between those who put their faith in the people and those who put their faith in dictators and tyrants. There have always been those who did not believe in the people, who attempted to block their forward movement across history, to force them back to servility and suffering and silence.

The people have now gathered their strength. They are moving forward in their might and power—and no force, no combination of forces, no trickery, deceit or violence, can stop them now. They see before them the hope of the world—a decent, secure, peaceful life for men everywhere.

I do not prophesy when this war will end.

But I do believe that this year of 1943 will give to the United Nations a very substantial advance along the roads that lead to Berlin and Rome and Tokyo.

I tell you that it is within the realm of possibility that this Seventy-eighth Congress may have the historic privilege of helping greatly to save the world from future fear.

Therefore, let us—all of us—have confidence, let us re-double our efforts.

A tremendous, costly, long-enduring task in peace as well as in war is still ahead of us.

But, as we face that continuing task, we may know that the state of this nation is good—the heart of this nation is sound—the spirit of this nation is strong—the faith of this nation is eternal.

ADDRESS TO CONGRESS [4]

WINSTON CHURCHILL [5]

With the persuasive eloquence with which he had addressed a joint session of Congress immediately after the United States entered the Second World War, Winston Churchill again defended Britain's part in the conflict and pledged his country's commitment to total victory against the Axis.

The immediate occasion for the Prime Minister's visit to America was his attendance at the War Council, then in progress at Washington between the outstanding spokesmen of the two nations. Now that the Tunisian campaign was so brilliantly concluded, the Americans were asking, How great was that victory? To what extent are we winning the war against the submarines? When and how will we strike on the continent? What of the military program for destroying the might of Japan?

Specifically, Senator A. B. Chandler of Kentucky, on Monday, May 17, had attacked the fundamental strategy of the British-American high command in its avowed aim to overthrow Germany first and to deal later with the Japanese. Senator Chandler argued that America should concentrate first on Japan, and second on Germany. The Nipponese, he contended, were making themselves invulnerable in conquered Asia and the East Indies; furthermore, after the collapse of Germany, Russia and Great Britain might leave America to engage singlehanded these Orientals.

Mr. Churchill, on Wednesday, May 19th, answered directly these arguments. His audience in the House Chamber, including both Senators and Representatives, was a distinguished one. Diplomats, Cabinet members were there. The Duke of Windsor was roundly applauded.

The speech was notable for the direct reply given to Chandler's arguments. Said the English speaker, in the persuasive style with which he appealed to the House of Commons, "And I am here to tell you that we will wage that war [against Japan] side by side with you in accordance with the best strategic employment of our forces, while there is breath in our bodies and while blood flows through our veins."

He stressed the Asiatic and European campaigns as constituting one global war. For the present, suggested Churchill, the field of

[4] Reprinted from the *Congressional Record*, v. 89, no. 91, p. 4690-4, May 19, 1943 (daily edition), proceedings of debates of the 78th Congress, first session.

[5] For biographical note see Appendix. See also Dorothy Thompson's "Let's Face the Facts," *Representative American Speeches: 1940-41* p. 137-48; also Winston Churchill's "Address to Congress," *Representative American Speeches: 1941-42*, p. 19-43.

military concentration that offered the best chance of decisive military triumph was Europe. The Tunisian triumph meant not only opening the Mediterranean, but also the intensification of the war in India and beyond.

"It was evident [in 1941] that while the defeat of Japan would not mean the defeat of Germany, the defeat of Germany would inevitably mean the ruin of Japan. The realization of this simple truth does not mean that both sides should not proceed together, and indeed the major part of the United States force is now deployed on the Pacific front."

Speaking for fifty minutes from loose notes, yet not restricted in delivery by his manuscript, the orator had almost all the features that have marked his previous addresses on the progress of the war. Characteristic was his strong personal reference and his reminiscent-autobiographical approach, ("In January 1942, I had that feeling of comfort—"); his frank recital of past defeats, ("One after another very heavy misfortunes fell upon us"); his skillful blending of ominous facts, ("At Singapore we ourselves suffered the greatest military disaster"); his unexpected humor, ("Now they have not traveled all this way simply to concern themselves about improving the health and happiness of the Mikado of Japan"); his continual identification of the British and American partnership; his eulogy of America, of China, of the anti-Axis French; his massing of concrete facts to buttress his assertions; his seeming frankness on all points ("friendly candor"); his resort to Biblical phrases ("in righteous work"); his use of invective and of appellatives and of sarcasm ("the master mind" of Hitler); his aphorisms couched in Anglo-Saxon ("It is a poor heart that never rejoices"); and his climaxes in thought and expression.

In general, the speech is a report of victory rather than an appeal for resistance in "England's darkest hour."

The reaction to the speech was, as usual, highly favorable. The audience continually cheered and applauded, and at the end gave him an ovation. Arthur Krock, in *The New York Times,* for May 20, stated, "By all indications, the Prime Minister's triumph was one of the greatest of his career." Both the Washington visible audience and the millions of radio listeners approved and continued to follow not only the President of this country, but also the Prime Minister of Great Britain. Such was the power of parliamentary oratory in 1943.

Mr. President, Mr. Speaker, Members of the Senate and the House of Representatives:

Seventeen months have passed since I last had the honor to address the Congress of the United States. For more than five hundred days—every day a day in which we have toiled and suffered and dared shoulder to shoulder against the cruel and mighty enemy—we have acted in close combination or concert in many parts of the world—on land, on sea, and in the air. The fact that you have invited me to come to the Congress again—a second time—now that we have settled down to the job, and that you should welcome me in so generous a fashion, is certainly a high mark in my life, and also shows that our partnership has not done so badly. I am proud that you should have found us good allies, striving forward in comradeship to the accomplishment of our task without grudging or stinting either life or treasure or indeed anything we have to give.

Last time I came at a moment when the United States was aflame with wrath at the treacherous attack upon Pearl Harbor by Japan and at the subsequent declarations of war upon the United States made by Germany and Italy. For my part I say quite frankly that in those days after our long, and for a whole year lonely, struggle I could not repress in my heart a sense of relief and comfort that we were all bound together by common peril, by solemn faith and high purpose to see this fearful quarrel through at all costs to the end. That was an hour of passionate emotion, an hour most memorable in human records, an hour, as I believe, full of hope and glory for the future.

The experiences of a long life and the promptings of my blood have wrought in me the conviction that there is nothing more important for the future of the world than the fraternal association of our two peoples in righteous work, both in war and in peace. So, in January 1942, I had that feeling of comfort and I therefore prepared myself in a confident and steadfast spirit to bear the terrible blows which were evidently about to fall on British interests in the Far East, which were bound to fall upon us from the military strength of Japan during a period when the American and British fleets had lost for the time being the naval command of the Pacific and Indian Oceans. One after another in swift succession very heavy misfortunes fell upon us and upon our allies, the Dutch, in the Pacific theater. The Japanese have seized the land and islands they so greedily coveted. The Philippines are enslaved. The lustrous, luxuriant regions of the Dutch East Indies have been overrun. In the

Malay Peninsula and at Singapore we ourselves suffered the greatest military disaster, or at any rate the largest military disaster, in British history.

Mr. President and Mr. Speaker, all this has to be retrieved and all this and much else will have to be repaid.

And here let me say this: Let no one suggest that we British have not at least as great an interest as the United States in the unflinching and relentless waging of war against Japan; and I am here to tell you that we will wage that war side by side with you in accordance with the best strategic employment of our forces while there is a breath in our bodies and while blood flows in our veins.

A notable part in the war against Japan must, of course, be played by the large armies and by the air and naval forces now marshaled by Great Britain on the eastern frontiers of India. In this quarter there lies one of the means of bringing aid to hard-pressed and long-tormented China. I regard the bringing of effective and immediate aid to China as one of the most urgent of our common tasks.

It may not have escaped your attention that I have brought with me to this country and to this conference Field Marshal Wavell and the other two commanders in chief from India. Now they have not traveled all this way simply to concern themselves about improving the health and happiness of the Mikado of Japan.

I thought it would be good that all concerned in this theater should meet together and thresh out in friendly candor, heart to heart, all the points that arise. And there are many. You may be sure that if it was necessary, if all that was necessary was for an order to be given to the great armies standing ready in India to march toward the Rising Sun and open the Burma Road, that order would be given this afternoon. The matter is, however, somewhat more complicated.

And all movement or infiltration of troops into the mountains and jungles to the northwest of India is very strictly governed by what your American military men call the science of logistics.

But, Mr. President and Mr. Speaker, I repudiate, and I am sure with your sympathy, the slightest suspicion that we should hold anything back that can be usefully employed, or that I and the government I represent are not as resolute to employ every man, gun and airplane that can be used in this business, as we have proved ourselves ready to do in other theaters of the war.

In our conferences, in January 1942 between the President and myself, and between our high expert advisers, it was evident that while the defeat of Japan would not mean the defeat of Germany, the defeat of Germany would inevitably mean the ruin of Japan.

The realization of this simple truth does not mean that both sides should not proceed together, and indeed the major part of the United States force is now deployed on the Pacific fronts. In the broad division which we then made of our labors in January 1942, the United States undertook the main responsibility for prosecuting the war against Japan, and for aiding Australia and New Zealand to defend themselves against a Japanese invasion, which then seemed far more threatening than it does now.

On the other hand, we took the main burden on the Atlantic, which was only natural. Unless the ocean lifeline which joins our two peoples can be kept unbroken, the British Isles and all the very considerable forces which radiate therefrom would be paralyzed and doomed.

We have willingly done our full share of the sea work in the dangerous waters of the Mediterranean and in the Arctic convoys to Russia, and we have sustained, since our alliance began, more than double the losses in merchant tonnage that have fallen upon the United States.

On the other hand, the prodigious output of new ships from the United States building yards has now for six months past overtaken and now far surpasses the losses of both Allies. And if no effort is relaxed, there is every reason to count upon a ceaseless progressive expansion of Allied shipping available for the prosecution of the war.

Our killings of the U-boats, as the Secretary of the Navy will readily confirm, have this year greatly exceeded all previous experience, and the last three months, and particularly the last three weeks, have yielded record results.

This, of course, is to some extent due to the larger numbers of U-boats operating, but it is also due to the marked improvement in the severity and power of our measures against them and of the new devices continually employed.

While I rate the U-boat danger as still the greatest we have to face, I have a good and sober confidence that it will not only be met and contained, but overcome. The increase of shipping tonnage over sinkings provides, after the movements of vital supplies of food and munitions have been arranged, that margin which is the main measure of our joint war effort.

We are also conducting from the British Isles the principal air offensive against Germany. And in this we are powerfully aided by the United States Air Force in the United Kingdom, whose action is chiefly by day, as ours is chiefly by night. In this war numbers count more and more, both in night and day attacks.

The saturation of the enemy's flak through the multiplicity of attacking planes, the division and dispersion of his fighter protection by the launching of several simultaneous attacks, are rewards which will immediately be paid through the substantial increases in British and American numbers which are now taking place. There is no doubt that the Allies already vastly outnumber the hostile air forces of Germany, Italy and Japan. And still more does their output of new planes surpass the output of the enemy.

In this air war, by which both Germany and Japan fondly imagined they would strike decisive and final blows and terrorize nations, great and small, into submission to their will, in this air war it is that these guilty nations have already begun to show their first real mortal weakness.

The more continuous and severe the air fighting becomes, the better for us, because we can already replace casualties and machines far more rapidly than the enemy and we can replace them on a scale which increases month by month.

Progress in this sphere is swift and sure, but it must be remembered that the preparation and development of airfields and the movement of the great masses of ground personnel on whom the efficiency of modern air squadrons depends, however earnestly pressed forward, is bound to take time.

Opinion, Mr. President and Mr. Speaker, is divided as to whether the use of air power could by itself bring about the collapse of Germany or Italy. The experiment is well worth trying, so long as other measures are not excluded.

There is certainly no harm in finding out. But, however that may be, anyhow we are all agreed that the damage done to the enemy's war potential is enormous. The condition to which the great centers of German war industry, and particularly the Ruhr, are being reduced, is one of unparalleled devastation. You have just read of the destruction of the great dams which feed the canals and provide power to the enemy's munition works. That was a gallant operation, costing eight out of the nineteen Lancaster bombers employed. But it will play a very far-reaching part in German munitions output.

It is our settled policy, the settled policy of our two staffs and war-making authorities, to make it impossible for Germany to carry on any form of war industry on a large or concentrated scale, either in Germany, in Italy or in the enemy-occupied countries. Wherever these centers exist or are developed, they will be destroyed and the munitions populations will be dispersed. If they don't like what's coming to them, let them disperse beforehand on their own.

The process will continue ceaselessly with ever-increasing weight and intensity until the German and Italian peoples abandon or destroy the monstrous tyrannies which they have incubated and reared in their midst.

Meanwhile our air offensive is forcing Germany to withdraw an ever-larger proportion of its war-making capacity from the fighting fronts in order to provide protection against the air attacks. Hundreds of fighter aircraft, thousands of antiaircraft cannon, and many hundreds of thousands of men, together with a vast share in the output of the war factories, have already been assigned to this purely defensive function. All this is at the expense of the enemy's power of new aggression or of the enemy's power to resume the initiative.

Surveying the whole aspect of the air war, we cannot doubt that it is a major factor in the process of victory. That, I think, is established as a solid fact. It is all agreed between us that we should at the earliest moment similarly bring our joint air power to bear upon the military targets in the homelands of Japan.

The cold-blooded execution of United States airmen by the Japanese government is a proof not only of their barbarism but of the dread in which they regard this possibility.

It is the duty of those who are charged with the direction of the war to overcome at the earliest moment the military, geographical and political difficulties, and begin the process so necessary and desirable of laying the cities and other munitions centers of Japan in ashes, for in ashes they must surely lie before peace comes back to the world.

That this objective holds a high place in the present councils is obvious to thinking men, but no public discussion would be useful upon the method or sequence of events which should be pursued in order to achieve it. Let me make it plain, however, that the British will participate in this air attack on Japan in harmonious accord with the major strategy of the war. That is our desire. And the cruelties of the Japanese enemy will make our airmen all the more ready to share the perils and sufferings of their American comrades.

At the present time, speaking more generally, the prime problem which is before the United States and to a lesser extent before Great Britain is not so much the creation of armies or the vast output of munitions and aircraft. These are already in full swing, and immense progress, prodigious results, have been achieved. The problem is rather the application of those forces to the enemy in the teeth of U-boat resistance across the great ocean spaces, across the narrow seas, or on land through the swamps, mountains, and jungles in various quarters of the globe. That is our problem. All our war plans must, therefore, be inspired, pervaded, and even dominated by the supreme object of coming to grips with the enemy under favorable conditions, or at any rate tolerable conditions—we cannot pick and choose too much—on the largest possible scale at the earliest possible moment, and of engaging that enemy wherever it is profitable and, indeed, I might almost say wherever it is possible to do so. Thus in this way we shall make our enemies in Europe and in Asia burn and consume their strength on land, on sea, and in the air with the maximum rapidity.

Now, you will readily understand that the complex task of finding the maximum openings for the employment of our vast forces, the selection of the points at which to strike with the greatest advantage to those forces, and the emphasis and priority to be assigned to all the various enterprises which are desirable, that is a task requiring the constant supervision and adjustment of our combined staffs and of the heads of governments. This is a vast and complicated process, especially when two countries are involved directly in council together, and when the interests of so many other countries have to be considered and the utmost good will and readiness to think for the common cause of all the United Nations are required from everyone participating in our conference. The intricate adjustments and arrangements can only be made by discussion between men who know all the facts, and who are and can be held accountable for success or failure. Lots of people can make good plans for winning the war if they have not got to carry them out. I dare say if I had not been in a responsible position, I should have made a lot of excellent plans, and very likely should have brought them in one way or another to the notice of the executive authorities. But it is not possible to have full, open arguments about these matters. That is an additional hardship to those in charge—that such questions cannot be argued out and debated in public, except with enormous reticence, and even then there is great danger that the watching and listening enemy may derive some profit from what they hear. In these circumstances, in my opinion, the American and British press and public have treated their executives with a wise and indulgent consideration, and recent events I think have vindicated their self-restraint. Mr. President and Mr. Speaker, it is thus that we are able to meet here today in all faithfulness and sincerity and friendship.

Geography imposes insuperable obstacles to the continuous session of the combined staffs and executive chiefs, but as the scene is constantly changing, and lately I think I may say constantly changing for the better, repeated conferences are indispensable if the sacrifices of the fighting troops are to be rendered fruitful and if the curse of war which lies so heavily upon almost the whole world is to be broken and swept away within the shortest possible time. I therefore thought it my duty, with the full authority of His Majesty's Government, to come here again with our highest officers, in order that the combined staffs may work in the closest contact with the chief executive power which the President derives from his office, and in respect of which I am the accredited representative of the Cabinet and Parliament.

The wisdom of the founders of the American Constitution led them to associate the office of Commander in Chief with that of the Presidency of the United States. In this they followed the precedents which were successful in the case of George Washington. It is remarkable that after more than 150 years this combination of political and military authority has been found necessary not only in the United States, but in the case of Marshal Stalin in Russia, and of Generalissimo Chiang Kai-shek in China. Even I, as majority leader in the House of Commons in one branch of the Legislature, have been drawn from time to time—not perhaps wholly against my will—into some participation in military affairs.

Modern war is total, and it is necessary for its conduct that the technical and professional authorities should be sustained and if necessary directed by the heads of governments who have knowledge which enables them to comprehend not only the military but the political and economic affairs at work, and who have the power to focus them all upon the goal. These are the reasons which compelled the President to make his long journey to Casablanca, and these are the reasons which bring me here. We, both of us, earnestly hope that at no distant date we may be able to achieve what we have so long sought—namely, a meeting with Marshal Stalin and if possible with Generalissimo Chiang Kai-shek. But how, when, and where this is to be accomplished is not a matter upon which I am able to shed any clear ray of light at the present time, and if I were I should certainly not shed it.

In the meanwhile, we do our best to keep the closest association at every level between all the authorities of all the countries who are engaged in the active direction of the war, and it is my special duty to promote and preserve this intimacy and concert between all parts of the British Commonwealth and Empire, and especially with the great self-governing Dominions, like Canada, whose Prime Minister is with us at this moment, and whose contribution is so massive and invaluable.

There could be no better or more encouraging example of the fruits of our consultations than the campaign in northwest Africa which has just ended so well.

One morning in June last, when I was here, the President handed me a slip of paper which bore the utterly unexpected news of the fall of Tobruk and the surrender of its garrison of 25,000 men in unexplained circumstances. That, indeed, was a dark and bitter hour for me. I shall never forget the kindness, the delicacy, the true comradeship which our American friends showed me and those with me in such adversity. Their only thought was to find the means of helping us to restore the situation, and never for a moment did they question the resolution or the fighting quality of our troops. Hundreds of Sherman tanks were taken from the hands of American divisions and sent at the utmost speed around the Cape of Good Hope to Egypt. When one ship carrying fifty tanks was sunk by torpedo, the United States Government replaced it and its precious vehicles before we could even think of asking them to do so. The Sherman tank was the best tank in the desert in the year 1942, and the presence of these weapons played an appreciable part in the ruin of Rommel's army at the battle of Alamein and in the long pursuit which chased him back to Tunisia.

At this time also, in June 1942, when I was here last, there lighted up those trains of thought and study which produced the memorable American and British descent upon French Northwest Africa, the results of which are a cause of general rejoicing today. We have certainly a most encouraging example here of what can be achieved by British and Americans working together heart and hand. In fact, one might almost feel that, if they could keep it up, there is hardly anything they could not do, either in the field of war or in the not less tangled problems of peace.

History will acclaim this great enterprise as a classic example of the way to make war. We used the weapon of sea power, the weapon in which we were strongest, to attack the enemy at our chosen moment and at our chosen point. In spite of the immense elaboration of the plan and the many hundreds, thousands even, who had to be informed of its main outline, we maintained secrecy and effective surprise. We confronted the enemy with a situation in which he had either to lose invaluable strategic territories or to fight under conditions most costly and wasteful to him. We recovered the initiative, which we still retain. We rallied to our side French forces, which are already a brave—and will presently become a powerful—army under the gallant General Giraud. We secured bases from which violent attacks can and will be delivered by our air power on the whole of Italy, with results which no one can measure, but which most certainly will be highly beneficial to our affairs. We have made an economy in our strained and straitened shipping position worth several hundreds of great ships, and one which will give us the advantage of far swifter passage through the Mediterranean to the East, to the Middle East, and to the Far East. We have struck the enemy a blow which is the equal of Stalingrad and most stimulating to our heroic and heavily engaged Russian allies.

All this gives the lie to the Nazi and Fascist taunts that parliamentary democracies are incapable of waging effective war. Presently we will furnish them with further examples.

Still I am free to admit that in North Africa we builded better than we knew. The unexpected came to the aid of what was designed and multiplied the results. For this we have to thank the military intuition of Corporal Hitler. We may notice, as I predicted in the House of Commons three months ago, the touch of the master hand. The same insensate obstinacy which doomed Field Marshal von Paulus and his army to destruction at Stalingrad has brought this new catastrophe upon our enemies in Tunisia. We have destroyed or captured considerably more than a quarter million of the enemy's best troops, together with vast masses of material, all of which had been ferried across to Africa after paying heavy toll to British submarines and to British and United States aircraft. No one could count on such follies. They gave us, if I may use the language of finance, a handsome bonus after the full dividend had been earned and paid.

At the time when we planned this great joint African operation we hoped to be masters of Tunisia even before the end of last year. But the injury we have now inflicted upon the enemy, physical and psychological, the training our troops have had in the hard school of war, and the welding together of the Anglo-American staff machine—these are advantages which far exceed anything which it was within our power to plan. The German lie factory is volubly explaining how valuable is the time which they bought by the loss of their great armies. Let them not delude themselves. Other operations which will unfold in due course, depending as they did upon the special instruction of large numbers of troops and upon the provision of vast technical apparatus, these other operations have not been in any way delayed by the obstinate fighting in northern Tunisia.

Mr. President and Mr. Speaker, the African war is over. Mussolini's African Empire and Corporal Hitler's strategy are alike exploded. It is interesting to compute what these performances have cost those two wicked men and those who have been their tools or their dupes. The Emperor of Abyssinia sits again upon the throne from which he was driven by Mussolini's poison gas. All the vast territories from Madagascar to Morocco, from Cairo to Casablanca, from Aden to Dakar are under British, American, or French control. One continent, at least, has been cleansed and purged forever from Fascist and Nazi tyranny.

The African excursions of the two dictators have cost their countries in killed and captured 950,000 soldiers. In addition, nearly 2,400,000 gross tons of shipping have been sunk and nearly 8,000 aircraft destroyed, both of these figures being exclusive of large numbers of ships and aircraft damaged. There have also been lost to the enemy 6,200 guns, 2,550 tanks, and 70,000 trucks, which is the American name for lorry and which I understand has been adopted by the combined staffs in Northwest Africa in exchange for the use of the word "petrol" in place of "gasoline." These are the losses of the enemy after three years of war. At the end of it all what is there to show? The proud German Army has by its sudden collapse, its crumbling, and breaking up—unexpected to all of us—the proud German Army has once again proved the truth of the saying: "The Hun is always at your throat or your feet."

That is a point which may have its bearing on the future. But for our part at this milestone in the war we can say: One continent redeemed.

The northwest African campaign, and particularly its Tunisian climax, is the finest example of the cooperation of the troops of three different countries and of the combination under one supreme commander of the use of sea, land, and air forces which has yet been seen. In particular, the British and American staff work, as I have said, has matched the comradeship of the soldiers of both our countries striding forward side by side under the fire of the enemy. It was a marvel of efficient organization which enabled the Second American Corps, or rather Army, for that was its size, to be moved three hundred miles from the southern sector, which had become obsolete through the retreat of the enemy, to the northern coast, from which, beating down all opposition, they advanced and took the fortress and harbor of Bizerte. In order to accomplish this march of three hundred miles, which was covered in twelve days, it was necessary for this very considerable army, with its immense modern equipment, to traverse at right angles the communications of the British First Army, which was already engaged, or about to be engaged, in heavy battle, and this was achieved without in any way disturbing the hour-to-hour supply upon which that army depended. I am told that these British and American officers work together without the slightest question of what country they belong to, each doing his part in a military organization which must henceforward be regarded as a most powerful and efficient instrument of war.

There is honor, Mr. President and Mr. Speaker, for all; and I shall at the proper time and place pay my tribute to the British and American commanders by land and sea who conducted or who were engaged in the battle. This only will I say now: I do not think you could have chosen any man more capable than General Eisenhower of keeping his very large, heterogeneous force together through bad times as well as good, and of creating the conditions of harmony and energy which were the indispensable elements of victory.

I have dwelt in some detail, but I trust not at undue length, upon these famous events, and I shall now return to the general war for a few minutes in which they have their setting and proportion. It is a poor heart that never rejoices, but our thanksgiving, however fervent, must be brief. Heavier work lies ahead, not only in the European but, as I have indicated, in the Pacific and in the Indian spheres; and the President and I and the combined staffs are gathered here in order that this work shall be, as far as lies within us, well conceived and thrust forward without losing a day. Not for one moment must we forget that the main burden of the war on land is still being borne by the Russian armies. They are holding at the present time no fewer than one hundred and ninety German divisions and twenty-eight satellite divisions on their front. It is always wise, while doing justice to one's own achievements, to preserve a proper sense of proportion, and I therefore mention that these figures of the German forces opposite Russia compare with the equivalent of about fifteen divisions which we have destroyed in Tunisia after a campaign which has cost us about 50,000 casualties. That gives some measure of the Russian effort and of the debt which we owe to her. It may well be that a further trial of strength between the German and Russian armies is impending. Russia has already inflicted injuries upon the German military organism which will, I believe, prove mortal. But there is little doubt that Hitler is reserving his supreme gambler's throw for a third attempt to break the heart and spirit and destroy the armed forces of the mighty nation which he has already twice assaulted in vain. He will not succeed. But we must do everything in our power that is sensible and practicable to take more of the weight off Russia in 1943.

I do not intend to be responsible for any suggestion that the war is won or will soon be over. That it will be won by us I am sure. But how or when cannot be foreseen, still less foretold. I was driving the other day not far from the field of Gettysburg, which I know well, like most of your battlefields. It was the decisive battle of the Civil War. No one after Gettysburg doubted which way the dread balance of war would incline. Yet far more blood was shed after the Union victory at Gettysburg than in all the fighting which went before.

It behooves us, therefore, to search our hearts and brace our sinews and to take the most earnest counsel one with another in order that the favorable position which has already been reached, both against Japan and against Hitler and Mussolini in Europe, shall not be let slip. If we wish to abridge the slaughter and ruin which this war is spreading to so many lands and to which we must ourselves contribute so grievous a measure of suffering and sacrifice, we cannot afford to relax a single fiber of our being or to tolerate the slightest abatement of our effort.

The enemy is still proud and powerful. He is hard to get at. He still possesses enormous armies, vast resources, and invaluable strategic territories. War is full of mysteries and surprises. A false step, a wrong direction of strategic effort, discord, or lassitude among the Allies might soon give the common enemy the power to confront us with new and hideous facts. We have surmounted many serious dangers. But there is one grave danger which will go along with us until the end. That danger is the undue prolongation of the war. No one can tell what new complications and perils might arise in four or five more years of war. And it is in the dragging out of war at enormous expense till the democracies are tired, or bored, or split that the main hopes of Germany and Japan must now reside.

We must destroy this hope as we have destroyed so many others. And for that purpose we must beware of every topic, however attractive, and every tendency, however natural, which turn our minds or energies from the supreme objective of the general victory of the United Nations.

By singleness of purpose, by steadfastness of conduct, by tenacity and endurance, such as we have so far displayed, by these, and only by these, can we discharge our duty to the future of the world and to the destiny of man.

WAR AIMS

AMERICAN WAR AIMS [1]

CARLTON J. H. HAYES [2]

The Hon. Carlton J. H. Hayes, Ambassador to Spain, gave this address before the Chiefs of Allied and Friendly Missions and the officials of the Spanish Government, at the Casa Americana, Madrid, on January 15, 1943.

With a Spanish army of perhaps 300,000 in Spanish Morocco to threaten the American troops assembled in Morocco and Algeria; with the possibility looming that Hitler's armies might flow through Spain to invest Gibraltar; and with Franco openly showing his friend-liness to the Axis cause, American diplomacy toward Spain assumed an important role in influencing the events in 1943 in North Africa.

American policy toward Spain had been one of "cautious appease-ment." We had offered Franco credits and had supplied Spain with considerable amounts of oil, gasoline, cotton, coal, and chemicals.

Ambassador Hayes framed a statement carefully calculated to re-assure the Spaniards, to invite their support of the United Nations cause, to make clear that America's participation was largely defensive, and yet one leading to the total defeat of the Axis. His remarks were thus conciliatory and yet sufficiently incisive to leave little doubt con-cerning our military and other intentions in areas where Spanish power and interests were concerned. The address represents a statement of the war aims of America, to which many Americans agreed. Many, however, looked askance at the remarks as insufficiently appreciative of Russian prestige, and as incomplete in delineation of a program for disposing of the defeated Hitler and Hirohito.

It is a curious fact that just as the United States began its national history as a federation of thirteen colonies, so now thir-teen sovereign states of the American continents are leagued together in a world war of colossal magnitude. These thirteen comprise one English-speaking country—the United States of America; one half English and half French—the Dominion of Canada; one great Portuguese-speaking country—Brazil; one

[1] Reprinted by permission from *The New York Times*, January 16, 1943.
[2] For biographical note see Appendix.

French-speaking country—Haiti; and nine Spanish-speaking countries—Mexico, Cuba, the Dominican Republic, Guatemala, Honduras, Nicaragua, El Salvador, Costa Rica, and Panama. All thirteen American nations are leagued together, moreover, in support of common objectives, and with these objectives certainly sympathize practically all the governments and peoples of the New World.

Why, then, to be specific, is the United States at war? Why are North American soldiers and sailors and airmen fighting alongside other Americans and also alongside British and Australians and French and Dutch and Belgians and Norwegians and Greeks and Poles and Czechoslovaks and Yugoslavs and Chinese and Russians? Why is the United States devoting all its manpower and material resources to the war and extending its battle fronts far away from America to North Africa, to New Guinea and the Solomon Islands, to Burma and China, to Iraq and Iran, to the coasts of France and the Low Countries, to the industrial nerve centers of Germany and Italy? And why is the United States determined not to accept a negotiated peace of compromise but to fight this war through, no matter what sacrifices it may entail, to a complete and overwhelming victory? In a word, what are the American war aims?

No nation is likely to plunge into a war of the extent and magnitude of the present global struggle without some powerful motivation. One does not risk everything for little stakes. Believe me, the government and people of the United States are no exception to that rule.

Let me, at the outset, correct some misapprehensions which our enemies have sedulously propagated and let me state clearly what American war aims are *not*. First, we do *not* aim at any extension of our national territory or seek any protectorate or other imperialistic sway over other peoples.

Whatever imperialistic impulse certain segments of my people may have exhibited or yielded to in the nineteenth century has quite disappeared in the twentieth century. To this, not only our words but our deeds bear witness. In 1918, when we had ample opportunity and even invitation, we established no protectorate, assumed no mandate, appropriated not a square inch of land anywhere. Long before the present war began, we promised independence to the Filipinos, and by the time Japan attacked us the sovereign Commonwealth of the Philippines was well on the road to full realization. With all our sister republics of the American continents we have developed, and we practice, the policy of the "good neighbor," and this policy we seek to apply to the Old as well as the New World. We have solemnly and specifically engaged to respect the territorial integrity of this Iberian peninsula together with the overseas possessions of both Spain and Portugal. And we have likewise engaged not to tarry longer in French North Africa or elsewhere on alien soil than military exigencies absolutely require. Imperialism is most emphatically *not* an American war aim. We fight not for conquest.

Second, we do *not* aim at imposing a particular form of government or a particular set of social institutions upon any other nation. As I said when I presented my credentials to His Excellency the Chief of the Spanish State last June, "We do not try to impose our system of government on any other people; equally, we are always quick to resist any attempt of another government to impose its system on us."

I know, alas, with what constancy and assiduity the factories of Axis propaganda manufacture stories to the contrary. I know, for example here in Spain, that they produce the most terrifying pictures of the consequences of Allied victory—intervention in behalf of some minority, resumption of civil war, reign of chaos and terrorism, triumph of Marxian Communism. This, Ladies and Gentlemen, is the main stock-in-trade of Dr. Goebbels and his associates, which should find market only among the timid and the gullible.

The United States is not Communist. Great Britain is not Communist. Brazil is not Communist. Among the great majority of the United Nations, the number of Communists and of sympathizers with Communism is very slight. Even the one country which is professedly Communist must be actuated in the magnificent and, I might add, successful defense it is now making less by Marxian doctrines than by the spirit of national freedom. What the United Nations will most want at the end of the present war is a continuity of traditional law and order, and any government which can maintain or establish such law and order will have the material as well as spiritual support of the United Nations. For in last analysis the best guarantee against Communism, for any nation which does not voluntarily choose it, is a government able to maintain order and to provide for the material needs of its people. Among the United Nations are the world's granaries and depots for supplying just those needs at the end of the present war.

The United States recognizes that no two nations have exactly the same historic traditions and that consequently no one form of government is equally suitable for all. Even the so-called democracies differ greatly in their democratic conceptions and usages. English democracy is different from American democracy, and both are different from Brazilian—or Polish—democracy. As the United States would not wish to impose its particular brand on Brazil, so much the more will it refrain from seeking to impose it upon an ancient country like Spain. If the political and social institutions of this country undergo change or modification in future years, it will be the work of Spaniards within Spain, not of the United States or of Spanish emigrés. No, American war aims are neither political nor socialistic.

Let me here refer, in passing, to yet another alleged war aim which is *not* American. I have occasionally heard it said—doubtless an echo of Axis propaganda—that the present war is simply a trade war, a capitalist war, a war for money stakes, by means of which the United States is trying to get a strangle hold on the world's riches. This seems to be a patently silly allegation. It staggers my imagination to conceive how, if my nation is fighting this war for capitalistic stakes, it can be accused simultaneously of favoring Communism. But that merely staggers imagination. What puts it to utter rout is one's inability to perceive how any financial gains from the present war can be at all commensurate with the fantastic expenditure involved. Already the United States alone—exclusive of its allies—is spending 250 million dollars a day, or, at the legal rate of exchange, 2 billion, 737 million pesetas a day, which in a year's time amounts to 91¼ billion dollars or almost a thousand billion pesetas. These, Ladies and Gentlemen, are astronomical figures. They have no relationship to any possible money return from an impoverished postwar world.

Actually in economics, as in politics, the United States is committed to the principle of asking nothing for itself which it is not willing to concede to others. It aims at no economic exclusiveness, at no monopolizing of natural resources or of the products of labor. It will undoubtedly be a creditor nation at the close of the war, but as such its own self-interest must dictate a policy of promoting the solvency and prosperity of the world at large. This can only be done, my government has said, by freeing international trade to the greatest possible extent and by making raw materials available to all peoples on an equal basis.

I have dwelt too long, perhaps, on what American war aims are *not*. To grasp what they really are, one must disabuse one's mind of the common but absurd fallacy that because my countrymen make a good deal of machinery—and pretty good machinery—they must be materialistic. Rather, one has to recognize the opposite truth that the people of the United States are intensely idealistic—incorrigibly idealistic. Americans have in them more of the Spanish than you might guess; they are, in their peculiar way, the Don Quixotes of the twentieth century.

For one thing, Americans love liberty—liberty for the individual, liberty for nations. This is not to say that they are necessarily sympathetic with everything which has gone by the name of liberalism, especially with that sectarian liberalism which in parts of Europe during the last century hardly disguised a selfish and pagan materialism. The liberty which Americans revere is the liberty of the seventeenth and eighteenth centuries, based on medieval Christian tradition and reinforced by New World life and experience. It is the liberty of St. Thomas Aquinas, of Suarez and Locke, and also of Washington and Jefferson, of Bolívar and Lincoln.

Then, too, despite what would seem to be very fundamental differences among them, Americans have learned to live together in peace and security, without liberty degenerating into license, and with growing mutual respect. The United States has attained to it, quite literally in accordance with its Latin motto, "E pluribus unum." It is a unity in which share a Protestant majority, Catholics more numerous than those in Spain, Jews more numerous than in any other country. It is a unity of Yankee New England, of originally Dutch and now cosmopolitan New York, of French Louisiana, of Scandinavian Minnesota, of historically Spanish California, Arizona, New Mexico, Texas and Florida, of peoples of the most diverse European extraction—Italian and German, Polish and Irish, English and Slav. The United States is a veritable association of nations, a very practical one; and Americans, recognizing that it has been achieved through cultivation of a good-neighbor policy at home, naturally glory in this policy and regard it as a proper article for export abroad.

Besides, Americans are peace-loving. They do not hanker after war and only grave and direct provocation will get them into war. They wanted very much to stay out of the present war, and they did stay out of it until they were treacherously attacked. They are, indeed, so used to adjusting differences among themselves by conference and debate and by a sporting rule of give-and-take that they have difficulty in understanding why the nations of the world should not settle their differences in like manner.

Yet once aroused, Americans can and will fight. And what most arouses them is resentment at being pushed around, or, almost equally, at seeing other people pushed around.

It is because the Axis Powers of Germany, Italy, and Japan have latterly been doing a good deal of pushing that the United States, in league with the other United Nations, is at war with the Axis. Our central war aim is to put a stop to the pushing.

The spectacle which the Nazi regime presents inside Germany is sufficiently disgusting and revolting, with its maltreatment of Jews, its persecution of the Catholic Church, its utilization of violence and terror to establish what Pope Pius XI characterized as "the grossest paganism." Yet while we have regretted and reprobated what the Nazis have done within their own country, we have long been patient and have felt that the responsibility and the remedy alike lay, not with us or any foreigners, but with the German people. According to our principles, it was for Germans to decide what domestic regime they would live under, provided only that they respected the right of other peoples to a like freedom.

But this is precisely what Germany and the other Axis Powers have not respected. For several years now, as everybody knows, they have employed force and violence not only to enslave their own peoples but also to conquer and despoil other peoples, to deprive them of their freedom and to impose upon them alien rule and the worst forms of vassalage and slavery. Nazi Germany has definitely run amok in Czechoslovakia, Poland, the Baltic countries, and the Ukraine, in Norway, Denmark, Holland, Belgium, and France, and, with ghoulish seconding from Fascist Italy, in Greece and Yugoslavia. Japan has similarly brought havoc and death to China, to the Spanish-speaking Catholic Philippines, to the Dutch East Indies, to Siam and Burma. In vain Great Britain and other powers tried to be reasonable and conciliatory; they found to their grief, one after another, that the only recourse left them was to oppose force with force. In vain, the United States and the other American republics protested their desire for peace; as they began preparations for defense, Japan descended with deadly bombs on Pearl Harbor, and Germany and Italy quickly joined in the attack on America.

Americans have long suspected—and now they know—that the so-called "New Order" which the Axis advertises as its supreme war aim is simply a gigantic pushing around and pushing down of practically all the peoples of the world in the selfish interest of a pair of swashbuckling and would-be "superior" powers—Nazi Germany and Imperial Japan. Even the original third partner is by now merely a silent partner, a kind of burned-out satellite helplessly held to its appointed course by solar Berlin.

The objectives of the German-Japanese "New Order" are clearly revealed in the war aims which I have previously said were *not* American and which indeed are absolutely antithetical to those of the United Nations. It is Nazi Germany and militaristic Japan which would blot out the independence of nations, annex territory far and wide, and establish imperialistic hegemonies, the one over Europe and Africa, the other over Asia and Oceania. It is the same Germany and Japan which would tear other peoples loose from their historic roots and compel them slavishly to imitate the political and social institutions and the de-Christianizing processes of the self-styled "master" peoples. It is, likewise, the same Germany and Japan which would exploit the world's economy to their own exclusive advantage, thereby impoverishing less favored nations and in the long run preparing them for Communist or other desperate adventures.

Against the menace of this German-Japanese world order, Americans wish ardently to retain their freedom—their freedom to determine their own form of governmnt, to live their own lives, to work and trade with some assurance of security and in an atmosphere of peace. In this sense American war aims are strictly defensive; they signify defense of the American continents against an alien and aggressive world order. But in a broader sense American war aims surely represent the aspirations and yearnings of all nations and people who want to be free and decent and self-respecting. They have been published to the world, let me remind you, in that solemn joint declaration of the President of the United States and the Prime Minister of Great Britain—the Atlantic Charter.

This Charter not only defines the war aims of the countries named, but to all others it conveys assurances of a future peace of justice and right. "Their countries," affirm the signatories of the Charter, "seek no aggrandizement, territorial or other. They desire to see no territorial changes that do not accord with the freely expressed wishes of the peoples concerned. They respect the right of all peoples to choose the form of government under which they will live; and they wish to see sovereign rights and self-government restored to those who have been forcibly deprived of them. They will endeavor . . . to further enjoyment by all states, great or small, . . . of access, on equal terms, to the trade and to the raw materials of the world

which are needed for their economic prosperity. They desire
to bring about the fullest collaboration between all nations in
the economic field, with the object of securing for all improved
labor standards, economic advancement, and social security.
After the final destruction of Nazi tyranny, they hope to see
established a peace which will afford to all nations the means
of dwelling in safety within their own boundaries, and which
will afford assurance that all men in all the lands may live
out their lives in freedom from fear and want. . . ."

These objectives accord perfectly with the best and highest
traditions of Christian civilization as expressed so clearly and
authoritatively in recent Christmas allocutions of the Sovereign
Pontiff. They accord likewise with the natural rights of man
and with the promptings of his conscience. Between these objectives and those of the Axis leaders, there can be no compromise.

There can be, then, no "negotiated" peace. The war must
be fought to a finish, for it is a war between freedom and en-
slavement, between civilization and barbarism.

I said at the beginning that no nation is likely to plunge
into a war of the extent and magnitude of this present global
struggle without some powerful motivation and that one does
not risk everything for little stakes. I conclude by stressing the
greatness of the stakes now involved and by pledging you that
Americans are firmly and unitedly determined to do their part
to win the war and to establish and maintain a just peace.

WHAT ARE WE FIGHTING FOR? [3]

EDUARD BENEŠ [4]

President Eduard Beneš, of Czechoslovakia, delivered this speech at the Chicago Stadium, in Chicago, on May 23, 1943.

Dr. Beneš was elected President of Czechoslovakia in 1935 after the resignation of T. G. Masaryk. Beneš attempted to help organize Europe against the threatening power of Hitler. France concluded with Prague a treaty of mutual assistance. Russia agreed also to protect the young Republic if France should take up arms in defense of that country. In 1938, at Munich, Beneš saw his country's rights stripped. He resigned and went into exile in England, and later became a professor at the University of Chicago.

In 1939 he returned to England to direct the program to restore his country. In December 1939, the British Government recognized the Czechoslovak National Committee; in 1940, Great Britain recognized the Czechoslovak Provisional Government, and in 1941 gave full recognition to it. In 1942 the United States followed suit. These governments also recognized Beneš as President, in acknowledgement of the fact that his resignation had been extorted from him.

During the year 1942-1943, President Beneš spoke repeatedly to Czechoslovakia from London. He continued also to add to his long list of publications in Czech, Slovak, English, and French.

In May 1943, he visited the United States. His public appearances included an address to Congress. In Chicago he talked before the Council on Foreign Relations, on May 22, on "The Future of the Small European Nations," and at the University of Chicago, on May 24, on "The Policy of the Present War and of the Future Peace."

At this mass meeting to welcome President Beneš, Senator Scott W. Lucas, of Illinois, said,

> It is a matter of personal appreciation for me to participate in this occasion when my fellow citizens of Chicago and Illinois gather to honor one of the world's leading citizens. In an era which has produced many of contemporary greatness and others whose names will long endure, one derives hope and renewed inspiration from the opportunity of joining in public acclaim for Eduard Beneš, the President of our sister democracy, Czechoslovakia.

[3] The text was supplied by the Czechoslovak Press Bureau, 1790 Broadway, New York. Reprinted here by permission of Dr. Jan Papánek, Chief of the Czechoslovak Information Service, New York.
[4] For biographical note see Appendix.

President Beneš is important to us Americans not alone because his countrymen are the ancestors of men and women who helped build our city and country; not alone because we have a heartfelt sympathy for the horrible trials which his people have undergone by virtue of the sadistic cruelties of the intuitive Hitler; not alone because Czechoslovakia is one of the children of that First World War which we, in our naivete, thought would bring a lasting democratic peace upon our planet. President Beneš stands out now, and will continue to stand out in history, because he symbolizes the fight for freedom, because he personifies our own historic perseverance at a cost of life and property to create and maintain the democratic institutions which are the bulwark of our existence. President Beneš is the token which reveals to us that in order to have democratic liberties we cannot sit still. We must fight for them. To be absolutely sure that no totalitarian poison will asphyxiate and overcome us, we must uproot the evils which generate those poisons wherever they may be, whether here or abroad. This is no idle statement. This is no platitude made in the heat of passion or vengeance. It is a truism that must be vigorously enforced after we have won a victory, if the civilization of free men is to survive.

It is particularly fitting that the people of this state of Lincoln, Douglas, and Grant should express their respect and esteem for Doctor Beneš, one of Europe's great apostles of liberty. As I have said, from Czechoslovakia have come many who, by dint of their diligent enterprise, their loyalty to the cause of democracy, and their culture, have added an ingredient of incalculable worth to the formula which ultimately produced this magnificent citadel of democratic achievement. We here know the value of that culture and that contribution to our own development, and thus we are eager to help make sure that no tyrant, surrounded by the hordes of intolerance and bigotry, shall be permitted to exterminate and destroy this worthwhile segment of civilization.

It is good to be back in Chicago, after an absence of almost four years—for it is like coming to an old, tried, trusted and true friend. I have often thought of this great city and its good people in the long interval with affection and gratitude. How could it be otherwise? In 1938, Nazi pressure compelled me to resign my office of President of the Czechoslovak Republic. Not content with this, Hitler's agents compelled me to leave my country. Before leaving, however, I had received an invitation to become a member of the faculty of the University of Chicago. At the time, it was like a friendly hand offered across the ocean and I grasped it gratefully. I left Czechoslovakia, where people loved the truth and lived by its light, a changed land, in which freedom had been violently crushed, where one free man after another was taken to a concentration camp, without warning or notice.

It seemed natural to take up teaching again for I had begun my life's work as a university teacher. The First World War sounded the call to liberate our country from Hapsburg bondage and with my great leader, Thomas Masaryk, we put aside our academic tasks to become, as it were, rebels against political absolutism and dictatorship. This interruption was one of four years, spent in Paris and elsewhere, and after Czechoslovakia's independence was proclaimed in October 1918, it stretched out to twenty more, while I served my country as Minister of Foreign Affairs and later as President.

The Munich dictate was a bitter, cruel blow to Czechoslovakia's every citizen—not less, but more so, to her president. The warmth of your hospitality, as well as my work here, made Chicago a home away from home. Like Prague, you have many of the same industries. There is a similar air of simplicity, purposefulness and common sense in both cities. There are faces in them, too, that bring to mind the bracing air of the Bohemian highlands. Political loyalties in Prague and Chicago are outwardly very different. You and your forebears have given your loyalty to the United States. There must be no nation within a nation. We in Prague give our loyalty to Czechoslovakia. Yet, we have a common loyalty—loyalty to freedom and to democracy. I could never go about Chicago without realizing that it had affinities and bonds of sympathy with Prague deeper even than those of race. These are cities made by, and for, men who are clear eyed and industrious, far-sighted and peace and freedom loving, yet men of energy and courage.

When I came, I expected to remain in the lectureroom for at least a year. I knew that Hitler would swiftly turn his attention to Poland after he had broken and destroyed the defenses of Czechoslovakia. I was certain that that attack would come in the fall of 1939. I assumed that a disillusioned and weakened Czechoslovakia would go to the aid of those powers which were prepared to resist the aggression against Poland. Hitler moved quickly, quicker than I anticipated, for on March 15th, 1939, the Germans were occupying Prague.

From that day on, my countrymen were at war with Nazi Germany and that day I put aside my professor's tranquillity and scientific labors. I hurried back to Europe. One dramatic event followed another in rapid succession. Little more than a year later, when France had signed her armistice with Germany and British fortunes were at their lowest ebb, Mr. Churchill showed his faith in us by formally announcing in the House of Commons that the British Government was according recognition to the new Czechoslovak Government, established in London.

Today, I bring you the best wishes of our government and officials in London, of our soldiers and airmen in Great Britain, Russia and North Africa and of our people at home.

Along with these wishes, I want to express the sincere thanks and appreciation of all, for the generous help of the American people and particularly those of Czechoslovak extraction, for the help which came when it was needed most, at the beginning of our struggle, and continued without interruption up to the present.

For four years our people at home have relentlessly resisted the Nazi invader. They have listened to the radio broadcasts from London, hearing news daily of the activities of our soldiers and airmen, of their government and their president in London and of all the Allied countries. Tonight, when they hear a broadcast version of my address here in the Chicago Stadium, they will wonder how many of their personal friends were present, for many are the families in Czechoslovakia that have one or more members living and working in the United States, or perhaps fighting with the United States land, sea, and air forces, in England, North Africa, the Near East, or some far-flung theater of war in the Pacific.

There is nothing unusual in an American citizen of Czechoslovak origin fighting in the Pacific against the Japanese, for his loyalty to the United States comes before all other loyalties, and America is at war with Japan. We Czechoslovaks are also at war with Japan. We are at war with all the countries with whom the United States, Great Britain and the other United Nations are at war. This is no idle gesture, though the enemy in our homeland is German. The aggressors have come together and joined forces. They must therefore be resisted together. The grand alliance known as the United Nations must go on, even if Germany and Italy should go down in defeat before the Japanese have been pushed back to their own islands. It is absolutely true that peace is one and indivisible. So long as Japan is undefeated, we in Czechoslovakia would not be safe. War has a habit of spreading. Would-be aggressors take advantage of the inevitable difficulties of those who are fighting aggression. Moreover, we are not merely at war with Japan, Germany, Italy and the other Axis countries. We are at war with a terrible and brutal ideology. Our enemies are men who insist that there is no freedom of thought and religion, that torture and the concentration camp are normal political weapons of the twentieth century, that schools and education are reserved only to members of the German master race, that the German *Herrenvolk* have the right to violate any and every treaty and pledge when it suits them, that dictatorship is the only normal regime of political life, that the most brutal terror is the best instrument of political discipline for a nation, that one master race, the German, Italian, or Japanese, is created to dominate the other nations.

Why do we fight? What are we fighting for and what are we fighting against? We do not ask this question because we do not know the answer, or because all these things are not clear to us, in spite of the complicated nature of contemporary international life. We ask this question in order to remind ourselves constantly of what must not be allowed to happen at any price after the war is over, and what we must do in the course of this war, and after victory has been achieved, so that it shall not happen again.

For nearly four years now the most terrible war which the world has ever seen has been raging. It is what the Nazis call total war. Men, women, and children are being slaughtered, towns and villages are being destroyed, ships are being sunk. Whole countries are being devastated, pillaged, and robbed.

Liberty and freedom have been suppressed by the brutal inter-loper, and entire populations terrorized in a most appalling manner. The whole world is threatened with the emergence of a regime in which the ruling power will be in the hands of people who have shown themselves to be international gangsters of the worst kind. And yet, even we, who know all this, ask each other: What are we fighting for?

We are fighting to eliminate the regimes of the Axis powers and the men responsible for those regimes that could sign a pledge at Munich, only to violate it a few months later when they treacherously occupied Prague; regimes and men that could negotiate in Athens, while they attacked Greece from Albania; regimes that were negotiating in Washington and at the same time treacherously attacking Pearl Harbor. We are fighting against the philosophy and action of international political gangsters.

It was our fate in Czechoslovakia to be a citadel of democracy placed next to a powerful country whose leaders believed in the totalitarian order. Our republic was founded at the end of the last war with the full blessing of the government and people of the United States. It was here in the United States that Masaryk and his friends issued the Czechoslovak Declaration of Independence. It was here that Masaryk was proclaimed the first President of the Czechoslovak Republic. We had thrown off the Hapsburg yoke, and were eager to lead a democratic way of life in Central Europe. We wanted to establish friendly relations with all our democratic neighbors, including the short-lived German Republic. One by one, our neighbors lost their faith in the democratic way of life, passed to authoritarianism and lost their freedom.

The evil genius was Hitler. He stood for the creed which he propounded in "Mein Kampf." His friends and followers were the men who have never abandoned their pan-German dream of world domination, and whose one desire was to reverse the military decision of 1918. It was unfortunate that his rise to power in Germany should have been taken so quietly by the rest of the world. His persecution of the Jews should have convinced the world that there could be no peace in Europe until Hitler had been driven from his seat of authority.

No doubt many well-intentioned people in America and elsewhere believed that the German people would rid themselves of Hitler as soon as he had destroyed certain features of the Versailles settlement which, rightly or wrongly, they disliked. But Hitler and his friends, always thinking of world domination, were not concerned mainly with the destruction of the Versailles settlement. They were determined to turn the whole German nation into one vast war machine. They stopped at nothing. All freedom of education, speech or thought was ruthlessly suppressed. The home itself was turned into a spying organization. Step by step the German leaders took all the strategic advantages they could before war actually began. The dispatch of German troops into the Rhineland in 1936 was the first military step. The occupation of Austria was the next. The demand for the German districts of Czechoslovakia followed, making possible the full occupation of Czechoslovakia in March 1939. Hitler believed with Bismarck that he who is master of Bohemia is also master of Europe. The taking of Austria imperiled Czechoslovakia. The taking of Czechoslovakia imperiled Poland. When he struck against Poland, he intended, as soon as possible, to swing his attack to the western democracies. The bastions of Czechoslovakia and Poland were thus the strongholds of France and Great Britain.

European democracy failed to realize its peril in time. We know now that in 1938 the western democracies were not ready for war. Public opinion in the whole world, though alert and very apprehensive, was not yet ready. Nazi propaganda successfully deceived opinion throughout the world as to the real aims of German policy. Many good men and women sincerely believed that the German minority in Czechoslovakia was the real reason and not a pretext for Hitler's attack against the happy and prosperous democratic Czechoslovakia. They took Hitler's word—for the last time—when he said that the cession of German districts in Czechoslovakia represented his last territorial demand in Europe. Six months later, when the Nazis marched into Prague, public opinion of the whole world knew better.

It knew that the sacrifice of Czechoslovakia had been made in vain. The policy of appeasement died overnight, and with British public opinion solidly behind him, Mr. Chamberlain gave Poland and Rumania the guarantees which had been denied to Czechoslovakia before the Munich dictate.

We in Czechoslovakia paid a very high price for the one extra year of so-called peace which the Munich decree gave to Europe. We do not say that the price was too high. We accepted the democratic way of life. We know that democracy has its drawbacks. A democratic government is answerable to its people. Public opinion is often slow to reach decisions. It can be persuaded, but not coerced. Democratic statesmanship must exercise endless patience. But when the mind of a democracy is made up nothing will deflect it from its course.

Democracy has a genuine hatred of war. It believes that the men who love peace are invariably greater than the men who love war. Its heroes are men who averted war or who went to war with the greatest reluctance. We had to face the Anglo-Saxon hatred of war at the time of the Munich crisis. It was perfectly understandable to me. But one year later the British people were mentally and physically ready for war. They have never turned back. They have magnificent leadership, and it is leadership of their own choosing. They will endure. I was with them during those heroic weeks beginning with the defeat of France up to the close of the Battle of Britain. They were in mortal danger, but they never admitted even the possibility of defeat.

They knew that the United States was arming for the defense of the democratic way of life. They knew that the American people were combating the philosophy of political gangsterdom. When Pearl Harbor came, it shocked the nation, but found it ready. You too will endure to the end. You too have magnificent leadership. Your soldiers bring comfort and encouragement to their friends, as they move along the bombed streets of London. They have won renown in North Africa. They are stubborn in defense and decisive in attack. Your great republic's will to victory is backing them. Against the combined strength of the United States, the Soviet Union, the

British Empire, China and the other United Nations, the Axis Powers *have never had* and *never will have* a chance for ultimate victory.

Through their own blundering and evil intentions the Axis Powers have brought into being a grand alliance known as the United Nations which is bound to be triumphant in the end. It will be triumphant, not merely because ·it represents the greatest aggregation of military power ever known in the world's history. It will be triumphant because the spirit of humanity and the trend of historical events are on its side. The Nazi creed represents reaction's last fling against the changing shape of things in the twentieth century. The new generations of the United Nations represent the new free and better postwar world. The new generation of the Axis Powers was educated for war and killing and to enslave others. That is one of the reasons why the Axis Powers are doomed beforehand.

And now for a few words about our collaboration with Soviet Russia. With the perspective of a quarter of a century after the event, we can see that the Russian Revolution of 1917 completed the work of the French Revolution of 1789. It was very violent. It had many features which the world outside the Soviet Union did not like. Time was needed before the barriers of misunderstanding could be removed. But Hitler was able—with remarkable success—to play against the democracies because of this hostility of the democratic world against the Soviet Union.

Hitler was not alone in underestimating the military preparedness, the ardor and the patriotism of the Russian people. It was he who finally brought the Russians and the English-speaking people together, for every American and every Englishman gloried in the defense of Moscow and the defense of Stalingrad, knowing that they were a curb to Hitler's evil and brutal domination. The Anglo-Soviet Pact brings to an end Soviet Russia's long exclusion from the affairs of Western Europe. Within its framework I believe all the outstanding problems of the European continent can be solved if the leaders are given sufficient time and have patience.

We in Czechoslovakia had worked for collaboration between the West and East of Europe for twenty years. We feared collaboration between Germany and Russia. We wished to prepare the way for the evolution of Soviet policy toward world democracy and collaboration with the democracies. Our republic was a liberal, socially advanced democracy, which differed profoundly from the Soviet Union. We intend to have a government responsible to the legislature again, and we mean to have a legislature which is in turn responsible to the electorate. We mean to have more democracy, if possible, than we had in the past, and to perfect a state in which a man can speak without fear and live without want. Our inspiration comes from George Washington, Abraham Lincoln, Woodrow Wilson, and from John Hus, Comenius and Masaryk. They worked for their own generation. We must work for ours. Our problems differ from theirs. Time has marched on, and a statesman who tries to put back the hands of the clock courts disaster. But all these leaders stand out in the minds of men because they lived, worked, in accordance with well established principles. Recurring upheavals seemed to undo the work they did, but the principles endure. If we are faithful to these principles, if we serve the cause of freedom with courage and singlemindedness, if we refuse to tamper with the true standards of democracy, we have no need to fear the future. Nor need we be afraid of the judgment of history.

We believe that the war collaboration with the Soviet Union will bring the United Nations into postwar collaboration in peace and democracy. We live in times which are almost without precedent, but with freedom as our goal we shall win. I sometimes hear the view expressed that the continent of Europe will be heavily policed when the war is over. I know well enough that the moral damage, let alone the material damage, will leave its mark upon Europe for a long time to come. Lives of millions have been broken. Men, once strong, will have to be nursed back to health. There are many pathetic casualties on the civilian front also. But I do not despair. No one who has faith in God and man need despair. Man, like nature, has an amazing recuperative power. In the stricken countries now under German occupation, men will make every effort to return to normal. They will be energetic again, hopeful and successful.

Returning to normal cannot, of course, mean returning to the state of affairs precisely as it was before Germany's aggressive march began. We have learned too much during the past four years of war. We must, somehow or other, overcome economic rivalry between nation and nation and between man and man. In my own country we shall not rest until we have reestablished our democratic way of life and secured freedom of speech, of assembly and press. Public opinion shall again be influential in Czechoslovakia. Our republic again will be one of the best democracies in Europe, happy and prosperous and perhaps one of the first completely restored and consolidated nations of Europe.

There has been no friction between the people of the United States and us at any time. Nor will there be any in the future. We know that your friendship for us is wholehearted and will remain so. The attitude which the United States adopts after the collapse of the Axis Powers and after the armistice is signed may determine the peace and happiness of generations to come. We hold your sympathy in high esteem; we admire your energy and determination in war. Your rocklike strength angers the Nazis. But the severest test still lies ahead. When it does come, your strength, your energy, your will, will be decisive for the victory, as they were in the First World War.

When four or five years after victory is ours, I come to Chicago again and when at some other great meeting we remember today and compare the conditions of Hitler's dominated Europe with the new postwar democratic peace, we shall be proud of what we have done for victory. We shall then better understand, too, what we are fighting for in this Second World War. Your historians will one day record your great fight against the Nazi-Fascist authoritarian powers and your victory over them, at the end of the first half of the twentieth century, as one of the greatest and most glorious periods in the national history of the United States of America.

WHAT IS IT THAT WE FIGHT? [5]

DENNA FRANK FLEMING [6]

Dr. D. F. Fleming gave this fifteen-minute broadcast over Station WSM, Nashville, Tennessee, on March 3, 1943, at 10:30 P.M. Central War Time. This talk was one of a weekly series begun by the speaker three years previously.

The series almost invariably treated a specific topic related to the war and our international relations. Topics in 1943 included "Geopolitics," "Toward Economic Peace in the Postwar Period," "Are the United Nations Due to Break Up?"

This commentator made it clear that "when it is clear to all Russians that we are punishing the German barbarians as much as they are, then we can talk to the Russians on a plane of sacrifice and performance." (Broadcast, March 10, 1943) He explained that Russia's apparent failure to cooperate with us at every point lay partly in the fact that "we can make war but not peace." (March 24, 1943) Concerning the break between the Polish exile government and Russia he said (April 28, 1943), "The vast bulk of us should be able to remember that there is no future whatever for Poland, and a very uncertain one for us, unless we win this world war, with the indispensable aid of Soviet Russia." The speaker (May 3, 1943) agreed with Willkie that "first, 'Russia is an effective society. It works. It has survival value'; second, 'Russia is an ally in this war'; and third, 'We must work with Russia after this war!' I do not see how anyone who has looked at the world lately can avoid these three conclusions about Russia."

Mr. Fleming as an undergraduate had excellent debate training. At the University of Illinois he was a member of the University teams debating the University of Wisconsin and Minnesota. His debate director was Lew Sarett, "one of the most stimulating teachers I ever had. I have always regarded my debate training as invaluable in the consideration of public issues. One is not likely to be effective in dealing with the controversial questions which crowd upon us unless one has the habit of keeping the opposition viewpoint in mind." [7]

Is Goebbels cracking our war front with his propaganda? Is he inducing us to forget which side we are on?

[5] By permission of Professor D. F. Fleming. Text provided through the courtesy of the speaker, and of Station WSM, Nashville, Tennessee.
[6] For biographical note see Appendix.
[7] Letter to the Editor, July 16, 1942.

In the winter of 1940 large and influential elements of the French people forgot which side of the war they were on. They forgot about the German-French war and went all-out against Russia in the Russian-Finnish war. By midsummer 1940 the same Frenchmen were surrendering France to Hitler, when she still had great fighting power left.

The recent Russian victories have enabled Propaganda Minister Goebbels to refurbish the old Bolshevik bogeyman and the effect, according to a *New York Times* dispatch from London, on February 27, has been "to unite various British and American elements which have always either feared or suspected the Soviet Union."

This is a distinctly alarming statement. It indicates that we had best ask ourselves what it is that we are fighting, because if we don't know with utter clarity we can lose our way, as France did.

We need to remember that we are fighting the cleverest attempt at world conquest ever made. Come with me for a moment back to that time from 1933 to 1936 when the Nazis were demanding "equality of rights." Wasn't that moderate of them? Just the right to have conscription and to fortify the Rhineland. The document proclaiming conscription oozed with peaceful words. The military seizure of the Rhineland, on March 7, 1936, was accompanied by fine words about friendly relations and by Hitler's statement, "We have no territorial demands to make in Europe."

But at once, in 1936, the Nazis raised a new demand: "the unification of all Germans." That, too, sounded quite reasonable to many Britishers and Americans. Under this banner Austria was conquered and the splendid Czech Republic broken to bits. "This," said Hitler on September 26, 1938, "is the last territorial demand which I have to make in Europe."

The German race had now been unified by two brutal conquests, so a third banner was raised in 1938—the cry for "living space"—*Lebensraum*. It was a false cry for Germany could have been highly prosperous if she had put half the zeal into peaceful work and trade that she was pouring into armaments and aggression. But the living-space cry fooled some of us. We said: "Well, Germany is a great industrial country. How can we keep her from dominating the agricultural states of Central Europe?" It took both the occupation of the rest of Czechoslovakia and the attack on Poland in 1938 and '39 to shock us into seeing that it wasn't living space the Germans wanted, but world domination.

It had been as clear as daylight all along, certainly since 1933, that this was the Nazi objective, but it was only after the fall of France in 1940 that the Nazis openly admitted it. Then they frequently and triumphantly proclaimed that that was it all along—world domination. A flood of boasts culminated in Hitler's speech of December 10, 1940, in which he declared that this is a war between two worlds, and that "one of them must break asunder." Which one it would be he left us in no doubt. It was the gullible democratic world which had still believed him when after seizing Austria he had said, "We want no Czechs," and when after smashing the Czechs he had assured the Poles that he stood firmly on his treaty of non-aggression with them. Are we now to be so simple as to forget this series of colossal deceptions and fall for the blandishments of the same set of Nazi liars?

But it is said that the Reds might spread Communism in Europe. Before we are unduly alarmed about that let us remember what the Nazis are doing to Europe. How can any man describe the Nazi crimes in a few minutes? But note some of the worst:

1. The Nazis are exterminating whole races. They are slaughtering the entire Jewish race in Europe. Enforced starvation does much of this work, but the Jews that remain are shipped to Poland for butchery. The Poles themselves have had their leaders massacred, their women prostituted, their people enslaved in both Germany and Poland, and their numbers greatly reduced by a dozen different means. The Serbs and the Greeks are undergoing similiar extermination. At least a million Serbs are already killed—men, women and children. Several million Russian civilians have been done to death and the German treatment of these people and of millions of Russian prisoners of war has been unspeakable.

It is the deliberate, often admitted, German policy to wipe out enough European peoples to make room for 250,000,000 Germans, just as soon as they can be bred by animal methods. The thing is so monstrous that it would be unbelievable if it were not actually being done. The Poles have been expelled in the dead of winter from large parts of their country. The French are being driven from Lorraine and the Germans have begun to move 3,000,000 Dutchmen from Holland to the wastes of Eastern Europe. France is being racially crippled by the Germans, deliberately, so that she will not recover for a century. All over Europe millions of children are dying or being warped for life because the Nazis will it.

2. The Germans have looted the whole wealth of Europe. Here again nothing is by accident. Everything is according to plan, from the wholesale pilfering of everything movable to the forced acquisition of land and factories. There are few business houses, banks, factories, or other properties anywhere in German Europe that have not been taken over by the master race. The loot passed fifty billion dollars' worth months ago, and it can never be measured in damage done to the people of Europe.

3. The Nazis intend to decivilize and paganize Europe. That is a serious charge, but it could be documented by the hour. Hitler declared to Rauschning his purpose to eradicate the thousands of years of human domestication from the youth of Germany and he has succeeded only too well. All youth is brutalized, pumped full of violent ideas to prepare them for permanent war and permanent rule over all the lesser races. Th full record is to be found in Gregor Ziemer's book, *Education for Death* (Oxford Press, New York, 1941).

Of course the Nazis intend to wipe out Christianity as a "Jewish invention." That only waits upon a German victory, but great progress has already been made. Fire worship has been revived and the worship of the ancient German gods, Thor and Wotan. A national anti-Christian church has been organized to feature Nazi rites under the swastika instead of the cross. The Catholic Church especially is marked for annihilation, because of its international connections and because of its strong resistance to Nazi barbarism.

Nor is there anything incidental about this. The Nazis are compelled to destroy Christianity, because their deeds violate every single Christian principle. Make a list for yourself of all the fruits of Christian teaching that you can think of: Belief in God, the brotherhood of man, honesty, fair dealings, truth, chastity, keeping one's word, respecting the rights and personality of others, tolerance of the views of other men, respect for property rights, advancement by one's own toil, helping the other fellow, obeying the laws, refraining from violence—extend the list as long as you can and you cannot find one single Christian way of living that the Fascists do not spurn and violate. They must destroy Christian civilization or give up their gangster ways of living.

Unless Europe can be released from the Nazi terror the whole continent is doomed to a terrible, strangling death. The birthplace and oldest center of European civilization will be blotted out.

That danger is so overwhelming and so acute that we can well afford not to lose too much sleep over what the Russians may do about this boundary or that. As compared to the conduct of the Germans, in every corner of Europe, the Russians have throughout this war conducted themselves as knights and gentlemen. If they should exact a terrible vengeance from Germany, no one could deny their right to do so or be certain that the world would be worse off. Nothing that the Reds could do in Europe could exceed barbarities which the Nazis have already committed. The German record is there—so black that nothing could exceed it.

Yet we have no evidence that the Russians will pursue a destructive policy in Europe. The Red leaders have demonstrated a high order of statesmanship during the past dozen years. They are certainly not to be compared to the maniacal perverts which rule Germany. We dislike the economics of the Soviets and believe our system is better, but that should not blind us to the evidence arising from the fires of this war that the Soviets are intent on creating a new civilization, instead of destroying an old one, as the Nazis are doing at breakneck speed.

THE MENACE OF JAPAN [8]

JOSEPH CLARK GREW [9]

The Honorable Joseph C. Grew gave this address before the Academy of Political Science, New York City, on November 10, 1942.

Mr. Grew returned in August after ten years as Ambassador at Tokyo. As soon as he landed from the exchange ship *Gripsholm* he began a series of speeches giving Americans the facts concerning the true character and aims of the Japanese and warning this nation of the immense latent military power of Nippon.

After Pearl Harbor an issue of military policy had constantly confronted not only our tacticians of the army and navy, but also of the American public: Shall we first whip Hitler and leave Japan for later punishment? Obviously, or so we believed, we had to do these jobs one at a time. Certainly Great Britain and Russia were to be supported in their holding operations against Germany; certainly, too, the United States was committed to a "second front" in Europe.

But those diplomats, military leaders, press representatives, and others well informed on the Far East felt strongly the apparent apathy of the American people toward the growing strength of Japan. Accordingly, the speeches pleading for more aggressive war in the Orient grew more numerous and more insistent in 1943. [10]

Ambassador Grew was an important contributor to the debate. He saw clearly both the favorable and the highly repulsive elements in Japanese character. In his "Last Hours in Tokyo" speech, broadcast from Washington on August 30, 1942, he said, "I have had many friends in Japan, some of whom I admired, respected, and loved. . . . For ten years I have broken bread in their homes and they in mine. . . . But there is another side to the picture—the ugly side of cruelty, brutality, and utter bestiality, the ruthlessness and utter viciousness of the Japanese military machine which brought on this war."

Mr. Grew was highly effective in his various appearances. He gave constant references to his own experience in Japan; he cited fact after fact concerning Japanese military methods; he diagnosed the psychological factors partly accounting for Japanese successes; he convinced by his own deep sincerity and by his somber but vigorous de-

[8] By permission of Mr. Grew. Text furnished through the courtesy of the speaker. See also *Vital Speeches*, Vol. 9, p. 155-7, December 15, 1942.

[9] For biographical note see Appendix.

[10] See introduction to Churchill's "Address to Congress," p. 30; also the introductions to Madame Chiang Kai-shek's addresses before Congress, p. 81, 85.

livery. Something of a Jeremiah was in his message and manner as
he addressed his responsive American audiences throughout the remainder of 1942.

For more than ten years it was my responsibility to act as
the representative of the United States in Tokyo. Throughout
that time I was aware of the portentousness of American-
Japanese relations. It is scarcely a confession for me to admit
to you that this responsibility was the weightiest—and at the
end, the most sorrowful—which I have ever borne. Yet in
coming before you tonight, I feel that I am carrying out a
mission even more urgent, even more weighty, than the one
I undertook in Tokyo. In Japan, I served as the representative
of the American people and government; with my colleagues
in the world-wide system of the Foreign Service, I sought to
hold America's diplomatic front against the threat of crisis
and war. But in coming before you tonight, I carry no formal
diploma. My mission is not to any one of you alone, but to
all of you. I am charged by my own knowledge of dangerous
truth to put that truth before you. I can succeed only if I
make this truth plain to each of you.

The truth I bring to you is simple. It is the story of the
power of our enemies, the Japanese. I bring this story to
you almost directly from Tokyo; it is not so many months
ago that I lived in the midst of our enemies, that I beheld
their power, and saw the "glory" which they thought their
weapons had achieved. Even in coming back to America, I
saw further evidences of the terrible power and successful
criminality of Japan. I saw one of the world's greatest naval
bases—Shonanko on Shonanto. A huge city fed the commercial and war fleets of victorious Japan. Rubber and oil
were plentiful—for Japan. Out of sight, but known to be
there, huge shipyards and drydocks worked for Japan. A cosmopolitan population, vast in number, and including thousands
and thousands of English-speaking prisoners, worked in bondage for Japan. That was *Shonan*—which is the Japanese phrase
for Southern Glory. Not so long ago, we knew it as Singapore.

We cannot and must not deceive ourselves about the war
in the Pacific. Japan launched the Northwestern and Far

Western Pacific campaigns. These were a war in themselves, and Japan has temporarily won that particular war. Japan has beaten us in the Philippines—and our allies in neighboring areas—as she has never beaten the Chinese in China. What we now face is a long, slow recovery of our own losses—only ultimately the attack on the enemy's own cities and bases—if we do not realize the magnitude of the task, and equip ourselves for it. We rejoice at each victory of our armed forces in the Solomons, forgetting that a few months ago the Solomons were uncontested British territory. We must remember that each victory won today is only a stepping-stone in the rolling back of Japan's advances.

Let me tell you why Japan succeeded. Let me present the case to you forthrightly and simply. To you, I am no representative of a foreign power, pleading for the recognition of a cause. I am your own former ambassador from Tokyo, and I plead for nothing but the truth. This truth can be put in three sentences:

Japan temporarily won the struggle for the Western Pacific because Japan was immensely strong—physically strong, technically strong, militarily strong, and most of all, psychologically strong.

Japan—the Empire of Nippon—was strong when the war started, but the new Japan—the great slave empire of the Greater East Asia—is today *potentially* the strongest power in the world.

Japan can be beaten; but Japan can be beaten only by physical and moral strength equal to or greater than her own, and that strength can be supplied only by the all-out effort of all Americans.

There you have it. These three sentences are all I have to tell. Some of you may see the picture, the whole picture, now. Others may prefer that I follow out, in general terms at least, the implications of these statements.

First, Japan is strong. Japan is not a little country. The Japanese are not a little people, except in stature, and they more than compensate for stature by vigor and skill. There are more Japanese than there are Englishmen, or Frenchmen, or Italians. Japan is about as populous as the German Reich, and each single Japanese is a part of an effective war machine. Man for man, nation for nation, Japan measures up to the highest standards of organized power in the modern world.

Japan is civilized, in her own way. This civilization is deep and beautiful, but its culture has a streak of brutality and subservience in it which makes Japanese ideals alien to ours or to the ideals of the Chinese, or any other of her neighbors. Japan was well ordered and metropolitan when New York, in our infant republic, was a small commercial port and Washington a scattered village in the thickets along the Potomac. At that time, the Emperor Napoleon never saw—perhaps never knew about—the largest city in the world he sought to conquer. That city was not his Paris, nor the London he sought to conquer, nor the Moscow where he met nemesis; that largest city was Yedo, which we know as Tokyo, where a vast dictatorship held a great urban culture under absolute and unrelenting control. Out of this old, big, rich, strange civilization, there emerged the power and brutality of modern Japan. It was no miracle that Japan adopted our machinery and our weapons so rapidly: Japanese civilization did it—despotic, sophisticated, military civilization.

Japan is unified, and pervasively governed. The Japanese live by their own rules. They swept ahead of Asia by the dictates of their rulers. They were accustomed to authoritarian, totalitarian government from the ages of their past growth. When Hitler was a maladjusted, unhappy student, and Mussolini an ardent young radical, the Japanese military leaders were men of foresight and ruthlessly cold vision. They already had an obedient, faithful people at their command— a people who believed in the rule of the warrior, in the *un*-freedom of the common man, in the superiority of the Japanese race to all others, and in the absolute incontrovertible rightness of what their government did. Japanese democracy never went behind these assumptions; Japanese freedom never included the freedom to challenge the *Kokutai*—literally the *national body*— of the Empire of Japan. Hitler fought the German people first, with the Stormtroopers and the SS., before he captured the German state and the German *Wehrmacht* as instruments of renewed attacks on free men; but the Japanese leaders never faced an effective opposition. They inherited their power from the dictatorial, military past of Japan; when the hour came for them to bid for wider power, perhaps for world dominion, they stepped smoothly into their inheritance. Today, we probably have spiritual allies among the German people; we have few among the Japanese. Whatever they may have believed, the Japanese today support their government. That is the difference between the raw new authoritarianism of Hitler, and the old suave authoritarianism of Japan. Germany will stand just so much, and will then collapse from within; the Japanese will stop fighting only when the last platoon of infantry, and the last torpedo-boat crew on the water, have no further hope. It is my considered opinion—and in the course of two years I have seen each at first hand—that as soldiers the Japanese are definitely superior to the Germans.

Civilized, unified, military, Japan is also up to date. In the big cities of Japan, skyscrapers float on pools of sand, ingeniously built to withstand the concussion of earthquake. The streets are asphalted, and clean. Busses and streetcars run regularly and well. Private homes are cheaply built, but simple and tasteful; the Japanese find them comfortable, and if one burns down, it costs a fraction of the cost of an equivalent American home to replace. The Japanese have extracted the best of their old thrift and the best of modern industrialism. They combine them. In the shadow of long-range electric power lines, the common peasants follow an intensive agriculture which keeps the home empire blockade-proof and self-sufficient. In the modern factories, which produce at speeds and standards equaling our own, the labor force lives by the old Japanese scale, and makes possible the price competition which we all knew before the war. This up-to-dateness of Japan, economically as well as psychologically, depends on the traditional Japan. The Japanese soldier or sailor who lives and fights like a Spartan is not undergoing privation; he has been a Spartan from birth. Just because a Japanese operates a battleship, a machine lathe, a modern locomotive, or a combat plane, he does not become un-Japanese; he is still a tough, simply satisfied man who believes in obedience and who is used to hard living because he has known no other. To call a Japanese worker or soldier a "coolie" is to forget the most dangerous thing about him: the fact that he, no less than you or I, is a man of the twentieth century and can fight, perhaps beat us at some of our own games and with some of our own weapons.

Such is the home Empire of Nippon. I do not have time to tell you of the internal sea communications which make of the Japanese Empire an immense, immobile and unmovable fleet—a fleet larger than the mind of man has ever dreamed of building—anchored forever close to the coast of Asia. Islands are unsinkable aircraft carriers, and Japan is all islands. Beyond this, I wish there were time to tell you of the newly built, up-to-date Japanese merchant marine, of the efficient navy, the huge army, the indispensable factories working at full time, the diversity and richness of the resources of Japan. You have known that these things were there; remember it now, keep it in mind, and consider with me what Japan has added.

To the home empire which I have described, Japan has added immense possessions in three wars of conquest—the war with China in 1895, the war with Russia in 1905, and the present war, which began in Manchuria in 1931. Japan has taken Korea, China's Manchurian provinces, the grain lands and coal and iron of North China, the dairy land of Inner Mongolia, the coast and main rivers of most of China, with the biggest cities of China; Japan has taken Formosa and Hainan, Indochina and Thailand, Burma and British Malaya, the vast empire of the Netherlands Indies, our daughter democracy of the Philippines, some of the British, Portuguese and Australian islands of the Southwest Pacific, and the strategic Andamans in the Bay of Bengal. Militarily and navally, this new and greater empire depends on internal communications, which—in simple language—means that we have to go the long way around while they work the short way through. To contain and roll back such an empire, the encircling forces cannot be merely equal; they must be superior, and be superior in geometric, not arithmetical, ratio. Economically—mark this, for here is the very essence of danger—*economically,* the so-called Greater East Asia contains everything, absolutely everything, which a great power needs. Grain, meat, fish, fruits, tobacco, palms for oil, sugar, rubber, oil, coal, iron, electric power, labor skilled and unskilled—all of this is there. The strong Japan which has defeated us and our allies momentarily in the Far East has become Japanese East Asia. If Japan could defeat indomitable China, organize her present holdings, consolidate her position, Japan—not Germany, not Britain, not Russia, not ourselves—*Japan* could become the strongest power in the world.

The Japanese need only one thing: time. They must try to correct their own political mistakes and military offenses. They must try to browbeat or cajole the peoples whose lands they have occupied. They must get the machinery, technical and financial, of exploitation going at full blast. Japan is entrenching herself in this empire of her conquests so rapidly that days are our most precious possessions in the war. To lose a day is as bad as losing a ship. We cannot wait. We cannot be leisurely. We cannot afford debate, or disunity, or indecison. Japan is getting stronger every hour, and this new Japan is not merely our equal; the new Japan is potentially our military superior. If we fight *there, soon,* and *hard,* we shall not have to fight here, later on, and with heavy handicap.

Do you not see the second of the truths I have stated: the fact that this new Japan, conceived in the invasion of China and born in the conquests of 1942, is a new, terrible power not known before in the world? We cannot let this slave empire become entrenched! I am sure that you cannot fail to see this.

As Americans, we can see the third truth in our own hearts. We know that there cannot be the slightest doubt of our own victory; but we must all see and understand that the task is a heavy one. China, the largest and most patient nation in the world, has stopped the thrust of Japanese invasion with the living bodies of her young men—indeed of men, women and children; she has built a new and unforgettable Great Wall with the heroic Chinese dead, who have died to protect free men in China and everywhere. But China has done her share, and more; China alone cannot defeat Japan. We must weigh and tip the scales to victory. We cannot accept an armistice or stalemate,—for the hours are with Japan, not with us. If we do not fight at our very hardest, and fight now, the period of our blood, sweat and tears may be *indefinitely and unnecessarily prolonged*. We cannot pause, or hesitate, or kill time— "as if you could kill time without injuring eternity!"

The Japanese are counting on our not being prepared to make great sacrifices. They have put great store in what they think to be our softness. They look upon us as constitutional weaklings, demanding our daily comforts and unwilling to make the sacrifices demanded for victory. The Japanese attach great importance to what they thought was our disunity over the war issue, and they count on us to delay before we develop a fighting spirit. That delay, they feel, will give them time to obtain complete control of all East Asia. When they struck, they made no provision for failure; they left no road open for retreat. Japan is counting on *you*—on each of us—one by one— to hold back and delay the American war effort long enough for Japan to consolidate her potential invincibility. Japan needs and relies upon your hesitation, or partial effort, or doubt. It is up to you and me to see that Japan does not get this.

If we act soon, we can strengthen our Chinese ally. We can, as Mr. Forrestal recently pointed out, continue to protect Russia's Asiatic flank by holding Japan's forces in the Pacific. We can restore hope and can carry the four freedoms to all the peoples now enslaved by Japan. If we fight and give aid now, we shall still have allies in Asia, bases in Asia, and an enemy not yet wholly prepared. Any advantages of delay to-day can be purchased only at one price: larger numbers of deaths of our own soldiers and our allies' today and tomorrow. We can buy additional hours for leisurely preparation with additional lives of our young men. We could buy peace only with our national honor and our own security. None of us wants to do this.

We must, therefore, be prepared to go forward against Japan with a full realization of the nature of our task and the gravity of our responsibility. Every adult in the United States, even every child that can walk and speak, can help in some way to promote the war effort. The troops are only the fighting front of the army which is America. We are all enlisted—of necessity—in this war for freedom. In this battle, we can do no better than to recall and to make our own resolve in the words of an American soldier, Martin Treptow, who fell at Chateau Thierry. He wrote in his diary,

"I will work; I will save; I will sacrifice; I will endure; I will fight cheerfully and do my utmost; *as if the whole struggle depended on me alone.*"

FIGHTING FOR THE COMMON CAUSE [11]

Madame Chiang Kai-shek [12]

Madame Chiang Kai-shek delivered this speech in the United States Senate on February 18, 1943. The address was given soon after twelve o'clock. Preceding her entry Senator Barkley of Kentucky said, "Mr. President, the Senate is to be honored by a visit from one of the outstanding women of the world and of this generation. I, therefore, ask unanimous consent that the Senate stand in recess subject to the call of the Chair, following the visit of Madame Chiang Kai-shek, and that the Chair appoint a committee of five to escort her into the Chamber. . . ."

The Chief Justice of the United States, Harlan Stone, Associate Justices Reed, Frankfurter, Jackson, and Rutledge, Jesse Jones, Secretary of Commerce, and Frances Perkins, Secretary of Labor; members of the party accompanying the distinguished visitor, including L. K. Kung, Dr. Wei Tao-ming, Ambassador of China to the United States, Madame T. V. Soong and others took seats to the right and left of Vice President Wallace's desk.

Madame Chiang was greeted with prolonged applause, the Senators and guests rising. Said Vice President Wallace, "Senators, Distinguished Guests: Madame Chiang Kai-shek, wife of the Generalissimo of the Armies of China, will now address you."

The talk was a splendid illustration of an effective extempore speech. It was personal, humorous, anecdotal, yet logical in its treatment of a highly important point—the necessity for American action as well as for purpose. Seldom does the Senate rise to its feet to applaud. For this speaker it both rose and thundered prolonged approval.

Mr. President, Members of the Senate of the United States, Ladies and Gentlemen:

I am overwhelmed by the warmth and spontaneity of the welcome of the American people, of whom you are the representatives. I did not know that I was to speak to you today at the Senate except to say "How do you do? I am so very glad to see you," and to bring the greetings of my people to the people of America. However, just before coming here, the

[11] From the *Congressional Record*, v. 89, no. 28, p. 1114-15, February 18, 1943 (daily edition), 78th Congress, first session.
[12] For biographical note see Appendix.

Vice President told me that he would like to have me say a few words to you.

I am not a very good extemporaneous speaker; in fact, I am no speaker at all. But I am not so very much discouraged, because a few days ago I was at Hyde Park and went to the President's library. Something I saw there encouraged me and made me feel that perhaps you will not expect over much of me in speaking to you extemporaneously.

What do you think I saw there? I saw many things, but the one thing which interested me most of all was that in a glass case there was the first draft of one of the President's speeches, a second draft, and on and on up to the sixth draft. Yesterday I happened to mention this fact to the President, and told him that I was extremely glad that he had to write so many drafts when he is such a well known and acknowledgedly fine speaker. His reply to me was that sometimes he writes twelve drafts of a speech. So my remarks here today being extemporaneous, I am sure you will make allowances for me.

The traditional friendship between your country and mine has a history of a hundred and sixty years. I feel and I believe that I am not the only one who feels this way, that there are a great many similarities between your people and mine, and that these similarities are the basis of our friendship.

I should like to tell you a little story which will illustrate this belief. When General Doolittle and his men went to bomb Tokyo, on their return some of your boys had to bail out in the interior of China. One of them later told me that he had to bail out of his ship, and that when he landed on Chinese soil and saw the populace running toward him, he just waved his arm and shouted the only Chinese word he knew, "Mei-kuo, mei-kuo," which means "America." Literally translated from the Chinese it means "beautiful country." This boy said that our people laughed and almost hugged him, and greeted him like a long lost brother. He further told me that he thought that he had come home when he saw our people; and that was the first time he had ever been to China.

I came to your country as a little girl. I know your people. I have lived with them. I spent the formative years of my life among your people. I speak your language, not only the language of your hearts, but also your tongue. So coming here today I feel that I am also coming home.

I believe, however, that it is not only I who am coming home; I feel that if the Chinese people could speak to you in your own tongue, or if you could understand our tongue, they would tell you that basically and fundamentally we are fighting for the same cause, that we have identity of ideals, that the Four Freedoms which your President proclaimed to the world resound throughout our vast land as the gong of freedom, the gong of freedom of the United Nations, and the death-knell of the aggressors.

I assure you that our people are willing and eager to co-operate with you in the realization of these ideals, because we want to see to it that they do not echo as empty phrases but become realities, for ourselves, for our children, for our children's children, and for all mankind.)

How are we going to realize these ideals? I think I shall tell you a little story which just came to my mind. You know China is a very old nation. We have a history of five thousand years. When we were obliged to evacuate Hankow and go into the hinterland to carry on and continue our resistance against aggression, the Generalissimo and I passed one of our fronts, the Changsha front.

One day we went into the Heng-Yang Mountains, where there are traces of a famous pavilion called "Rub-the-Mirror" pavilion, which was built over two thousand years ago. It will perhaps interest you to hear the story of that pavilion.

Two thousand years ago near that spot was an old Buddhist temple. One of the young monks went there, and all day long he sat cross-legged with his hands clasped before him in an attitude of prayer, and murmured "Amita-Buddha! Amita-Buddha! Amita-Buddha!" He murmured and chanted day after day, because he hoped that he would acquire grace.

The Father Prior of that temple took a piece of brick and rubbed it against a stone hour after hour, day after day, and week after week. The little acolyte, being very young, sometimes cast his eyes around to see what the old Father Prior was doing. The old Father Prior just kept on his work of rubbing the brick against the stone. So one day the young acolyte said to him, "Father Prior, what are you doing day after day rubbing this brick on the stone"?

The Father Prior replied, "I am trying to make a mirror out of this brick." The young acolyte said, "But it is impossible to make a mirror out of a brick, Father Prior." "Yes," said the Father Prior, "it is just as impossible for you to acquire grace by doing nothing except 'Amita-Buddha' all day long, day in and day out."

So, my friends, I feel that it is necessary for us not only to have ideals and to proclaim that we have them, it is necessary that we act to implement them. And so to you, gentlemen of the Senate, and to you ladies and gentlemen in the galleries, I say that without the active help of all of us our leaders cannot implement these ideals. It is up to you and to me to take to heart the lesson of "Rub-the-Mirror" pavilion.

I thank you.

JAPAN IS FIRST UNITED STATES FOE [13]

Madame Chiang Kai-shek [14]

Soon after 12:30 o'clock, on February 18, following her address to the Senate, Madame Chiang Kai-shek was escorted to the Speaker's rostrum in the House of Representatives. Speaker Samuel Rayburn, of Texas, introduced her: "Members of the House of Representatives, it is a proud day for the United States of America to receive and do honor to one of the outstanding women of all the earth. She is the helpmeet and the coworker of one of the outstanding figures of the world. It is my great pleasure, my high privilege, and my distinguished honor to present to you Madame Chiang Kai-shek."

She spoke from a manuscript. It had been weeks in the making. Her technique of audience adaptation and persuasion was highly effective. Obviously, she was an experienced speaker.

She began by complimenting the Congressmen. Then she referred to the pride Americans should have in "their fighting men in so many parts of the world," and dwelt at some length on those "unsung heroes of the war." Subtly she referred to the American army as composed of "first-generation Germans, Italians, Frenchmen," and so on—"but there they were—all Americans." Her application was obvious: "The identity of ideals is the strongest possible solvent of racial dissimilarities." Her approach to her theme, "We must now so prosecute the war that victory will be ours decisively and with all good speed," was thus gradual and disarming.

She stated directly and without qualification that Japan should be the Number-One Enemy in this war. She thrust directly at America's indecisive military policy in the Far East; she gave no special plea for help. She spoke as an equal. Her references to the planning for a postwar world were statesman-like.

The entire speech was logically woven together, reasonable in its analysis, progressing to its solution of the inevitable connection between the immediate military and later political victories in the Orient, couched in personal terms, interspersed with quotations from Chinese philosophy, and expressed in language somewhat stilted (e. g. "gallant allies will not be obtunded by the mirage of contingent reasons of expediency").

Her English articulation had little foreign trace; present was the inflection of Georgia, where she spent part of her girlhood. Her voice

[13] From the *Congressional Record*, v. 89, no. 28, p. 1142-43, February 18, 1943 (daily edition), 78th Congress, first session.
[14] For biographical note see Appendix.

had excellent carrying power; was modulated, yet intense; it conveyed her deep conviction. "It was the woman, the way she clutched her handkerchief and brought her tight hand on the desk for emphasis, the flash in her eyes which reflected something deep in her experience." (*Time,* March 1, 1943, p. 23)

The speech was dramatically moving in its effect upon the Congressmen. At least one member testified that he was "on the verge of bursting into tears." (*Time,* March 1, 1943, p. 23.) Wrote Edward Angly, of the *Chicago Sun* (February 19, 1943), "Madame Chiang was both a stunning and appealing figure. . . . Her English was impeccable. Indeed so perfect was her command of the language that there seemed nothing strange that a Chinese woman should be telling an American Congress about American soldiers whose accents struck her as 'so thick one could not cut them with a butter knife.' . . . And the whole was spoken with such firmness, dignity and charm that afterward Senators and Congressmen alike went about the remainder of the day using their most rhapsodic rhetoric in praise of her."

Following this day of speech-making in Washington, Madame Chiang gave highly successful speeches in Madison Square Garden, New York, in Chicago, in San Francisco, and elsewhere across the nation. Thus did she, through the spoken word, strengthen American public opinion in support of China and in the full prosecution of our war against Nippon.

At any time, it would be a privilege for me to address Congress, more especially this present august body which will have so much to do in shaping the destiny of their world. In speaking to Congress I am literally speaking to the American people. The Seventy-seventh Congress, as their representatives, fulfilled the obligations and responsibilities of its trust by declaring war on the aggressors. That part of the duty of the people's representatives was discharged in 1941. The task now confronting you is to help win the war and to create and uphold a lasting peace which will justify the sacrifices and sufferings of the victims of aggression.

Before enlarging on this subject, I should like to tell you a little about my long and vividly interesting trip to your country from my own land which has bled and borne unflinchingly the burden of war for more than five and a half years.

I shall not dwell, however, upon the part China has played in our united effort to free mankind from brutality and violence. I shall try to convey to you, however imperfectly, the impressions gained during the trip.

First of all, I want to assure you that the American people have every right to be proud of their fighting men in so many parts of the world. I am particularly thinking of those of your boys in the far-flung, out-of-the-way stations and areas where life is attended by dreary drabness—this because their duty is not one of spectacular performance and they are not buoyed up by the excitement of battle. They are called upon, day after colorless day, to perform routine duties such as safeguarding defenses and preparing for possible enemy action. It has been said, and I find it true from personal experience, that it is easier to risk one's life on the battlefield than it is to perform customary humble and humdrum duties which, however, are just as necessary to winning the war.

Some of your troops are stationed in isolated spots, quite out of reach of ordinary communications. Some of your boys have had to fly hundreds of hours over the sea from an improvised airfield in quests, often disappointingly fruitless, of enemy submarines. They, and others, have to stand the monotony of waiting—just waiting. But, as I told them, true patriotism lies in possessing the moral and physical stamina to perform faithfully and conscientiously the daily tasks so that in the sum total the weakest link is the strongest.

Your soldiers have shown conclusively that they are able stoically to endure homesickness, the glaring dryness and scorching heat of the tropics, and keep themselves fit and in excellent fighting trim. They are among the unsung heroes of this war, and everything possible to lighten their tedium and buoy up their morale should be done. That sacred duty is yours.

The American army is better fed than any army in the world. This does not mean, however, that they can live indefinitely on canned food without having the effects tell on them. These admittedly are the minor hardships of war, especially when we pause to consider that in many parts of the world, starvation prevails. But, peculiarly enough, oftentimes it is not the major problems of existence which irk a man's soul; it is rather the pinpricks, especially those incidental to a life of deadly sameness, with tempers frayed out and nervous systems torn to shreds.

The second impression of my trip is that America is not only the cauldron of democracy, but the incubator of democratic principles. At some of the places I visited, I met the crews of your air bases. There I found first-generation Germans, Italians, Frenchmen, Poles, Czechoslovakians, and other nationals. Some of them had accents so thick that, if such a thing were possible, one could not cut them with a butter knife.

But there they were—all Americans, all devoted to the same ideals, all working for the same cause and united by the same high purpose. No suspicion or rivalry existed among them. This increased my belief and faith that devotion to common principles eliminates differences in race, and that identity of ideals is the strongest possible solvent of racial dissimilarities.

I have reached your country, therefore, wth no misgivings, but with my belief that the American people are building and carrying out a true pattern of the nation conceived by your forebears, strengthened and confirmed. You, as representatives of the American people, have before you the glorious opportunity of carrying on the pioneer work of your ancestors, beyond the frontiers of physical and geographical limitations. Their brawn and thews braved undaunted almost unbelievable hardships to open up a new continent.

The modern world lauds them for their vigor and intensity of purpose, and for their accomplishment. You have today before you the immeasurably greater opportunity to implement these same ideals and to help bring about the liberation of man's spirit in every part of the world. In order to accomplish this purpose, we of the United Nations must now so prosecute the war that victory will be ours decisively and with all good speed.

Sun-tse, the well-known Chinese strategist, said: "In order to win, know thyself and thy enemy." We have also the saying: "It takes little effort to watch the other fellow carry the load."

In spite of these teachings from a wise old past, which are shared by every nation, there has been a tendency to belittle the strength of our opponents.

When Japan thrust total war on China in 1937, military experts of every nation did not give China even a ghost of a chance. But, when Japan failed to bring China cringing to her knees as she vaunted, the world took solace in this phenomenon by declaring that they had overestimated Japan's military might.

Nevertheless, when the greedy flames of war inexorably spread in the Pacific following the perfidious attack on Pearl Harbor, Malaya and lands in and around the China Sea, and one after another of these places fell, the pendulum swung to the other extreme. Doubts and fears lifted their ugly heads and the world began to think that the Japanese were Nietzschean supermen, superior in intellect and physical prowess, a belief which the Gobineaus and the Houston Chamberlains and their apt pupils, the Nazi racists, had propounded about the Nordics.

Again, now the prevailing opinion seems to consider the defeat of the Japanese as of relative unimportance and that Hitler is our first concern. This is not borne out by actual facts, nor is it to the interests of the United Nations as a whole to allow Japan to continue, not only as a vital potential threat, but as a waiting sword of Damocles, ready to descend at a moment's notice.

Let us not forget that Japan in her occupied areas today has greater resources at her command than Germany. Let us not forget that the longer Japan is left in undisputed possession of these resources, the stronger she must become. Each passing day takes more toll in lives of both Americans and Chinese.

Let us not forget that the Japanese are an intransigent people. Let us not forget that during the first four and a half years of total aggression China has borne Japan's sadistic fury unaided and alone.

The victories won by the United States Navy at Midway and the Coral Sea are doubtless steps in the right direction— they are merely steps in the right direction—for the magnificent fight that was waged at Guadalcanal during the past six months attests to the fact that the defeat of the forces of evil, though long and arduous, will finally come to pass. For have we not on the side of righteousness and justice staunch allies in Great Britain, Russia and other brave and indomitable peoples? Meanwhile the peril of the Japanese juggernaut remains. Japanese military might must be decimated as a fighting force before its threat to civilization is removed.

When the Seventy-seventh Congress declared war against Japan, Germany and Italy, Congress, for the moment, had done its work. It now remains for you, the present representatives of the American people, to point the way to win the war, to help construct a world in which all peoples may henceforth live in harmony and peace.

May I not hope that it is the resolve of Congress to devote itself to the creation of the postwar world? To dedicate itself to the preparation for the brighter future that a stricken world so eagerly awaits?

We of this generation who are privileged to help make a better world for ourselves and for posterity should remember that, while we must not be visionary, we must have vision so that peace should not be punitive in spirit and should not be provincial or nationalistic or even continental in concept, but universal in scope and humanitarian in action, for modern science has so annihilated distance that what affects one people must of necessity affect all other peoples.

The term "hands and feet" is often used in China to signify the relationship between brothers. Since international inter-dependence is now so universally recognized, can we not also say that all nations should become members of one corporate body?

The hundred and sixty years of traditional friendship between our two great peoples, China and America, which has never been marred by misunderstandings, is unsurpassed in the annals of the world. I can also assure you that China is eager and ready to cooperate with you and other peoples to lay a true and lasting foundation for a sane and progressive world society which would make it impossible for any arrogant or predatory neighbor to plunge future generations into another orgy of blood.

In the past China has not computed the cost to her manpower in her fight against aggression, although she well realized that manpower is the real wealth of a nation and it takes generations to grow it. She has been soberly conscious of her responsibilities, and has not concerned herself with privileges and gains which she might have obtained through compromise of principles. Nor will she demean herself and all she holds dear to the practice of the market place.

We in China, like you, want a better world, not for ourselves alone, but for all mankind, and we must have it. It is not enough, however, to proclaim our ideals or even to be convinced that we have them. In order to preserve, uphold and maintain them, there are times when we should throw all we cherish into our effort to fulfill these ideals, even at the risk of failure.

The teachings drawn from our late leader, Dr. Sun Yat-sen, have given our people the fortitude to carry on. From five and a half years of experience we in China are convinced that it is the better part of wisdom not to accept failure ignominiously, but to risk it gloriously. We shall have faith that, at the writing of peace, America and our other gallant allies will not be obtunded by the mirage of contingent reasons of expediency.

Man's mettle is tested both in adversity and in success. Twice is this true of the soul of a nation.

AMERICA AND GREAT BRITAIN IN THE POSTWAR WORLD [10]

AMERICA'S PART IN WORLD RECONSTRUCTION [1]

HENRY A. WALLACE [2]

This address was broadcast by the National Broadcasting Company under the sponsorship of the Woodrow Wilson Foundation, on the eighty-sixth anniversary of the birthday of Woodrow Wilson, December 28, 1942. The address was originally prepared for delivery at the joint annual meeting of the American Society for Public Administration and the American Political Science Association in Chicago. When transportation difficulties led to the cancellation of the meeting, Mr. Wallace consented to give his paper by radio.

The speaker expressed the typical philosophy of those American liberals who stood squarely for postwar international cooperation. Here are found the suggestions that (1) the situation at the end of the war will more or less parallel that of America in 1787; (2) the League of Nations failed because it "was not strong enough"; (3) Woodrow Wilson was a great leader, the F. D. Roosevelt of his day; (4) the isolationists, not ready for world unity, were through their "action or lack of action" responsible for the anarchy and the huge losses of the Second World War; (5) an international organization of the United Nations must be set up to disarm Germany, Japan, and Italy; (6) the organization must allow a maximum of home rule, but with sufficient central authority to preserve peace and to supervise trade relations; (7) the organization must supervise or "inspect" the educational systems of Germany and Japan; (8) the United States and the world must protect themselves from inflation and the "economic storms"; (9) from motives of self-interest alone, we must attempt to raise world-wide economic standards of living; (10) in this country we must continue to provide full employment, both in cities and on farms; (11) we must keep prices under control; (12) industry must cooperate in this program of maximum production and of full employment; (13) under this program of the "new democracy," liberty and freedom for the common man will result.

[1] From the *Congressional Record,* v. 89, no. 2, p. 25-7, January 7, 1943 (daily edition), 78th Congress, first session. Reprinted by permission of Vice President Wallace. Text furnished through the courtesy of the speaker.
[2] For biographical note see Appendix.

The address covered too much ground, contained too many ideas, for the average radio listener to assimilate. Each proposition or principle enumerated needed concrete and plausible analysis and explication. Mr. Wallace himself followed in other speeches with further interpretations of his postwar world philosophy. [3]

For the people of the United States, the war is entering its grimmest phase. At home, we are beginning at last to learn what war privations mean. Abroad, our boys in ever greater numbers are coming to grips with the enemy. Yet even while warfare rages on, and we of the United Nations are redoubling our great drive for victory, there is dawning the hope of that day of peace, however distant, when the lights will go on again, all over the world.

Adolf Hitler's desperate bid for a Nazi world order has reached and passed its highest point and is on its way to its ultimate downfall. The equally sinister threat of world domination by the Japanese is doomed eventually to fail. When the Hitler regime finally collapses and the Japanese warlords are smashed, an entirely new phase of world history will be ushered in. The task of our generation—the generation which President Roosevelt once said has a "rendezvous with destiny"— is so to organize human affairs that no Adolf Hitler, no power-hungry warmongers, whatever their nationality, can ever again plunge the whole world into war and bloodshed.

The situation in the world today is parallel in some ways to that in the United States just before the adoption of the Constitution, when it was realized that the Articles of Confederation had failed and that some stronger union was needed.

Today, measured by travel time, the whole world is actually smaller than was our little country then. When George Washington was inaugurated, it took *seven* days to go by horse-drawn vehicle from Mount Vernon to New York. Now army bombers are flown from the United States to China and India in less than *three* days.

[3] Cf. "The Price of Free World Victory," *Representative American Speeches*: *1941-42*, p. 47-55 ; see also "Practical Religion for Tomorrow," infra, p. 276.

It is in this suddenly shrunken world that the United Nations, like our thirteen American states in 1787, soon will be faced with a fundamental choice. We know now that the League of Nations, like our own union under the Articles of Confederation, was not strong enough. The League never had American support, and at critical moments it lacked the support of some of its own members. The League finally disintegrated under the successive blows of world-wide economic depression and a second World War. Soon the nations of the world will have to face this question: Shall the world's affairs be so organized as to prevent a repetition of these twin disasters—the bitter woe of depression and the holocaust of war?

It is especially appropriate to discuss this subject on this particular date, because it is the birthday of Woodrow Wilson, who gave up his health and eventually his life in the first attempt, a generation ago, to preserve the world's peace through united world action. At that time, there were many who said that Wilson had failed. Now we know that it was the world that failed, and the suffering and war of the last few years is the penalty it is paying for its failure.

When we think of Woodrow Wilson, we know him not only for his effort to build a permanent peace but for the progressive leadership he gave our country in the years before that First World War. The "New Freedom" for which Wilson fought was the forerunner of the Roosevelt "New Deal" of 1933 and of the world-wide new democracy which is the goal of the United Nations in this present struggle.

Wilson, like Jefferson and Lincoln before him, was interested first and always in the welfare of the common man. And so the ideals of Wilson and the fight he made for them are an inspiration to us today as we take up the torch he laid down.

Resolved as we are to fight on to final victory in this world-wide people's war, we are justified in looking ahead to the peace that will inevitably come. Indeed, it would be the height of folly not to prepare for peace, just as in the years prior to December 7, 1941, it would have been the height of folly not to prepare for war.

As territory previously overrun by the Germans and the Japs is reoccupied by the forces of the United Nations, measures of relief and rehabilitation will have to be undertaken. Later, out of the experience of those temporary measures of relief, there will emerge the possibilities and the practicalities of more permanent reconstruction.

We cannot now blueprint all the details, but we *can* begin now to think about some of the guiding principles of this world-wide new democracy we of the United Nations hope to build.

Two of these principles must be liberty and unity, or in other words, home rule and centralized authority, which for more than a hundred and fifty years have been foundation stones of our American democracy and our American union.

When Woodrow Wilson proposed the League of Nations, it became apparent that these same principles of liberty and unity—of home rule and centralized authority—needed to be applied among the nations if a repetition of the First World War was to be prevented. Unfortunately the people of the United States were not ready. They believed in the doctrine of liberty in international affairs, but they were not willing to give up certain of their international rights and to shoulder certain international duties, even though other nations were ready to take such steps. They were in the position of a strong, well-armed pioneer citizen who thought he could defend himself against robbers without going to the expense and bother of joining with his neighbors in setting up a police force to uphold civil law. They stood for decency in international affairs, but in the world of practical international politics the net effect of their action or lack of action was anarchy and the loss of millions of lives and hundreds of billions of dollars in a second world war.

The sturdy pioneer citizen, proud of his own strength and independence, needed to be robbed and beaten only once by bandits to be ready to cooperate with his law-abiding neighbors. I believe the United States also has learned her lesson and that she is willing to assume a responsibility proportionate to her strength. England, Russia, China, and most of the other United Nations are perhaps even more eager than the United States to go beyond the Charter which they have signed as a declaration of principles. The United Nations, like the United States a hundred and fifty-five years ago, are groping for a formula which will give the greatest possible liberty without producing anarchy and at the same time will not give so many rights to each member nation as to jeopardize the security of all.

Obviously the United Nations must first have machinery which can disarm and keep disarmed those parts of the world which would break the peace. Also there must be machinery for preventing economic warfare and enhancing economic peace between nations. Probably there will have to be an international court to make decisions in cases of dispute. And an international court presupposes some kind of world council, so that whatever world system evolves will have enough flexibility to meet changing circumstances as they arise.

As a practical matter, we may find that the regional principle is of considerable value in international affairs. For example, European countries, while *concerned* with the problems of Pan America, should not have to be *preoccupied* with them, and likewise Pan America, while *concerned,* should not have to be *preoccupied* with the problems of Europe. Purely regional problems ought to be left in regional hands. This would leave to any federated world organization problems involving broad principles and those practical matters which affect countries of different regions or which affect the whole world.

The aim would be to preserve the liberty, equality, security, and unity of the United Nations—liberty in a political sense, equality of opportunity in international trade, security against war and business depression due to international causes, and unity of purpose in promoting the general welfare of the world.

In other words, the aim would be the maximum of home rule that can be maintained along with the minimum of centralized authority that must come into existence to give

the necessary protection. We in the United States must remember this: If we are to expect guarantees against military
or economic aggression from other nations, we must be willing
to give guarantees that we will not be guilty of such aggression ourselves. We must recognize, for example, that it is
perfectly justifiable for a debtor, pioneer nation to build up
its infant industries behind a protective tariff, but a creditor
nation can be justified in high-tariff policies only from the
standpoint of making itself secure in case of war.

A special problem that will face the United Nations
immediately upon the attainment of victory over either Germany or Japan will be what to do with the defeated nation.
Revenge for the sake of revenge would be a sign of barbarism
—but this time we must make absolutely sure that the guilty
leaders are punished, that the defeated nation realizes its
defeat and is not permitted to rearm. The United Nations
must back up the military disarmament with psychological
disarmament—supervision, or at least inspection, of the school
systems of Germany and Japan to undo so far as possible
the diabolical work of Hitler and the Japanese warlords in
poisoning the minds of the young.

Without doubt, in the building of a new and enduring
peace, economic reconstruction will play an all-important role.
Unless there is careful planning in advance, the return of
peace can in a few years bring a shock even worse than the
shock of war.

The magnitude of the problem here in the United States,
for example, is indicated by the probability that in the peak
year of the war we shall be spending something like 90
billion dollars of public funds in the war effort, whereas two
years later we may be spending less than 20 billion dollars
for military purposes. In the peak year of the war effort,
it is probable that we shall have around 10 million men in
the armed services and 20 million additional men and women
producing war goods for the armed services. It would seem
that within the first two years after the peace at least 15
million of these 30 million men and women will be seeking
jobs different from those which they had when peace came.

Our expenditures have been going on at a rate fully seven times as great as in World War No. 1 and the conversion of our industry to wartime uses has been far more complete. Thousands of thoughtful businessmen and economists, remembering what happened after the last war, being familiar with the fantastic figures of this war, and knowing the severity of the shock to come, have been greatly disturbed. Some have concerned themselves with plans to get over the first year. Others have given thought to the more distant future.

It should be obvious to practically everyone that, without well-planned and vigorous action, a series of economic storms will follow this war. These will take the form of inflation and temporary scarcity, perhaps, followed by surpluses, crashing prices, unemployment, bankruptcy, and in some cases violent revolution. If there is lack of well-planned and vigorous action, it is quite conceivable that the human misery in certain countries after the war may be even greater than during the war.

It is true that in the long run any nation, like any individual, must follow the principle of self-help, must look to its own efforts to raise its own living standards. But it is also true that stronger nations, like our own, can provide guidance, technical advice, and in some cases capital investment to help those nations which are just starting on the path of industrialization. Our experience with the Philippines is a case in point.

The suggestions I have made with a view to promoting development and encouraging higher standards of living are necessarily fragmentary at this time. But in some quarters, either knowingly or unknowingly, they have been grossly distorted and misrepresented. During the recent political campaign one member of Congress seeking reelection made the flat statement that I was in favor of having American farmers give away a quart of milk a day to every inhabitant of the world. In other quarters these suggestions have been referred to by such terms as "utopian," "soggy sentimentality," and the "dispensing of milk and honey." But is it "utopian" to foresee that South America, Asia, and Africa will in the future experience a development of industry and agriculture comparable to what has been the experience in the past in Europe and North America? Is it "soggy sentimentality" to hold out hope to those millions in Europe and Asia fighting for the cause of human freedom—our freedom? Is it the "dispensing of milk and honey" to picture to their minds the possible blessings of a higher standard of living when the war is over and their own productivity has increased?

Among the self-styled "realists" who are trying to scare the American people by spreading worry about "misguided idealists" giving away United States products are some whose policies caused us to give away billions of dollars of stuff in the decade of the twenties. Their high tariff prevented exchange of our surplus for goods, and so we exchanged our surplus for bonds of very doubtful value. Our surplus will be far greater than ever within a few years after this war comes to an end. We can be decently human and really hardheaded if we exchange our postwar surplus for goods, for peace, and for improving the standard of living of so-called backward peoples. We can get more for our surplus production in this way than by any high-tariff, penny-pinching, isolationist policies which hide under the cloak of 100 per cent Americanism.

Self-interest alone should be sufficient to make the United States deeply concerned with the contentment and well-being of the other peoples of the world. For, as President Roosevelt has pointed out, such contentment will be a practical guarantee of world peace and it is only when other peoples are prosperous and economically productive that we can find satisfactory export markets among them for the products of our factories and our farms.

A world family of nations cannot be really healthy unless the various nations in that family are getting along well in their own internal affairs. The first concern of each nation must be the well-being of its own people. That is as true of the United States as of any other nation.

During the war we have full employment here in the United States, and the problem is not to find jobs for the workers but to find workers for the jobs. After the war it will be vital to make sure that another period of unemployment does not come on. With this end in view, the suggestion has been made that Congress should formally recognize the maintenance of full employment as a declared national policy, just as it now recognizes as national policies the right of farmers to parity of income with other groups and the right of workers to unemployment insurance and old-age annuities.

Full employment is vital not only to city prosperity but to farm prosperity as well. Nothing contributes more to stable farm prosperity than the maintenance of full employment in the cities and the assurance that purchasing power for both farm and factory products will always be adequate.

Maintenance of full employment and the highest possible level of national income should be the joint responsibility of private business and of government. It is reassuring to know that business groups in contact with government agencies already are assembling facts, ideas, and plans that will speed up the shift from a government-financed war program to a privately financed program of peacetime activity.

This shift must be made as secure against mischance as if it were a wartime campaign against the enemy. We cannot afford either a speculative boom or its inevitable bust. In the war we use tanks, planes, guns, and ships in great volume and of most effective design. Their equivalents in the defense against postwar economic chaos will be less spectacular but equally essential. We must keep prices in control. We must have continuity in the flow of incomes to consumers and from consumers to the industries of city and farm. We must have a national system of job placement. We must have definite plans for the conversion of key industries to peacetime work.

When the war is over, the more quickly private enterprise gets back into peacetime production and sells its goods to peacetime markets here and abroad, the more quickly will the level of government wartime expenditures be reduced.

No country needs deficit spending when private enterprise, either through its own efforts or in cooperation with government, is able to maintain full employment. Let us hope that the best thought of both business and government will now be focused on this problem which lies at the heart of our American democracy and our American way of life.

The war has brought forth a new type of industrialist who gives much promise for the future. The type of business leader I have in mind has caught a new vision of opportunities in national and international projects. He is willing to cooperate with the people's government in carrying out socially desirable programs. He conducts these programs on the basis of private enterprise, and for private profit, while putting into effect the people's standards as to wages and working conditions. We shall need the best efforts of such men as we tackle the economic problem of the peace.

This problem is well recognized by the average man on the street, who sums it up in a nutshell like this: If everybody can get a job in war work now, why can't everybody have a job in peacetime production later on? He will demand an answer, and the returning soldier and sailor will demand an answer—and this will be the test of statesmanship on the home front, just as ability to cooperate with other nations for peace and improved living standards will be the test of statesmanship on the international front.

How thrilling it will be when the world can move ahead into a new day of peaceful work, developing its resources and translating them as never before into goods that can be consumed and enjoyed! But this new day will not come to pass unless the people of the United Nations give wholehearted support to an effective program of action. The war will have been fought in vain if we in the United States, for example, are plunged into bitter arguments over our part in the peace, or over such fictitious questions as government versus business. Such bitterness would only confuse us and cloud our path. How much more sensible it would be if our people could be supplied with the facts and then, through orderly discussion, could arrive at a common understanding of what needs to be done.

I have heard the fear expressed that after the war the spirit of self-sacrifice which now animates so many of our people will disappear, that cold and blind selfishness will supplant the spirit which makes our young men willing to go thousands of miles from home to fight—and die if need be—for freedom. Those who have this fear think that a return of blind selfishness will keep the nations of the world from joining to prevent a repetition of this disaster.

We should approach the problem objectively from the standpoint of finding the common meeting ground on which the people of the world can stand. This meeting ground, after all, should not be hard to find—it is the security of the plain folks against depression and against war. To unite against these two evils is not really a sacrifice, but only a common-sense facing of the facts of the world in which we live.

Now at last the nations of the world have a second chance to erect a lasting structure of peace—a structure such as that which Woodrow Wilson sought to build but which crumbled away because the world was not yet ready. Wilson himself foresaw that it was certain to be rebuilt some day. This is related by Josephus Daniels in his book, *The Life of Woodrow Wilson,* as follows:

> Wilson never knew defeat, for defeat never comes to any man until he admits it. Not long before the close of his life Woodrow Wilson said to a friend: "Do not trouble about the things we have fought for. They are sure to prevail. They are only delayed." With the quaintness which gave charm to his sayings he added: "And I will make this concession to Providence—it may come in a better way than we propose."

And now we of this generation, trusting in Providence to guide our steps, go forward to meet the challenge of *our* day. For the challenge we all face is the challenge of free world democracy. In the new democracy there will be a place for everyone—the worker, the farmer, the businessman, the house-wife, the doctor, the salesman, the teacher, the student, the store clerk, the taxi driver, the preacher, the engineer—all the millions who make up our modern world. This new democracy will give us freedom such as we have never known, but only if as individuals we perform our duties with willing hearts. It will be an adventure in sharing—sharing of duties and responsibilities, and sharing of the joy that can come from the give-and-take of human contacts and fruitful daily living. Out of it, if we all do our part, there will be new opportunity and new security for the common man—that blend of liberty and unity which is the bright goal of millions who are bravely offering up their lives on the battle fronts of the world.

ECONOMIC FREEDOM FOR THE WORLD [4]

WENDELL L. WILLKIE [5]

Wendell Willkie gave this address on Monday evening, November 16, 1942, before the Eleventh Forum on Current Problems, under the auspices of the New York *Herald Tribune*.

The theme of the conference, held during November 16 and 17, was "Our fight for survival in a free world." Mrs. Ogden Reid, in introducing the speaker, said, "The concluding speaker on this program needs no introduction from me. At a time when our minds and hearts are with the A. E. F. in North Africa, I shall simply present him to you as a former captain in the 325th Field Artillery in that earlier A. E. F. of 1918. It has been said that the most American thing about America is Wendell Willkie. This is the way he is known the world 'round, and we are proud of the fact. I have the great honor to present to you Wendell Willkie."

On August 26, 1942, in a four-engine Consolidated Liberator bomber, "Gulliver," operated by United States army officers, Wendell Willkie took off from Mitchell Field, New York, to see "the world and the war, its battle fronts, its leaders, and its people." [6]

On October 14, 1942, forty-nine days later, he had encircled the world and landed in Minneapolis, Minnesota. He had touched Puerto Rico; Natal, Brazil; Accra and Kiano, West Africa; Cairo, Khartoum and El Alamein, Egypt; Ankara, Turkey; Bagdad and Teheran, in the Middle East; Moscow and Kuibyshev, Russia; Chungking, Chengtu, and elsewhere in China; Chita and Yakutsk, in Siberia; Fairbanks, Alaska; and Edmonton, Canada. He had travelled thirty-one thousand miles. He had talked with Joseph Stalin, Chiang Kai-shek, and many another leader, as well as with American soldiers and many "common men" of these countries. His views, therefore, on any phase of his recent observations, were found to have wide interest.

The address as given on November 16 was subject to official censorship. The section referring to the Vichy French situation was toned down to read, "For instance, shall we be quiet when we see our State Department's long appeasement of Vichy? I tell you we cannot fight this war in silence, whatever our experts say. . . ."

[4] By permission of Wendell L. Willkie. The text was furnished through the courtesy of Mr. Willkie.
[5] For biographical note see Appendix.
[6] Wendell Willkie, *One World*, p. 3, Simon and Schuster, New York, 1943.

Even in its deleted condition the speech was not permitted to be sent abroad "for twelve hours after the delivery." (Jay B. Hayden, North American Newspaper Alliance, *Chicago Sun,* November 20, 1942)

Officials at the State Department were reported as saying, "If you make that speech, you will endanger the lives of thousands of American soldiers." British newspaper correspondents were also excited over the speech because of its criticism of Churchill's "We mean to hold our own" statement. The address was not released for foreign transmission until the next day.

On that afternoon President Roosevelt at his press conference declared, "I thoroughly understand and approve the feeling in the United States and Great Britain and among all the other United Nations that in view of the history of the past two years no permanent arrangement should be made with Admiral Darlan. People in the United States likewise would never understand the recognition of a reconstituting of the Vichy government in France or in French territory. We are opposed to Frenchmen who support Hitler and the Axis."

The assassination of Darlan a month later, the destruction of the Axis forces in Tunisia in May, and the consolidation of the North African De Gaullist and the Giraud followers were some of the later developments related to this Willkie speech.

Mr. Willkie's book, *One World,* appeared in March, 1943. By May 30, 1943, almost a million copies had been sold. "No book ever published in this country," according to Dr. D. F. Fleming, "has sold so fast, fiction or otherwise." Why? Partly because Willkie was popular, partly because Americans believed in his sincerity, partly because he vividly interpreted the case for each country he visited, and partly because millions of Americans responded to the writer's suggestion that this is "one world."

The importance of the military in today's struggle is clear to us all. My concern tonight is with an even more powerful weapon than the gun, and that is, the idea.

For, however important the role of bayonets and guns may have been in the development of mankind, the role of ideas has been vastly more important—and, in the long run, more conclusive. In historical times, at any rate, men have not often fought merely for the joy of killing each other. They have fought for a purpose. Sometimes that purpose has not been very inspiring. Sometimes it has been quite selfish. But a war won without a purpose is a war won without victory.

A most outstanding example of a war fought with a purpose was our own American Revolution. We did not fight the Revolution because we hated Englishmen and wanted to kill them, but because we loved freedom and wanted to establish it. I think it is fair to say, in the light of what that freedom has meant to the world, that the victory won at Yorktown was the greatest victory ever won by force of arms. But this was not because our army was large and formidable. It was because our purpose was so clear, so lofty, and so well defined.

Unhappily this cannot be said of the First World War. It has become almost an historical truism that that was a war without victory. Of course, it is true that, while we were engaged in it, we thought, or said, that we were fighting for a high purpose. Woodrow Wilson, our Commander in Chief, stated our purpose in eloquent terms. We were fighting to make the world safe for democracy—to make it safe, not just with a slogan, but by accepting a set of principles known as the Fourteen Points, and by setting up a full-fledged international structure to be known as the League of Nations. That was a high purpose, surely. But when the time came to execute it in a peace treaty, a fatal flaw was discovered. We found that we and our allies were not really agreed upon that purpose. On the one hand some of our allies had entangled themselves in secret treaties; and they were more intent upon carrying out those treaties, and upon pursuing traditional power diplomacy, than upon opening up the new vista that Mr. Wilson had sought to define. And on the other hand, we ourselves were not as deeply dedicated to our declared purpose as we had led the world to believe. The net result was the abandonment of most of the purposes for which the war had supposedly been fought. Because those purposes were abandoned, that war was denounced by our generation as an enormous and futile slaughter. Millions had lost their lives. But no new idea, no new goal, rose from the ashes of their sacrifice.

Now I think that these considerations lead us inescapably to one conclusion. I think we must conclude that, generally speaking, nothing of importance can be won in peace which has not already been won in the war itself. I say nothing of importance. It is quite true, of course, that many details must be worked out at the peace table and at conferences succeeding the peace table—details which cannot be judiciously worked out under the pressure of war. We—we and our allies, of course—cannot, for instance, stop fighting the Japs to make a detailed plan of what we intend to do about Burma when victory is won. Nor can we relent in our pressure against Hitler to decide the detailed future of Poland now.

What we must win now, during the war, are the principles. We must know what our line of solution will be. Again, let me use the American Revolution as an example. When we fought that war, we had no inkling of the actual structure of the United States of America. No one had ever heard of the Constitution. The federal system, the three branches of government, the brilliant bicameral compromise by which the small states were induced to come into the Union—all these innovations lay as yet in the future, nourished only by the brains of a few great political thinkers—who, themselves, were not entirely clear. And yet the basic principles of that great political structure that was to become the United States of America were, surely, contained in the Declaration of Independence, in the songs and speeches of that day, in after-dinner discussions and private arguments around soldiers' camp fires and everywhere along the Atlantic Coast. Even though the great states of Massachusetts and Virginia were held together by the vaguest pronouncements and the flimsiest of political contraptions (the Continental Congress), their citizens were in substantial agreement as to the cause they were fighting for and the goal they wished to achieve.

Had they not agreed during the war, Massachusetts and Virginia, surely, would have failed to agree concerning the principles of the peace. They won in the peace exactly what they won in the war—no more and no less. This truth, if it were not self-evident, could be proved by citing one calamity. The people of those states did fail to agree concerning the freedom or slavery of the Negro. The result was that there grew up around the enslaved Negro in the South an entirely different economy from that which grew up in the North.   And this resulted in another, and far bloodier, war.

Can we not learn from this simple lesson, and from similar lessons of history, what our task is today?   I say to you, we must learn.   We must know that we shall win in the future peace only what we are now winning in the war—no more and no less.

That being profoundly true, we are faced today with two problems: How shall we determine what we want to win in the next peace?   And how shall we prepare ourselves to win it during the war?

First, to determine our aims it is clearly necessary to reach substantial agreement with our allies.   Here, as in our Revolution, agreement in detail is not necessary, or even desirable. But unless we are to repeat the unhappy history of the First World War, agreement in principle must be won.   Moreover, it must exist, not just among the leaders of the Allies.   The basic agreement I am thinking of must be established among the allied peoples themselves.   We must make sure that these peoples are fighting for essentially the same thing.

Now what does this mean?   It means that every one of us has the obligation to speak out, to exchange ideas, freely and frankly, across the Pacific, across the Atlantic, and here at home.   Unless the British people know the way we are thinking in America, and take it to heart, and unless we have a similar idea of what they are thinking in England and in the Commonwealth, there can be no hope of agreement.   We must know what the people of Russia and China aim for and we must let them know our aims.

It is the utmost folly—it is just short of suicide—to take the position that citizens of any country should hold their tongues for fear of causing distress to the immediate and sometimes tortuous policies of their leaders.

Shall we in America be quiet, for instance, when our leaders, after promising freedom to the French people, put into control over them the very man who has helped to enslave them? Shall we be quiet when we see our government's long appeasement of Vichy find its logical conclusion in our collaboration with Darlan, Hitler's tool? Such collaboration outrages the spirit of free peoples everywhere, whatever expediency dictated it. I tell you we cannot fight this war in silence, whatever our experts say. Because if we fight in silence those same experts will, in the end, even winning the war, win nothing but blood and ashes.

Thus, in order that we may win a real victory, we must encourage the utmost amount of discussion among ourselves and with our allies. Moreover, we must be very clear as to what this word "allies" means. We have many allies—roughly, I should estimate them at a billion people. Britain and the United States are great powers, but they are not the only powers involved in this struggle, nor even necessarily the greatest powers. Russia and China have each already suffered greater losses in this war than all the rest of us put together. Those two enormous nations are also our allies, and consequently, when we talk about reaching agreement among allied peoples, we must mean the Russian people and the Chinese people as well as the British people and the American people.

Indeed, we must go further. We must try to find out and openly to express the desires and hopes of hundreds of millions of other peoples—in the torn heart of Europe, in India, on the embattled shores of the Mediterranean, in Africa, on the southern shores of Asia, and in our own hemisphere. For, if some of these people are not now our allies, they are potential allies, and they are necessary participants in the world that is to follow this war. We must win substantial agreement with them also. If we do not, we cannot win substantial peace.

That then is our first problem—to discuss, and to discuss openly and frankly, the desires and needs of the allied peoples so that we may all come into substantial agreement concerning what we are fighting for.

Just as you have listened this evening to representatives of government, of industry, of labor, to aviators of peace and of war, to producers and scientists, so men and women all over the world must discuss and learn and exchange ideas and purposes with which to direct the future.

But discussion alone is not enough. Having discussed what we want to win in the peace, having set our goals, our second problem faces us: How, during the war, shall we prepare ourselves to attain those goals in the peace? The answer to that is plain: We must learn to work together; we must learn to work with all our allies that we may win both the war and the peace. We must work together today; tomorrow will be too late. Our most immediate common need is of course a united military plan arrived at by a board of strategy representative not alone of the United States and Great Britain but representing likewise our other allies. Even such obviously essential cooperation has not yet been brought about. It is true we are beginning to work with the British. That is comparatively easy, for we are possessed of the same linguistic and cultural heritage. But we must learn equally well to work with Russians and Chinese in the arduous task of today. And that task is not merely the task of military cooperation, however pressing that may be; it is also the task of working together now for a world at peace. For as I have already said, military victory is fruitless unless on the anvil of war we hammer out joint and honorable purposes.

And now about the goals for which we work. Here again perhaps we may learn from past failures.

After the last war the peace failed because no joint objectives upon which it could be based had been arrived at in the minds of the people. The League of Nations was created full blown; and men and women, having developed no joint purpose, except to defeat a common enemy, fell into capricious and irrelevant arguments about its structural form. Likewise, it failed because it was primarily an Anglo-French-American solution, retaining the old colonial imperialisms under new and fancy terms. It took inadequate account of the pressing needs of the Far East, nor did it sufficiently seek solution of the economic problems of the world. Its attempts to solve the world's problems were primarily political. But political internationalism without economic internationalism is a house built upon sand. For no nation can reach its fullest development alone.

There were those among us prior to this war who entertained the notion that America was an exception to this economic law; that America was economically self-sufficient. The war must surely have dissipated such ideas. We have seen our domestic economy and habits dislocated by a shortage of rubber. We have had cause to fear that even our war requirements could not be met. Sugar and coffee rationing have come. Our military and production experts fight frantically to find the methods of allocating our inadequate supplies of copper and tin. Submarines have taught us hideously how dependent America is upon the rest of the world's products, just as the aeroplane has dramatically shown us how the problems of all men are close and interrelated. If, with our great resources, our boasted self-sufficiency disappears so quickly when the flow of goods from the outside world is reduced, it becomes doubly clear that less fortunate nations, in order to develop, must have access to basic raw materials.

Therefore, we should work today to make available presently to all the United Nations and, when the war is over, to all the world, access to the materials indispensable to economic self-development. This cannot be accomplished by mere declarations of our leaders, as in an Atlantic Charter, particularly when one of the two principals to that instrument has in the last few days seemingly defended the old imperialistic order and declared to a shocked world: "We mean to hold our own." Its accomplishment depends primarily upon acceptance by the peoples of the world. For if the failure to reach international understanding after the last war taught us anything it taught us this: Even if war leaders apparently agree upon principles, when they come to the peace time they make their own interpretations of their previous declarations. So unless today, while the war is being fought, the people of the United States and of Great Britain, of Russia and of China, and of all the other United Nations, fundamentally agree on their purposes, fine and idealistic expressions of hope such as those of the Atlantic Charter will live merely to mock us as have Mr. Wilson's Fourteen Points. The Four Freedoms will not be accomplished by the declarations of those momentarily in power. They will become real only if the people of the world forge them into actuality.   And political internationalism alone will not accomplish them.   Real freedom must rest on economic internationalism.

Take a specific and difficult example of what lies before us if we are to give reality to those freedoms we have proclaimed. The Malayan Peninsula and the islands of the Southwest Pacific are areas containing, among other things, the principal source of the rubber supply of the world.   They are inhabited in part, at least, by unlettered, and, in some instances perhaps, savage people.   Those who sneer when it is suggested that freedom and self-government can be brought to all men feel that such areas must be ruled perpetually by some nation's colonial imperialism.   Now assume that the allies reconquer those areas— shall we return them to their previous status, where their defense was courageous but inadequate and their peoples undeveloped under the governmental custody of some one nation?   Or shall they be wards of the United Nations, their basic commodities made freely available to the world, their safety protected by an international police force; the full yield of their resources used for their own health, their own education and development, and for their training—no matter how long it may take—in the practices of self-government?   It is the principles upon which we shall base the solution of such problems that we must begin now to determine for ourselves.

There is another economic condition about which we must be thinking for it is the most necessary of all goals to the accomplishment of real freedom.   Not only must people have access to what other peoples produce but their own products must in turn reach men all over the world.   There will be no peace, there will be no real development, there will be no economic stability unless we find the method by which the trade barriers hampering the flow of goods are removed.   I know there are many men, particularly in America, where our standard of living exceeds the standard of living in the rest of the world, who shudder at such a prospect, who believe that any such process will only lessen our own standard of living.   The reverse of this is true.

Many reasons might be assigned for the amazing economic development of the United States—the abundance of our national resources, the freedom of our political institutions, the character of our population have all undoubtedly contributed. But in my judgment, the greatest factor has been that by the happen-stance of good fortune, there was created here in America the largest area in the world in which there existed a free exchange of goods and ideas.

And I should like to point out to those who are fearful an inescapable fact. Today in a world reduced in size by industrial and transportation developments, even our present standard of living in America cannot be maintained unless the exchange of goods flows more freely over the whole world. On the other hand, to raise the standard of living of men anywhere in the world is to raise the standard of living by some slight degree of every man everywhere in the world.

You have heard tonight an account of the economic world of today and its possibilities for the future. Mr. Byrnes has expressed the hope that the regimented economy of wartime will expand freely when peace comes. Mr. Kaiser and Dr. Moore have told you there are no frontiers in the laboratory and the factory and the shipyard. That all we have heretofore known of potential productivity will seem slight compared with what can be produced tomorrow.

Mr. Johnston and Mrs. Hamilton and Mr. Watt have pointed out clearly how, under modern industrial conditions, labor and management must find a road to economic stability in order to satisfy the aspirations and the needs of men.

Mr. Trippe and Major Seversky have pictured the amazing developments of aviation and its possibilities for war and for peace. They have shown you what became so clear to me on my recent trip around the world—that the peoples of the world are closer together geographically and physically than were the residents of the thirteen colonies at the time of the establishment of the United States of America.

These are all testaments to the fact that the vibrant forces of modern science and industry are but awaiting the chance to break forth into ever-widening streams of well-being for all mankind. The potential markets for the goods and ideas of the East in the Western world are unlimited; and the demands of the East for the materials and the machinery and the skills of the West are beyond imagination.

But—let me impress on you—the forces that open these streams will come only if the people of the world agree on the methods of their release. We cannot wait until after the war when the already developing spirit of rampant nationalism may hold sway and then expect by some miracle to accomplish what history teaches us must be accomplished while we fight. We must not listen to those who say "Win the war now" and leave postwar solutions to our leaders and to our experts.

We, the people, must begin to solve these problems today, not tomorrow. For we know that bayonets and guns are feeble as compared with the power of the idea.

A FRUITFUL APPROACH TO A PROLONGED PEACE [7]

HENRY CABOT LODGE, JR. [8]

Senator Henry Cabot Lodge, Jr., delivered this speech in the United States Senate on Friday, June 18, 1943.

In the midst of many a prolonged discussion of postwar plans and programs, this address gave new arguments for the necessity of American international cooperation after the armistice. Mr. Lodge's close analysis of the need for such cooperation was based upon many concrete data (for complete data consult the *Congressional Record* of June 18, 1943). This country, according to the speaker, was likely to become a "have not" nation. In view of limited minerals and other resources, what should be our foreign policy?

The obvious conclusion was that limited international exchange, trade restrictions, and isolationism in general would only engender more wars or make for the United States a most awkward economy.

This realistic approach, as contrasted with a primarily "cosmic" analysis of the argument for cooperation, distinguishes this debate.

The speech is temperate, is free from name calling, and yet takes its listeners squarely into the fold of those who espouse various concrete forms of intergovernmental concerts.

Young Senator Lodge, then, in contrast to Henry Cabot Lodge, Senior, who heavily contributed to the wrecking of Woodrow Wilson's League of Nations program in 1919, becomes a constructive internationalist.

Said Senator Vandenberg, of Michigan, "[Mr. Lodge] made one of the ablest speeches I have heard in my time." Mr. Johnson, of Colorado, followed Lodge's speech with the observation, "Mr. President, I desire to commend and congratulate the Senator from Massachusetts on the address he has just delivered. It is timely, challenging, and thought provoking, and relates to a subject which should be called to the attention of the country and the Senate."

The press widely acclaimed the debate. The Lowell (Massachusetts) *Sun,* of June 19, 1943, for example, said, "This is one of the most convincing commentaries that has originated in Washington since the war began, and the American people owe Senator Lodge a debt of gratitude,

[7] Reprinted from the *Congressional Record,* v. 89, no. 113, p. 6138-43, June 18, 1943 (daily edition), 78th Congress, first session. Mr. Lodge graciously approved this reprinting.
[8] For biographical note see Appendix.

for speaking in defense of America of the future and coming generations of Americans."[9]

Mr. President: It has become plain as day and it is common sense to recognize that our British and Russian allies are not only dedicated to the broad purpose of crushing Nazism and Fascism, but that they have a number of very definite and very practical national aims which have been frankly revealed to the world. These great nations are not only committed to defeat of the common enemy and to cooperation for peace thereafter; one of them—Britain—frankly intends to maintain the Empire, and the other one—Russia—has clear intentions regarding eastern Europe.

We in the United States, on the other hand, are committed to speedy victory and to effective measures to preserve peace thereafter. But in the field of definite and practical aims there seems to be a vacuum. Why this vacuum exists, I cannot say; but I suggest that it is not because there is any lack of matters lying outside our borders in which we have a vital interest. I further submit that the clear statement of these aims is not only in our own interest, but is also a frank act to which our allies and our own people are entitled, and is an essential step—nay, the most fruitful approach—toward discharging the overshadowing obligation of effective postwar collaboration.

What are some of these matters outside of our borders in which we must have a definite interest?

It will, for example, come as a surprise to many Americans to be told that we are actually facing the prospect of an America materially depleted of some of its magnificent natural resources. The great demands of our own fighting forces and those of our allies have cut deeply into our reserves of vital, basic materials. We are not in the habit of regarding the United States as a "have not" nation—and now is the time to think of steps to avert such a catastrophe. These thoughts are also expressed in an article appearing in the St. Louis *Post-Dispatch* for Sunday, January 10, 1943, and written by Richard L. Stokes, its Washington correspondent, from which I desire to quote certain excerpts:

[9] For other comments see *Congressional Record,* v. 89, no. 116, p. A 3388-9, June 22, 1943 (daily edition), 78th Congress, first session.

Another legend exploded since Pearl Harbor was the idea that the United States had inexhaustible natural resources. The country has been at war for only thirteen months, but the fury with which its material wealth is being ransacked has already perturbed the government's scientific agencies.

Chairman Donald M. Nelson, of the War Production Board, predicted recently that manufacture of armament goods in the current twelvemonth will surpass that of 1942 by two thirds. He defined 1942 as the year of the battle of facilities, which was won, and promised that 1943 would bring victory likewise in the battle of materials.

If so, the triumph may be a Pyrrhic one, because of the headlong greed with which Mars is rifling the nation's material stocks, even of clay and sand.

On the presumption that World War No. 2 will continue several years and that depletion of this country's natural reserves will accelerate rather than decline, the following question, of portentous significance for the destiny of the American people, is now being raised:

Is the United States headed toward an economy of scarcity, which will replace its historic economy of abundance?

And, if the answer to the first question is yes, there are these further considerations: Must regimentation of materials become national policy in time of peace as well as war? Will there be a leveling down of American wage and living standards, with a proportionate leveling up of such standards in countries from which essential supplies are imported? Is a revolution in our trade and tariff systems bound to follow? Will the United States, out of its own resources, ever again be able to fight a big-time war?

On the verge of exhaustion or serious impoverishment, according to scientists in the Department of the Interior, are the domestic stores of materials having such ultra-vital combatant importance as lead, zinc, mercury, and iron, for which there are no substitutes; and copper, bauxite, and petroleum as well. Alternatives for the last three are known, but they are either at a primitive stage of development, exorbitant in cost or relatively inefficient.

In the *Reader's Digest* for April appears a condensation of an article from the *United States News* entitled "Will War Make Us a 'Have-Not' Nation?"

We are digging deep into our natural resources to make bombs and bullets that will be shot away; to make tanks, planes and ships some of which will never return. As a result, the United States may become a "have not" nation in many materials basic to our economy.

The vast expenditure of irreplaceable riches is leading thoughtful people in and out of the government to ask if the United States will be left with enough basic resources to fight another big-time war. They ask if present material shortages aren't just the forerunners of permanent shortages in the future. They ask whether this country should not eventually develop resources in other areas of the world and conserve its own.

War costs astronomical amounts of all materials. Copper is a good example. A 37-millimeter antiaircraft gun shoots away a ton every twenty minutes of action. The Army Signal Corps uses five thousand tons a month in communications equipment. Once plentiful deposits of high-grade copper ore are now reduced to a single big deposit near Butte, Montana.

The same applies to oil. Until recently, 60 percent of the supplies going to the African front were petroleum products. Government officials warn that our oil supply is not inexhaustible. In 1942, output of oil was greater than reserves discovered. This is a reversal of a trend that lasted until 1938, and comes just when oil reserves are subjected to the greatest strain in history. While new fields have been found, they average less than half the size they did before. There seems to be little question that the United States eventually will be dependent on foreign sources.

We are running out of high-grade ores in certain metals. Supplies of bauxite, best source of aluminum, may be used up within three years. The great Mesabi Range of iron ore in Minnesota, which supplies 80 to 85 percent of our needs, may be exhausted by 1950. Lead deposits in the tri-state area centering at Joplin, Missouri, are nearing their end. Mercury deposits are expected to be exhausted for good before this war is finished. The possibility of opening new zinc mines is small. Depletion of these ores is the price paid for all-time record production of metals and minerals.

I, therefore, undertook an investigation of my own. I addressed an inquiry to Dr. R. R. Sayers, Director of the Bureau of Mines, in which I asked him to give me the facts bearing on the exhaustion of our supply of vital minerals. Under date of March 2, 1943, Dr. Sayers wrote me as follows:

March 2, 1943.

DEAR SENATOR LODGE: In your letter of February 17 you made inquiry concerning the status of domestic resources of ores of some of the common metals and of petroleum, and to what extent depletion has been accelerated by war production.

The volume of our mineral resources cannot be evaluated with precision because of the multitude of factors that affect the definition of ore, price being usually the major consideration. Under wartime conditions even that factor may be of subordinate importance, need being the governing criterion. However, a reflection of the relative reserve positions of the minerals you named is provided by the classification given in the list of material substitutions and supply issued by the Conservation Division of the War Production Board, February 1, 1943.

Iron ore and petroleum as such are not listed, but numerous iron and petroleum products are in the extremely short-supply category and are completely subject to allocation. That is, currently and for the near future, raw material resources are ample to meet anticipated demands although the rapid depletion of direct shipping open-cut iron ores and restrictions of wildcat oil drilling are causing some concern. The immediate problems connected therewith are primarily those of conversion and distribution. Our internal ability to meet the requirements now does not however imply that the current high rates of production can long be maintained unless discovery be kept in pace with extraction.

Lead is now among the noncritical materials and is available in sufficient volume to serve as a substitute for scarcer materials. In the early part of last year shortages were feared. Thus it may be a borderline case as far as domestic supply is concerned. Mercury remains in the critical class, with supply approximately in balance with war and essential civilian needs. Although domestic production rose approximately one third from 1940 to a half-century peak in 1942, it is doubtful if that rate, which was just about sufficient to meet domestic needs, can be maintained for more than a year. The relatively satisfactory and fair current positions of these metals are in large measure owing to substantial volumes of imports from Canada and Mexico during the past year.

The situation with respect to the other minerals is in varying degree precarious. Aluminum, copper, and zinc are, respectively, second, third, and sixth in the most critical metals group, viz., those essential for war, but in insufficient supply for war and essential civilian demands and in many cases, including those named, insufficient for war purposes alone. We are highly dependent on overseas resources for major portions of our total supply, and since ocean transport has become increasingly difficult while demand pyramided domestic production capacity has been strained and appears about to reach its peak or a point of rapidly diminishing returns. Ore reserves in a major zinc-producing area are close to exhaustion, and reserves of bauxite that can be treated in existing plants will last but a few years at the contemplated rate of extraction; a condition so serious that this Bureau has recently proposed a greatly expanded exploration and research program. Although our copper store has a potentially longer life, its concentration in a few large ore deposits precludes further expansion of output except at the expense of production of war end products.

The exploratory programs of the Bureau of Mines and Geological Survey and the Bureau's research work with those that could be carried out by industry have indeed added much to our known natural resources, but although these results are impressive they still have failed to keep step with extraction, and it is to be noted that for virtually all the minerals most of the deposits explored have been smaller in size and lower in tenor than those being exploited. Except for petroleum and iron ore there have been also marked declines in grade of ore mined, another definite marker of impoverishment. Thus our ore reserves are being depleted at a rate even greater than accelerated production might indicate because in more normal times much of what remains may be submarginal.

In the attached pages are given more detailed statements concerning each of the minerals you named. Since virtually all the data have been furnished in confidential reports to the Bureau, you will understand, I am sure, that their use is restricted.

Sincerely yours,

R. R. SAYERS.

I then became interested in discovering the minerals which the United States needed but which it did not possess within its own borders. I requested the Bureau of Mines to make a compilation listing these minerals together with principal world sources. The list includes antimony, arsenic, asbestos, bauxite, beryllium ore, chromite, graphite, industrial diamonds, lead, manganese ore, mercury, mica, natural nitrates, nickel, platinum, quartz crystals, tin, titanium ore, tungsten, vanadium, and zinc.

Mr. President, I ask unanimous consent that this tabulation be printed in the *Record* at this point as a part of my remarks. . . . [Table deleted]

I have been told about it, but the figures which I have been shown I am not permitted to use in public. The knowledge as to the exact location of all the oil deposits is somewhat of a military secret; and while the authorities will allow a Member of Congress to examine the figures, they will not authorize him to use them in public.

It is undoubtedly true that we can improve our position by using low-grade ores, of which we have a large supply in the case of certain metals. We have, during our short national life, lived off the cream. We may not be able to skim off the cream much longer. We must take careful stock of our domestic resources and stand ready to develop them. Military considerations indicate that these resources should be freely available and that at the same time we should encourage importations and stock piles of scarce materials.

In the case of those metals of which we are entirely deficient, however, we have no choice but to import them.

While considering this subject of matters outside our own borders in which the welfare of the American people compels us to have a strong national interest, let us take a somewhat longer look at oil.

The importance of insuring a supply of oil adequate to maintain the domestic economy of this country is painfully apparent to every citizen today. Competent opinion is that our domestic reserves are inadequate. The world supply of oil is ample for all if efficiently developed and distributed. Present American concessions abroad are sufficient for our needs and trade, if preserved. Responsibility for this preservation could be left with the oil companies as in the past, or could be taken in some degree by the government. History does not give us confidence that private company policy alone will adequately safeguard the national public interest, particularly with the prospect of circumstances in the future even more difficult than those which the private companies have failed to cope with in the past. How should this government move to achieve the security of so important a factor in our national life? This responsibility is a real one, and those entrusted with it cannot dismiss it with fair promises.

The importance of oil from the standpoint of the armed forces is also vital. Responsible and forward-looking Navy officers, experienced in oil-supply problems, have been asking what assurance have we—if any—that our fleet and air force will have certain supplies for maintenance or police duty. This question extends itself to include supplies for such cargo shipping as this government may choose to keep under its own administration following the war for implementation of its security or economic policies until a stabilized world economy makes this unnecessary. These officers bear and keenly feel a high responsibility. They know better than most the price paid for empty bunkers and do not intend to find them empty. They are waiting impatiently for our solution.

I shall not enter into the details of what the answers are to these two challenging questions. The suggestion has been made by thoughtful men that a petroleum reserve corporation should be established to provide an agency in which many related functions could be centered and through which much might be accomplished. Certain it is, however, that we must have oil, that the average citizen insists that he have oil, and that he looks to us who are public servants to see that he gets it. . . .

In my remarks up to this point I have listed some of the mineral resources which are vital to our existence and for which we are to a greater or lesser degree dependent on the outside world.

Then, of course, there are vast vegetable resources, such as rubber, coffee, and quinine. I wish to emphasize that we are also vitally interested in the world outside our borders for other things—for services as well as goods. Think of the merchant marine which we have so suddenly built. Think of radio, telegraph, and telephone communications, a field in which we have a natural proficiency, and in which I do not think we are on an equality throughout the world. Think of aviation. After the war we shall have at least three million young men who will be well versed in the fields of aviation, merchant marine, and communications. They will probably look to their government to give them an opportunity to exercise these skills. These are activities which rest on international agreements if they are to exist at all. You cannot have free air transportation without international understanding. You cannot have a large merchant marine without agreements. You cannot operate either of these things without a communications system at least on an equal basis with that possessed by other countries. In these fields, therefore, other countries have things to give, things which we want to get. I hope we can get them—of course, by just, peaceful means, for under no condition can this war ever become an imperialistic one.

Then there are the broad questions of currency, international exchange, and beyond these the still broader questions of international commerce as a whole.

These are vital matters in the long view, as we well know. They will also have great immediate urgency. There is a deep conviction in men's minds today that the powers of government, now being used to win the war, can and must be used after the war to promote prosperity, while at the same time preserving and encouraging free enterprise. . . .

I think we can all agree that there will be no patience with a postwar world of doles and bread lines. There must be a gradual transition from a war to a peace footing. In all this the goods and services which we must get from abroad will play a vital part—a part which cannot be postponed.

Mr. President, we pride ourselves on having the highest material living standard of any nation in the world, and we boast of it not merely in a materialistic spirit. We know that a society of free men, with free speech, free worship, free institutions, and equal opportunity cannot exist in a country which is in a state of abject poverty. If you are to have democracy you must have a certain amount of prosperity.

Therefore, both our standard of living and our spiritual freedom are based on the fact that Providence has blessed us with so many natural resources.

In this war some of us have been privileged to observe our young American fighting man. In a very true sense he represents the justification of our democratic system, for his hardihood, his quickness of thought, his self-reliance, and his courage under the most severe tests life holds are the results not only of the food and clothing which he received as a child, but of the education which he received and the spiritual climate in which he grew to manhood. All these things rise and fall together. An America without a plentiful supply of natural resources would not be the America of democracy. It would be a bitter irony if we were to shoot away our natural resources in the name of democracy and lose democracy while we were doing it.

After the last war it was stated many times that the United States wanted nothing, and we magnanimously refused to accept any territory. If it is true that we are becoming a "have not" nation, it is a very open question indeed whether we should not at the end of this war seek to acquire, in a just and peaceful manner, some things which we might lack. We hear it often said—and with admiration in some quarters—that our allies know exactly what they want out of this war. Should we not be equally definite in making our wants known? Is not such frankness on all sides the best guarantor of fruitful agreement and true understanding?

What will be the result of a conference at which two parties know exactly what they need whereas the third wants everything in general and nothing in particular? As a fervent believer in the pressing need of effective international collaboration after the war, I submit that the United States owes it to the world as well as to herself to define her needs.

Mr. President, these are the questions which bring me to the last part of this speech.

In the part just ended I tried to list the goods and services which we must obtain from outside our borders if we are to maintain either our democratic life or a respectable military establishment, or our influence for peace in the family of nations.

I now submit that if these problems are solved—if we have a satisfactory set of treaties assuring us, for example, proper supplies of oil and tin and our fair share of our shipping and communications rights, that the framework of our relationship with the rest of the world would be fixed—and that it would be fixed on a sound basis, a true basis, a basis which took into account the differences between nations, a basis which saw the different needs of different peoples and sought to satisfy those needs—instead of a basis which assumed that all nations and peoples are alike when actually they are not.

Mr. President, I have very little faith in what I call the cosmic or transcendental approach to the question of American foreign relations. I cannot see why it is necessary to treat the relations between peoples of different nationalities on a highly theoretical, political, and emotional basis when the relations between peoples of the same nationality are not treated that way. True, the airplane has changed commerce and revolutionized military science; it has not, however, automatically created a universal state of brotherly love. I have some good friends, of whom I am personally fond, both in and out of the Senate who believe in the cosmic approach, and I respect their sincerity. But the more I think about it the more convinced I become that it is an approach which can only do harm to the very cause which its proponents espouse.

One method produces agreement on the part of the American people; the other method divides the American people. And have we not learned by this time that one of the first considerations in forming any foreign policy in this country is that it must be a policy on which the American people can unite?

Such a policy must be based on national interest, guided by justice. Would that we had had a clear policy of national interest to guide us in the past. I am very much afraid that we have not had such a policy for quite a little time. We have had momentary policies based on emotion, such as the Neutrality Act, the purpose of which was to keep us out of war by legislation and which circumstances then caused us to repeal. We then had a vacuum instead of a true policy based on national interest, and that was all too often—and all too naturally—filled by old hatreds and old attachments relating to countries in the Old World. I do not hesitate to say that if a policy based on national interest had been in existence in the past in the prewar period it would have been wholeheartedly supported by all Americans regardless of racial extraction. Such a policy in the future would weld Americans together—regardless of racial differences—more than any other single act of government.

In his book entitled "U. S. Foreign Policy," Walter Lippmann makes some true observations on the mentality prevailing in the administrations of two Presidents holding office before and during the First World War. He says:

Both were idealists who habitually rejected the premises of the politics of power. Both disliked armaments. In them the idealism which prompts Americans to make large and resounding commitments was combined with the pacifism which causes Americans to shrink from the measures of force that are needed to support the commitments. Neither promoted the preparation of armaments in time of peace. Both accepted reluctantly and tardily the need to arm. Both abhorred as inherently vicious and unnecessary, and as contrary to American principles, the formation of alliances. But both favored a league of nations in which the United States assumed the obligation to enforce peace.

This eagerness to accept commitments and reluctance to arm also characterized our conduct before World War No. 2.

In a later discussion of the failure of the United States to enter the League of Nations, Mr. Lippmann says:

The United States did not go to war because it wished to found a league of nations; it went to war in order to preserve American security. And when the war was over, the nation would almost certainly have accepted in some form or other the scheme of the League of Nations if President Wilson had been able to demonstrate to the people that the League would perpetuate the security which the military victory had won for them. Mr. Wilson failed to make this demonstration. He failed because in leading the nation to war he had failed to give the durable and compelling reasons for the momentous decision. The reasons he did give were legalistic and moralistic and idealistic reasons, rather than the substantial and vital reason that the security of the United States demanded that no aggressively expanding imperial power, like Germany, should be allowed to gain the mastery of the Atlantic Ocean.

Mr. Lippmann here points out the dangers of what he calls a legalistic, or a moralistic, or an idealist policy, rather than a substantial and vital policy. I have used the phrases cosmic, transcendental, theoretical, and political. We both mean the same thing.

I believe we have made some progress toward a truly national policy. For instance, we are determined that never again shall we find ourselves unprepared as we were on the outbreak of this war, and that we must have a military force which is manifestly ready to function at any moment. We believe that if we had had such a force Hitler might never have started. We hold that there must be practical plans for a rapid expansion of our army and navy, that there will have to be limited compulsory military training, that never again must we be dependent on others for essential war materials, and that the approaches to the United States must be safeguarded.

Robert Moses has expressed this new feeling about the foreign policy of the future in these words:

We will go along with feeding the starving and undernourished everywhere, binding up the world's wounds, canceling debts and making loans, perhaps with some kind of League and World Court which do not require the surrender of our sovereignty and which frankly separate ultimate from immediate objectives, with moderate tariff barriers not involving the lowering of our living standards, and with immigration restricted in order to prevent the rushing in of the vast hordes who will attempt to seek escape from painful readjustments abroad.

Our people will favor cooperation with other nations in the many benefits to be derived from improvement of communications, but they won't give up nationalism. They will be for sufficient American armament to insure respect, and for an internal economy which will not again make us dependent on others for vital needs. They will be for spreading democratic doctrine by example rather than by forcing conformity upon those to whom democracy is still a new experience. Does any sane person seriously contend that with the signing of the peace our armed forces should be quickly reduced to skeletons and stripped of appropriations and respect? Not after this war. This time we shall be more prudent. We shall not disarm until we see how sincere the rest of the world is about the new Utopia.

Uncle Sam is neither a skinflint nor a fool. The middle road in world affairs may not be melodramatic, but it has always looked good to him. He knows this at least—that in the long run he will win the widest respect by refusing to overpromise and by being scrupulously careful to keep his word.

Mr. President, I do not mean to ignore or belittle the fact that thorny military and political decisions will have to be made. They will be difficult decisions, no matter how successfully we settle our material questions about which I have been speaking. The matter of control of any international military organization and our reaction to the continuation, resurrection, and extension of imperialism are two out of many thorny questions from which we cannot escape. The question of restoring small nations without also restoring the European crazy-quilt of quarreling nationalities is another. There are many more.

But the fact still remains that the approach is important. The more matters are agreed on, the easier agreement becomes even on these thorny problems. And it is so very plain that there are things which we need in the world outside our borders, things which we must have in order to maintain not only our material standard of living but our democratic way of living— things which we need to maintain our influence for peace in the family of nations. These are the things which should be the basis of prompt agreements based on national interest, because these are the things on which Americans can agree among them-

selves and regarding which reasonable men of differing nationalities should be able to come to terms. For fifty years the American people have been divided on questions of foreign policy.
I submit that the test of a sound foreign policy is "that those
who have disagreed are brought toward agreement."

Let me summarize:

First. It is a sacred duty to achieve effective international
collaboration after the war to prevent the recurrence of these
slaughters. Only thus can we be worthy of the sacrifice of our
fighting men.

Second. The political and theoretical approach to the peace
divides the people and defeats its own purpose. We cannot
assume that the aeroplane has automatically created a state of
universal brotherly love. The touchstone of any American
foreign policy must be that it unites the American people.

Third. We must develop a policy based on national interest
guided by justice which will bring people together as Americans
regardless of racial differences.

Fourth. Such a policy can be based on those things which
we must have from outside our borders to maintain our democracy, our military establishment, and our influence for peace in
the family of nations.

Fifth. Some of the things which should be the objects of
international agreement are:

(a) Vital natural resources which we either lack completely
or of which our supply is growing scarce. For example, we will
soon be dependent on the rest of the world for oil.

(b) Equality with other nations in international radio, telegraph, and telephone.

(c) An opportunity for free competition in international
aviation.

(d) A real chance for our new, big merchant marine.

(e) Equitable arrangements in the field of international exchange.

(f) Naval, military, and air bases to safeguard the approaches to the United States.

Sixth. Agreement on these practical matters will make agreement easier on the great political problems. It is a fruitful approach which will unite the people.

Indeed the challenge of making a conclusive peace is too compelling to be met in any other spirit. The sacrifices made by American fighting men impose the duty of developing world relations which will work, which will be accepted, and which will meet the issues of our time. We simply cannot afford the pride of opinion which says that it must be done a certain way or not at all. That the cosmic approach is attractive to many people cannot be denied. Certain aspects of it are attractive to me. In a less important cause we might tolerate it. But in the vital, soul-stirring task of making a just and lasting peace for our children and grandchildren we cannot afford this dubious luxury. We have the stern duty of being practical, of making a peace which will work. Only thus can we be worthy of the sacrifice of our fighting men.

AMERICA AND GREAT BRITAIN IN THE
POSTWAR WORLD [10]

ANTHONY EDEN [11]

Anthony Eden, British Foreign Secretary, and heir-apparent to election as Prime Minister, gave this address before a joint session of the Maryland General Assembly, at Annapolis, on March 26, 1943. Mr. Eden had been in this country about two weeks, and he departed for England a few days later. This was his most important public utterance in the United States.

This speech followed quickly on the heels of other highly significant addresses and of Parliamentary or Congressional debates that analyzed directly or indirectly the problems of (1) America's habitual relations with Russia now and in the postwar era; (2) the relations, military and political, of the United States and Great Britain with China; (3) America's role in any postwar international political policy. In spite of the Casablanca conference between Roosevelt and Churchill in January 1943, both the British and American public felt that many of the political issues raised above should be specifically answered. Eden's trip to the United States aimed to tackle these same problems.

Any agreement between the United States and Great Britain, for example, should take account of the existing twenty-year treaty of alliance between Great Britain and Russia. Eden's political job was to have a definite and continued understanding with Stalin concerning such settlements as those having to do with Yugoslavia (where rival parties were contending for control), of Poland (Should it be restored to independent nationhood?), of Franco's Spain (certainly a government with which Russia would have no traffic). The Foreign Secretary, moreover, was obliged to secure some understanding with the United States that would provide a postwar working agreement among these three nations, as well as China.

Why should Eden be the British spokesman to grapple with these matters? Partly because he was a protégé of Stanley Baldwin and of Winston Churchill. The latter described Eden as "the one fresh figure of magnitude" among Britain's young men to survive World War I.

In one of his 1942 speeches, Eden gave the fundamentals of British foreign policy: "We are determined to keep in close touch with the United States in all matters of policy, and we have also specifically

[10] Reprinted from *Congressional Record*, vol. 89, no. 57, p. 2817-19, March 30, 1943 (daily edition), 78th Congress, first session.
[11] For biographical note see Appendix.

pledged ourselves in the Anglo-Soviet treaty to collaborate fully in post-war reconstruction with Soviet Russia".

On March 15, Mr. Eden arrived in Washington's airport in a Liberator bomber. It was his first trip to America since 1938, when he had been out of public life. Mr. Eden dined at the White House, conferred with leaders, but above all his trip was designed, according to popular impression, to help solve the problem of America's relations with Russia.

On March 21, Winston Churchill delivered from London a notable address on "Postwar Councils on World Problems," in which he expounded specifically a four-year plan for England, including his categorical statement that, upon the defeat of Hitler, "We shall immediately proceed to transport all the necessary additional forces and apparatus to the other side of the world" to punish Japan and to rescue China. He further proposed the setting up in Europe of a "Council of Nations," somewhat along the lines of the League of Nations. "It [the Council] certainly cannot be accomplished without their [Britain, the United States, and Russia] cordial and concerted agreement and direct participation."

Mr. Eden's speech was thus a supplement to the Churchill speech of March 21. The significance of Eden's address lay in its subtle attack on American isolation; its suggestion that the four countries of Britain, Russia, China, and the United States must act in concert, both in the war and postwar world; its specific designation of "our partner China" (the Churchill speech ignored positive reference).

The speech was delivered with Mr. Eden's usual parliamentary skill. The speaker has extempore ability and effectiveness in audience adaptation, both in delivery and in subject matter. He, of course, fails in parliamentary adeptness to measure up to Churchill but ranks high in speaking ability, in knowledge of international and domestic affairs, and in leadership in the House of Commons, qualities promising well for the supreme cabinet post.

The address was well received by the American listeners and press, and by the members of the British Commonwealth of Nations. Senator George, of Georgia, in commenting on it before the Senate, called it a "very noteworthy address" and "altogether worthy" and praised the references to "our Chinese allies" and the need for concerted action. Strongly dissenting voices, as usual, came from India, because of Churchill's and Eden's silence on that country's clamor for freedom.

Doubtless, one direct result of Eden's visit was the highly successful trip by Prime Minister Churchill himself seven weeks later. [12]

First let me say that I feel at home here. From my earliest years I have been steeped in the atmosphere of Maryland. It

[12] See pages 30-46.

is a keen personal pleasure to stand in Annapolis on the spot where Robert Eden once stood.

A few miles away, in the City Hall at Baltimore, now hang the pictures of the Calvert family from whom I am proud to be descended. They are friendly faces which I recognize from my childhood days, when they looked down on me from the walls of my father's house.

I am even prouder of the fact that one of the Calverts, the third Lord Baltimore, was the prime mover in the great Act of 1649, by which the early settlers were assured of full freedom to worship God according to their conscience. That was nearly three hundred years ago, but our times have given new significance to that event.

Four and a half years have passed since I last stood on American soil. They are years that have changed the face of the world and brought much suffering to the human race. Some of us in Europe thought we saw the catastrophe approaching and felt the chill of the coming storm, while many, both of my countrymen and yours, were still clinging to the precarious hope of peace. This was, no doubt, excusable enough. There is always a strong temptation for countries to try to preserve their own peace of mind by turning a deaf ear to the first warnings of danger from abroad.

We know now how vain were these hopes and efforts. So far as we were concerned, Hitler finally destroyed any possibility of illusion by his repeated violation of treaties, by his open repudiation of any rule but that of force. It was plain beyond argument that not Poland, not Europe itself, would satisfy his mad ambitions. His purpose was the conquest and domination of the world.

Thus for the second time within a generation we are at war to redeem our pledged word.

The decision to take up the challenge was a decision of a united people at home. It was endorsed at once by the Parliaments and peoples of the great overseas dominions—Canada, Australia, New Zealand and South Africa—and by all parts of the British Empire. From that day in early September, 1939, there has been no turning back; there will be no turning back until victory is won.

We are not yet at the climax of the struggle; and I must repeat the warning I uttered when I first arrived here a fortnight ago. We have yet far to travel before the final triumph over our enemies in the West and in the East. In the interval, there will be strains and stresses, setbacks and disappointments. But if we nerve ourselves to meet these, if we work to the utmost of our strength, the result is not in doubt.

In a struggle of this nature, it is clearly desirable that those upon whom the responsibility lies in each of the Allied belligerent states should meet in personal conference as often as they can. There is, in truth, no substitute for such meetings. Men who do not know each other well cannot exchange views by dispatch or cable to the best advantage. I was therefore happy to accept the invitation of your government to pay this visit to the United States.

Nothing could have exceeded the kindness and hospitality that have been shown to me by every one—by the President, by Mr. Hull, by the Members of Congress and by all with whom I have been privileged to work. We have done much work together and we are both well pleased at the result.

For myself I can only say this: In my life it has fallen to my lot on many occasions to visit foreign capitals, and I am sure that never in my experience has a journey been more worth while. You will not expect, I trust, sudden and sensational developments, for there will be none. But there has been a meeting of minds between us about the present and the future that will, we are sure, bear fruit.

During my brief visit it has been my good fortune to spend some days in visits to your army and navy. I can assure you in all sincerity that I have never known a more inspiring experience. It is at once evident that your methods and organization are thoroughly well planned, but there is much more to it than this. Wherever I went, from the Deep South to the neighborhood of Washington, I found the same virile spirit of dauntless determination. Your young men are truly splendid. You have every cause to be proud of them and they to be proud of the country and the cause they serve.

Let me now for a moment look back to our experience in this war and see if we may gain from it guidance for the future. I have said that we declared war to defend the sanctity of treaties, and we have tried in the ebb and flow of battle to keep this high purpose clear and constant before our eyes. There have been some dark moments—the darkest probably being those of Dunkerque and the weeks that followed. Then for the first time in our remembered history we as a people faced national extinction. Every horror seemed possible. We walked through the fire.

Yet that ordeal strengthened us and brought us a new spirit of fellowship and of endurance and of simple living, which I pray may remain with us long after the peril is passed. We gained then, I believe, a new sense of what our national life could be. Nor shall we ever forget your sympathy and your active help in the days when it needed an act of faith to believe even in our own survival.

One incident in particular will be vivid in my recollection to my dying day. It had been my duty as Secretary of State for War at that time to call upon the nation to enroll in a new force, the Local Defense Volunteers, since renamed by the Prime Minister the Home Guard.

The men responded in numbers far exceeding our calculation. They were eager to drill and to fight, but we had no weapons for them. We had not equipment enough for the divisions of our regular army saved from Dunkerque. Our industry, though working as it had never worked before, could not meet this demand.

It was then that you made your first great gesture. In a brief span, you sent us more than a million rifles, guns, machine guns and other weapons from your arsenals to arm our volunteers. I can recall today the anxiety with which we watched the voyage of those ships, and the relief with which we signaled each consignment safely brought to port by the gallant men of the Royal Navy and the merchant marine. Those weapons might well have meant the difference between life and death for us. Such acts of generosity and faith mean more in the history of two nations than all the speeches of statesmen or the labors of diplomacy.

In that year when we stood alone against Germany and Italy, we had to take great risks. The collapse of France, with her overseas empire, had laid bare our strategic positions, not only in Europe, but over the whole of that area loosely called the Middle East, and in the Far East also. As a result, perilously weak as we were at home, we had to take armed divisions from our undermanned citadel of Britain and send them round the Cape to reinforce our threatened defenses. Even so, we tried to keep faith with our friends.

We had given our pledge to the people of Greece, and the world will not forget their epic resistance. We, for our part, did all in our power to help them. We failed, but that was not a failure of which we shall ever feel ashamed.

It was in this same spirit that, on behalf of our Chinese allies, we reopened the Burma Road in 1941.

Let China not misdoubt us. We shall not forget how for years she resisted aggression singlehanded. The Japanese brought against her all the terrors of mechanized war and she had little with which to oppose them. They burnt her cities. They tore from her large tracts of territory. They forced her armies inch by inch into the interior. But never for a moment did her resolution falter. Never has there been a thought of parley, and China no longer stands alone.

The day will come when the Burma Road will once again be open. It will carry to China an ever-increasing volume of supplies, which the efforts of your country and mine are turning out daily from the assembly lines.

As I have explained, with the fall of France we lost our reserves of material which had been transported there. If we were to rearm our trained divisions and to expand our forces and equipment, our own production could not suffice.

It was in such an hour that lend-lease was born, that great conception by which once again the mighty resources of the New World were called in "to redress the balance of the Old."

In that hour, we knew, finally and beyond a doubt, that we were not alone in the cause for which we stood.

Lend-lease began as a one-way traffic. It brought American tanks and guns and aircraft to the battlefields of North Africa and for the defense of Britain. It brought American ships to strengthen the Atlantic lifeline. It brought American supplies of every kind, wherever they could be carried and the need was greatest.

Today the picture is changing. Lend-lease has become the machinery for pooling the war effort of the United Nations, the material equivalent of the combined strategic planning of our armies and navies. It is no longer a one-way traffic. Each nation gives to the others what it can send and they need.

The United States will remain the greatest arsenal of democracy, but Britain in her turn is sending supplies to Russia, to her other allies, to the American forces abroad and even to the United States itself. But if we are glad to take our part in this common effort, we are none the less grateful for what we have received.

Life is hard for many people in Britain today. Shortages, discomforts, privations even, have been accepted by our people in a spirit of which they have a right to be proud. Yet we have still to ensure that they have a minimum of rations required for total war. We have to supply our fighting men with weapons to wage war to best advantage. We could not do these things without the food produced by your farms and industries and exported to us by your ships.

You have been generous to those of our people who have come among you. Today we in our turn are happy to welcome your sons, brothers, husbands and your daughters, too, in our cities and our homes. We are learning from them how alike are our peoples on both sides of the ocean in the things that matter most. London, scarred and seared and blacked-out though it is, yet presents an inspiring sight today. The youth of the world is there, united in the common garb of war.

Your young men and ours rub shoulders with each other and with the young men of the nations united against a common enemy. There they achieve in a short span that national sympathy and understanding which years of diplomatic exchanges could never give. On five continents and seven seas, soldiers and sailors of the United Nations are living and fighting side by side. May they cherish in peace the friendship that they learned in war.

May our young airmen who have renewed an old comradeship of the air carry that spirit with them on errands of peace. Upon them and their like, upon their friendship with one another, rests both the burden and the hope of mankind. Where our generation failed, I pray that theirs may succeed. It may be our last chance. It may be in very truth "the last best hope of earth."

In the period between the two wars the intentions of the peace-loving nations were excellent, but their practice was weak.

If there is one lesson we should have learned from the distresses of those years, it is surely this: that we cannot shut our windows and draw our curtains, and be careless of what is happening next door or on the other side of the street. No nation can close its frontiers and hope to live secure.

We cannot have prosperity in one country and misery in its neighbor, peace in one hemisphere and war in the other. And if we try to have these things we shall be back on the old road to world war. We shall never find security or progress within heavily defended national fortresses. We shall only find them by the greatest possible measure of cooperation. The United Nations, and in particular the United States, the British Commonwealth, China and the Soviet Union, must act together in war and in peace.

The greatest of all peace aims is to insure that never again shall unscrupulous leaders be able to carry their peoples into war and bring tragedy on the world. We shall accordingly take steps for the physical prevention of this danger by the enforced disarmament of these gangster nations. We must insure that this protection of peace-loving peoples is maintained in full effectiveness for whatever period may be necessary.

We must therefore be ready to protect and maintain whatever settlement we devise, and one thing, I am sure, is, above all, essential. Never again must the civilized world be ready to tolerate unilateral infraction of treaties. For that would be to sap the whole foundation of the secure international life which it is our principal purpose to restore.

We must prosecute the war to a final victory. We must determine together to take steps to make sure that neither Germany nor Italy nor Japan can commit a like aggression again. We can do this if we will. If we do, we will fulfill the first condition of peace.

And I take this opportunity once again to make plain that we have no secret engagements with any country, nor do we seek as a result of this conflict to extend our boundaries or increase our possessions.

We in the British Commonwealth have grown up in the thought of cooperation. Some parts of the Commonwealth—the self-governing Dominions—enjoy complete independence, while others are moving toward this goal. Our enemies have looked to this war, as they have looked to the last great war, to sound the death knell of this great association. Nothing in the world is more unlikely.

The Commonwealth is a voluntary union. Its bonds are the will of peoples and races with a common past and a common purpose to travel the same way. Theirs is no static society, shrinking from change or fearful of the future. On the contrary, the British Commonwealth is capable of continuing development. We have sought to learn by our mistakes. The British Empire is the first in history to evolve the idea of self-governing Dominions. That is an entirely new conception in the world. We believe that it can help us to reach our common aim—man's freedom and self-government under the rule of law.

It is in this spirit that we shall administer our trust for the peoples in our empire, whom it is our duty and our pledge to lead to full membership of our community of nations.

I maintain that these principles of our Commonwealth are not of limited application. They are inseparable from the kind of world for which we are fighting, the kind of world we hope to see. That hope is today gathering strength in North Africa, the Pacific, China, through enslaved Europe and on the wide plains of Russia.

Today more than ever war is one and indivisible. The enemies of your country are our enemies. A danger to us is a threat to you, as it is a threat to China and Russia. Let there be no mistake; we shall not rest upon our arms until every one of our enemies has unconditionally surrendered.

We, no less than you and our partner China, have a score to settle with the Japanese; nor shall we cease fighting until that evil growth in the Pacific has been cut back. We shall be with you in this to the end.

When the defense of one is the defense of all, security and peace have no frontiers. Our common safety demands that overwhelming force be brought to bear against the aggressor wherever he may be. And what applies to war applies even more to the peace that is to come. I can say with confidence that today the men and women of Britain are alive to the fact that they live in one world with their neighbors. Only within an international system which is backed with sufficient force can the enterprise and liberty of the individual find protection.

After the last war, the lack of power behind the international system led to the triumph of the dictators. This has more often been said than understood or heeded. On one side, we have the idea of a narrow and covetous nationalism which destroys the life of its own people first, and then the life of its neighbors.

On the other, we have the idea of a close-knit framework of free nations—free as we in Britain, and you here, understand the word. We believe that it is only in such a framework as this that the individual can rise to the full height of his powers and call his soul his own. And we believe that it has been the world's failure to create such a framework which has twice led to war in our time. This at least is certain: if we do not find the common ground on which to build this time, we shall not have deserved victory.

Any new international authority that we may agree to set up can only succeed if it is backed by sufficient strength. It will not be enough for one country, or even two, to display the qualities necessary to protect the peace. The work will take all that America and Britain, Russia and China, and the United Nations can offer.

Your country is justly proud of the wide vision and the boldness and youthful vigor with which it thinks and acts. You will not find my countrymen bound by any narrower horizon.

In the common performance of this task you will find the peoples of our Commonwealth—for I am sure that in this I speak for them all—full and worthy partners. You will find in them a toughness, a resolution, an unsuspected fund of energy, a vitality of spirit, such as have more than once surprised the world.

Our joint task will be hard. But, for our part, we are proud of the company with which we march. No one flag, no one government, no one language unite the peoples of our great alliance. We have one passport, freedom; one objective, victory, total and unmistakable; and one purpose, a just and lasting peace.

DESIGN FOR A PEOPLE'S PEACE [13]

FREDERICK L. SCHUMAN [14]

Dr. Frederick Schuman, Woodrow Wilson Professor of Government, Williams College, delivered this notable address before the Institute of Public Affairs, University of Virginia, Charlottesville, on July 11, 1942.

The Institute was conducted during July 5-11, and included such lecturers as Harold D. Lasswell, Director of War Communications Research, Library of Congress; Leonard Doob, Office of the Coordinator of Inter-American Affairs; Stuart Chase, writer and lecturer; Stringfellow Barr, President of St. John's College; Dean G. Acheson, Assistant Secretary of State; Senator Elbert D. Thomas; Dr. Louis Quintanilla, Minister from Mexico; Louis P. Lochner; Walter Nash and Senator Alben W. Barkley, of Kentucky.

At the session of July 11, the theme was "The Organization of Power in the Postwar World." On this program Percy E. Corbett discussed "Conflicting Trends in Postwar Planning."

Professor Schuman analyzes the problem of ways and means of securing a permanent "people's peace" and outlines clearly his proposed pattern of world government. He ignores the innumerable practical problems arising out of the armistice—the specific policies to be followed in handling a defeated Germany, Italy, Japan; the policies of international credit, trade, geographical boundaries, problem of securing concurrent participation of Great Britain and Russia, and other United Nations in this world government. His statement, nevertheless, is logically reasoned, and deserves close analysis in relation to the other discussions of the postwar world included in this volume and in the preceding volumes of this series.

In all transactions involving profit or loss, it is simple common sense for buyers to bargain for the lowest price. But in all transactions involving the values men live by and die for, it is everywhere deemed wise and right to spare no expense and shrink from no sacrifice, even unto life itself, to preserve them from destruction. The total war in which we are engaged is

[13] Reprinted from *Vital Speeches*, 8:656-61, August 15, 1942. By permission of the author and of the publishers of *Vital Speeches*.
[14] For biographical note see Appendix.

clearly not a matter of gain or deficit but a mortal struggle for the annihilation or survival of all that has hitherto given meaning to the lives of freemen. We know this surely. We say this often. With high resolve we repeat the words of Patrick Henry, "Is life so dear, or peace so sweet, as to be purchased at the price of chains and slavery? Forbid it, Almighty God! I know not what course others may take, but as for me, give me liberty, or give me death!"

And yet, in their deeds if not in their words, most Americans and most of the peoples and leaders of the other United Nations are still dealing with the dangers and opportunities of their self-inflicted tragedy by a niggardly effort to balance accounts on an unseen ledger. Unacknowleged questions trouble our spirits more than the burden and grief of war itself. What is the lowest possible price we must pay for victory? How cheaply can the war be won? How little must we pay to win the peace? By such a miser's reckoning as this our generation bartered away the peace of yesterday and squandered utterly the victory of the day before for which so much was paid in wasted blood and tears. By such penny-pinching bookkeeping the war of today and the peace of tomorrow may be lost beyond recovery, along with the fairest and final promise of our century.

Our miserliness does not lie in the value we place upon our money or our lives. If the lavish expenditure of gold and blood would give us victory, then victory would already be within our reach instead of looming doubtfully beyond some dark horizon we cannot see. What we have hitherto been unwilling to give up for the fulfillment of our purpose are the goods of the mind and heart which men always part with far less willingly than they part with their fortunes or their flesh. The goods we clutch at gaspingly, as if they were the most priceless of treasures, are pride and prejudice, old habits and time-worn grooves of thought and action, familiar superstitions and beloved myths, and all of the confused legacy of loyalties left us by our forebears. Because we know that most of our inheritance of beliefs and practices is worth preserving against the barbarians, we cling grimly to all of that inheritance. In stubborn desperation we refuse to see that much of our cherished past has brought us to this monstrous present and that we are more than likely to lose it all unless we exchange some of it for newer and better ways.

This much most of us are ready to grant—in words. We applauded Vice President Wallace's evaluation of the war as a People's Revolution to inaugurate the Century of the Common Man. We cheered Sumner Welles' denunciation of "unenlightened selfishness," his condemnation of imperialism and his plea to rectify past mistakes by undertaking "the maintenance of an international police power" and by making the United Nations "the nucleus of a world organization of the future to determine the final terms of a just, an honorable and a durable peace." We nodded assent when Mr. Welles, seconding Mr. Wallace, said, "This is in very truth a people's war. It is a war which cannot be regarded as won until the fundamental rights of the peoples of the earth are secured."

We are none the less unwilling still to translate words into deeds if the deeds which are called for conflict with our fixations on the symbols of a dead yesterday. We know in our hearts that words without deeds are the empty mouthings of hollow men. But let anyone propose concrete action to achieve the objectives we say we desire and he will at once be assailed by a host of critics, complaining that his suggestions are contrary to diplomatic precedent, that they are revolutionary or un-American, or that they are politically impracticable and probably subversive. Our political leaders still strive for unity and re-election by resting their appeals on the lowest common denominators of mass support. Our tradition-ridden diplomats remain earnest and small-minded men, wedded to the past and afraid to face the future boldly, lest by so doing they lose friends and alienate people or jeopardize their own stake in the *status quo*.

Yet our leaders in fact represent us. Even our diplomats, albeit less touched by the dynamic forces of our time than many other groups of public servants, are but reflections of ourselves. Responsibility for sluggishness and indecision in the face of the challenge of change lies in our preoccupation with ancient magic and obsolete rituals. Confronted with danger, we take fearful refuge in old formulas which seem somehow less terrifying than the perils of novelty, even in the presence of the disasters to which they have brought us.   Like Hamlet, we prefer to suffer the evils that we know rather than fly to others we know not of.   The enemy, however, has no fear of what is strange and new.   And he has given his oath to his pagan gods to rebuild the world, after his own Satanic design, over the ashes of our homes and the earth of our graves.

We say, as we do battle with his fanatic hordes, that we want freedom of religion everywhere in the world.   But we are timid and furtive about the practical implications of the Fatherhood of God and the Brotherhood of Man, lest we be summoned to treat all men and women of all colors and creeds as truly our fellows, entitled to the rights and opportunities which we claim as our own.   We say we desire freedom of speech everywhere in the world.   But we prefer that the speech be limited to feeble phrases, since bold words calling us to new deeds are disturbing to the contentment which goes with avoidance of thought.   We say we wish freedom from want everywhere in the world.   But we shun the burden of planning a world economy of abundance, and some of us hope against hope for a return to normalcy and for a plenty to be miraculously gained by a restoration of economic anarchy.   We say we wish freedom from fear everywhere in the world.   But we show small eagerness to accept the duties of organizing the world society for security and peace.

We want democracy, but not too much and not for everybody.   We want self-determination for ourselves and for the good Europeans, but we display no sign of desiring self-determination for the people of Hong Kong or Indo-China or Java or Burma or Syria or Madagascar or even Puerto Rico.   We want victory for the United Nations.   But we scarcely want them wholly united or permanently united, lest we be obliged to surrender the fond belief that we can live alone and like it.   Some of us want America to win the war but have no desire for Britain to win it or for China or Russia or Roosevelt to win it.   We still fear communism because we lack faith in our own capacity to offer a betrayed generation anything better.   We are still desperately jealous of our national sovereignty because we refuse to lift our vision to anything broader and more hopeful than national sovereignty. We wish peace and safety, but we seek to keep the attitudes and habits that destroy peace and safety. We are entangled and trapped, now as before, by the narrow provincialisms and the entrenched interests, material and spiritual, of an epoch upon which the morticians hold a mortgage that is already foreclosed.

No easy prescription is at hand for resolving this dilemma, nor is it helpful to dwell upon it in any spirit of melancholy satisfaction or pessimism nor to search for scapegoats or villains to whom it may be ascribed. Our most dangerous enemies are those within our minds and hearts. Those who want things which are incompatible and mutually exclusive must either make up their minds as to what they want most and accept the consequences, or they must remain forever frustrated, forever unable to reconcile ends and means, forever irresolute and doomed to defeat at the hands of those who know what they want. The English-speaking peoples among the United Nations, along with their pathetic house guests of governments-in-exile, have not yet decided what they want most. Until they do, they will remain incapable of formulating war aims and peace plans in any terms more substantial than such devalued words as "freedom" and "survival."

Here again we all agree, in principle, that a concrete declaration of goals and programs for building the world of tomorrow is an indispensable and perhaps a decisive weapon for waging the war itself. Without it we cannot persuade the enemy peoples and the conquered peoples and the colonial peoples and even many of our own people that we are fighting for a future better than the past and better than that promised by the foe. And we know, or will presently know, that until we have carried this conviction far and wide over the world as a burning faith, we will be lacking in the political and psychological prerequisites for a second front, for successful military attack anywhere, for ultimate victory itself.

But, like diplomats bargaining with our own consciences, we shrink from practicing the principles we accept. We cannot formulate an effective declaration of our purposes because we cannot choose sharply among our own conflicting desires.

So long as we refuse to choose, so long will our every move be hampered by our own confusions, so long will we continue to believe blindly that the war can be won by money and blood, or by mass production, or by the frantic fear of defeat in our souls, or by the loathing to which decent men and women everywhere are moved by the crimes of the enemy. Yet every day the voice within and the news without tell us that the cost of the triumph we pray for is quoted in different figures on some quite different price list.

The invisible barriers to victory within our heads are reflected in the organization, in the obligations and in the stated objectives of the United Nations—or, to put it bluntly, in the lack of organization, in the confusion of obligations and in the absence of clearly stated objectives. The weaknesses of our coalition are too many and varied for brief enumeration. Suffice it to say that our grand alliance still has no common central organs with powers of decision, no unified high command, no adequate representation of many peoples whose aid is essential for victory, no universal commitments beyond a pact to fight together and make no separate peace, no program whatever for winning the peace, and no common statement of goals beyond the Atlantic Charter. The Charter itself, whatever we may think of its pale platitudes and however frequently it may be mentioned in new agreements among the United Nations, has no meaning to the subject peoples and the enemy peoples save as a reckless formula to restore the world of yesterday by putting Humpty-Dumpty back on the wall. It is a statement of desirable ends wholly devoid of any indication of relevant means by which the ends are to be attained. It is a declaration, noble in purpose, of the rights of men and nations, unaccompanied by any suggestion of those duties of the world community without which no rights can be maintained. If these judgments seem harsh and dismal, they are less so than the facts themselves or the fruits of the facts in the course of the war which is plain for all to see.

The question of whether the war can be won through the use of such weapons of the spirit as we now have available is almost "academic," a word which is the layman's euphemism for unanswerable and unimportant. The war is in fact being lost. The enemy is conquering ever wider spaces and ever longer time intervals within which to prepare for us the irreparable defeat, preceding the final kill. It is clear, or should by now be clear, that our succession of defeats is due less to lack of courage or of arms or of resources than to lack of willingness to undertake new departures in the conduct of war and the planning of peace and to resultant lack of ability to move the peoples of the world to that measure of purposeful devotion which is needed for victory. If nevertheless, as all of us hope, the tide of battle can yet be turned by the sheer brute power of our production of soldiers and guns, unaccompanied by political imagination to reshape the world, then the further question of whether we can win the peace will have found its own answer. In this event, at once welcome and heartbreaking, we shall prepare our children as best we can for the next epoch of power politics with its renewal of the sickening cycle of concert and balance, disunity and unbalance, aggression and appeasement, futile evasions and ultimately world-shattering war once more.

The alternative to this prospect is willingness to pay the price of victory now. The price of victory is, in the largest sense, the price of peace. For it is almost as certain as death and taxes, despite widespread belief to the contrary, that the winning of the war will not precede, but will follow, the formulation of our plan for winning the peace. That plan will be the principal weapon of our victory. The price of peace has been stated over and again in sundry shapes and is everywhere being discussed in many tongues, thus far without agreement. The way of freemen, however, is to arrive at a consensus through discussion. Everyone whose mind is clear and whose will to victory is firm therefore owes it to himself and his fellows to think through the issue, while there is yet time, and to state the price as best he can, with humility and full awareness of the obstacles in the way of its payment, but also with frankness and with hope that wisdom and action will flow from debate.

The first step toward winning the war through a program for winning the peace is to obtain general acceptance of a few simple and familiar propositions which may be stated quite briefly, even at the risk of appearing dogmatic. The basic premise has been constantly reiterated through the centuries by all who have ever given serious thought to the issue. As good a statement as any is that of Alexander Hamilton, "To look for a continuation of harmony between a number of independent and unconnected sovereignties in the same neighborhood would be to disregard the uniform course of human events and set at defiance the accumulated experience of the ages." Armed violence between nations is not a consequence of tyranny or sin but a concomitant, invariable and inevitable, of the presence of a multiplicity of sovereignties in the same community, whether that community be as small as ancient Greece and medieval Italy or as large as all our shrunken globe. Such sovereignties, so long as they are wholly sovereign, independent, and unconnected through any supreme law or higher authority, must necessarily play power politics with one another. For power politics is the only possible form of politics in a society whose members live in a condition of anarchy. War is the final and inescapable form of power politics. Its abolition is impossible without the abolition of power politics. The abolition of power politics is impossible without the abolition of anarchy among rival sovereignties. The abolition of anarchy is impossible without the establishment of government. The prerequisite of government in the world community is the merging of sovereignties into a permanent world authority, created by all for the protection of each and so devised that its agents will have power to maintain a world order, to enforce a world law, and to prevent or suppress all violence save the organized violence of the world community against evil-doers. Only in this fashion can world politics be made an orderly process of compromise and planning for welfare and justice rather than a hideous nightmare of fraud and force.

However dim their perceptions may be of the relationship between ends and means, however deep their affections may be for the tribal divinities and the local absolutisms making for world anarchy, the vast majority of men and women everywhere are now so weary of ruin and slaughter that their deepest hunger is for harmony, order, and peace. They want world order more than they want national sovereignty, though they see no means as yet for attaining the former without destroying the latter. They want world order more than they want freedom, a value which we have all but emptied of content by our refusal to organize the security and the opportunity without which freedom is meaningless. Because all of humankind now needs and wants world order with such imperative urgency, it is reasonable to believe that a way will be found in our time to establish world government and therewith to abolish international anarchy, power politics and the war.

The hard journey towards the world commonwealth can follow one of two routes. World government is possible through the armed subjugation of the many by the few, with the freedom and sovereignty of all sacrificed to conquerors who keep peace and order by the sword and the lash. World government is also possible through the voluntary establishment of a free world order on the basis of the consent of the governed, incorporated in a new world law, with all citizens enjoying a new freedom and with all nations participating in a new interdependence affording their peoples true independence and security. The first way is the way of our foes. We are fighting against it with all our strength. We can never make it our own, now or in the future, without betraying all the values we live by. The second way is the only way open to freemen. We cannot pursue it with any hope of accomplishing our purpose, however, through the mere cooperation of sovereign governments with sovereign governments, through diplomatic conferences and military alliances, or through any new effort to establish an international government composed of national governments pledged to keep the peace by coercing those national governments which break it. All such attempts, from the Achaean League of the Greeks to the American Articles of Confederation and the Wilsonian League of Nations, have invariably failed and must always fail. Sovereign governments by their nature pursue their own interests and not the commonweal, whether they act alone or together. The old conception of the sovereign independence of nations, so dear to the framers of the Atlantic Charter, is a formula for anarchy. The ancient principle of the sovereign equality of nations, so dear to those who sing the praises of Pan Americanism, is a prescription for irresponsibility and inaction. Never can world government be attained by bringing local governments together but only by bringing peoples together through their directly chosen representatives into a larger mansion of freedom wherein human fraternity will become politically possible.

How then, granted the ultimate acceptance of these propositions, can the enterprise be launched? One possible method was resorted to in an hour of disaster by Prime Minister Winston Churchill in mid-June of 1940 when he perceived that the Anglo-French alliance, with its bonds as firm and tightly drawn as the present alliance of the United Nations, was about to crack asunder under the blows of the enemy. He proposed to Premier Paul Reynaud the formation of an Anglo-French union with a written constitution, a joint cabinet, a common citizenship, a single supreme command and a pooling of all the sovereign powers of the two nations in the fields of defense, foreign affairs and financial and economic policies. This daring proposal was the product of a bold mind, spurred to a truly creative effort by the imminence of catastrophe. The proposal was not too little, but it was assuredly too late. It was forthwith rejected by the French defeatists who surrendered to the Axis in preference to continuing the war from the colonies in close union with Britain. Yet the proposal itself, which reappears in greatly diluted form in the agreements between the Polish and Czechoslovak Governments-in-Exile and between the Greek and Jugoslav Governments-in-Exile, offers a workable basis of permanent unity for all the states of Europe, for the United States and Britain, for the American Republics and perhaps, if one may venture on large hopes, for all the United

Nations. But such a forward step as this is still pronounced dangerous and utopian by all conservative diplomats and patriots, who prefer to believe that defeat and slavery are less dangerous and utopian. No such program of reconstruction can apparently be expected on the part of governments now in power save in the face of further disasters or in the aftermath of collapse and exile when the hour for action will have passed.

What steps short of this and yet still relevant to the task in hand might be currently urged upon our leadership with some chance of success? Most urgently needed now is a supreme political council of the United Nations to direct the war as a global struggle requiring an effective common demand. Such a supreme political council, already urged by Mr. Walter Nash, Deputy Prime Minister of New Zealand, must be established before we can hope to begin winning the war. If we are also to win the peace, such a council must be envisaged as a provisional world executive to function in peace and war alike for the organization and direction of a world police force and for the rational planning of a postwar economy.

The broad conditions for successful achievement on the part of such a council deserve to be stated clearly. Its members should not be professional diplomats or soldiers but, wherever possible, elected representatives and majority leaders in their respective countries. Under their direction there should be brought into being three indispensable administrative agencies: a United Nations military general staff, composed of experts in the science of arms, for the management of coming campaigns and the planning of the world police force: a United Nations psychological general staff, composed of experts in the skills of education propaganda and psychological warfare, for the waging of the war of ideas and for the reeducation of the citizenry of the world community; and a United Nations economic general staff, composed of experts in the arts of business administration (with employers and workers perhaps represented along with governments, as in the International Labor Organization), for the conduct of economic warfare and the development of the controls and practices needed in the world economy of the days to come. The officials in these lesser bodies should be regarded not at all as spokesmen for national states but as professional administrators and members of a world secretariat, answerable only to the supreme political council.

On the council itself a majority of votes must be held by the great powers, namely, the United States, the British Commonwealth of Nations, the Soviet Union, China and ultimately Free France and a self-governing India, each with equal representation. All the lesser belligerents should be represented equally, with their combined votes in a minority. Let no one contend that the rights of small nations demand that they control the enterprise. There can be no possible security for the lesser countries without an effective union for security among the great powers. There can be no possible security for any one great power without a union with the other great powers in which all assume equal responsibilities. Equality of rights is impossible without equality of duties, and great and small nations alike must assume equal duties if they would share in the benefits of equal rights. But in the planning and execution of duties there can be no equality among communities which differ enormously in population, resources, and power. To treat the microcosms of world politics as the sovereign equals of the great continental states is to defeat the project and negate the democratic principle of popular representation. To permit the pretensions of lesser sovereignties to interfere with the efforts of the greater sovereignties to devise a world order in which all sovereignties will be pooled for the good of all is to invite the destruction of all.

Let there be further established now a world commission of jurists, consisting of eminent authorities of various nationalities chosen by the supreme political council to represent the major legal systems of the world. Let this commission prepare plans for a new world court, modeled upon the old and having obligatory jurisdiction over all legal controversies among states, but envisaged also in bolder terms as a court of appeal from the highest national courts for the protection of fundamental rights of individuals. If such a world court is to be effective as the judicial branch of the world government to come, it must have appellate jurisdiction in constitutional questions. Only thus can the world order of the future be enforced through the rule of law and the orderly processes of litigation and judgment.

Now, or at latest tomorrow, is also the time for an intercontinental congress of legislators, made up of delegates from the Congress of the United States, the British Parliaments, the All-Union Congress of Soviets, and such lawmakers of China, India and the lesser United Nations as their governments may care to designate. Let such an intercontinental congress of the United Nations act as a convention to draw up a world bill of rights, defining and safeguarding the elementary human freedoms everywhere, as part of a world constitution, establishing a permanent world executive responsible to a permanent and popularly elected world parliament. That constitution should in no sense supersede the national constitutions of the United Nations, save insofar as they are inconsistent with its terms, but it should be planned as a supreme public law for mankind, binding on all national governments and their citizens and enforceable in national courts. It must grant limited but effective powers of world legislation to the world parliament, established as a permanent and continuous peace conference for the rational governance of the planet. Those powers must include authority to administer all the non-self-governing colonial territories of the earth, held in trust by the world parliament as mandatory, pending their admission to the ranks of the United Nations as equal and autonomous communities. Those powers must embrace the right and duty of discussing and settling by statutory enactment all political disputes among the nations, including all questions of frontiers, disarmament obligations, provisional administration of occupied and enemy territories, admission of the vanquished to the ranks of the United Nations, reparation for damage inflicted by past aggression, and indictment for trial before the world

court of all individuals charged with international or inter-
racial crimes against their fellow men.   These powers must
encompass the maintenance and direction of the world police
force under the command of the world executive.

The central function, and at the outset the only function,
of the world parliament, the world executive and the world
court of the United Nations should be the abolition of international violence.   The means thereto must not be sought in
old ways which have tragically failed so often and so utterly.
They must be sought in the acceptance of the principle that
the fabrication and the use of heavy armaments must never
again be a function of national governments, large or small,
but only of the United Nations, acting through the world
executive and the world police force.   This principle must
be at the core of the world constitution, enforceable on
individuals through judicial procedures, with anything to the
contrary thereto in the laws or practices of the member states
to be held invalid through judical review.   On this basis, and
in all likelihood only on this basis, can the United Nations
effectively forbid any state henceforth to take up arms against
another.   On this basis, and only on this basis, can international security and justice be achieved through the adjudica-
tion of legal disputes and the legislative settlement of political
controversies, with all the armed might of an organized world,
resolved upon the defense of freedom and order, turned
against any individual or group seeking by self-help or
violence to break the law and defy the common will.   Beyond
this goal, and as a result of its achievement, stretch limitless
vistas for the enrichment of human experience and the further
liberation of all peoples from fear and want and frustration.
In this enterprise the world government of the United Nations
will have great and growing opportunities for creative service.
But the first step, without which our only future may well
be a return to the Dark Ages, is victory over the hosts of
tyranny through the replacement of international anarchy by
a world constitution of freedom and peace.

Is the task too hard?   Is our vision too warped, our imagination too fettered, our talent for agreement and construc-

tion too feeble to vanquish the obstacles and master the details attendant upon such a project as this? Perhaps so, if we choose so to believe out of inertia or despair. If so, we shall, beyond the slightest peradventure of a doubt, lose the war or the peace or both. The most dangerous defeatists among us are those who say these things cannot be done. The most vicious, because the most unwitting, enemy agents among us are those who say these things must not be done and that we must cling to our last black hour to the bloody rags and tatters of an age long dead and now in full decay.

These things can and must be done by leading the people of the United States and of the United Nations to tell their leaders that the time is now. This is the test of our worthiness to survive and of our fitness for freedom. Let us take courage from the words of George Washington, who said of another liberating enterprise in human unification, "Is there a doubt whether a common government can embrace so large a sphere? Let experience solve it. To listen to mere speculation in such a case were criminal. We are authorized to hope that a proper organization of the respective subdivisions will afford a happy issue to the experiment. It is well worth a fair and full experiment."

Here is our best hope, and perhaps our last hope, to win the war by winning the peace through a free world order now. Here is our chance to build the temple of tomorrow on such foundations that no conference of diplomats need ever be held, no "long armistice" or transitional period to chaos need ever be risked, no entangling alliances need ever be made, no punitive and patched-up treaties need ever be debated by neo-isolationists and neo-internationalists. All our war aims will be reduced to one: to defend, to extend and through the years to perfect our program-in-action for the emancipation and self-fulfillment of the human family. Our allies and friends will be with us from the outset, inspired with new courage to crush the foe. Many neutrals will be eager to join, lest they be left in limbo. The enemy peoples will be required to join, once they have laid down their arms, cast out their despots and cleansed their souls. The requirement will be for them a challenge, an invitation and an opportunity, at once our road to victory and their road to redemption. Here, beyond the valley of the shadow, is the new day. Those with eyes for the dawn, those who can turn the vision of men and women everywhere toward the promise it offers them, will ultimately win the gratitude of their fellows all over the flowering planet and the thanks of all posterity during the bright generations ahead. To fail in the duties of this task is to forfeit not only our honor and our lives but all the legacy of liberty that has been given us to cherish, to enrich and not to cast away. To succeed is to conquer the future and inherit the earth.

INSIDE WARRING EUROPE

THE SOUL OF FRANCE [1]

JOHN W. VANDERCOOK [2]

Mr. John W. Vandercook gave this radio commentary over the National Broadcasting Company network on November 27, 1942. Mr. Vandercook, like other news analysts, came to radio after considerable experience as reporter and journalist. He has both facility in composition and impressiveness in delivery. His rich voice with its wide pitch-range suggests the actor that he was for a short time.

Early in the morning of November 27, Marshal Petain at Vichy was aroused to receive a letter from Adolf Hitler. The Fuehrer explained that because of the "treachery" of high French officers the remaining units of Vichy's army and navy would be demobilized. The great naval base at Toulon, the last important stronghold of French defense, would be occupied and the warships then would be taken or "annihilated."

For two and one half years sixty-two vessels of the French navy, battleships, cruisers, submarines, destroyers and one airplane carrier, had been at anchor.

At daybreak of the twenty-seventh the German armored forces poured into the town and onto the docks. German bombers swooped over the docks and warships. Parachute mines were dropped in the channel to block any exit to the sea. Vice Admiral Jean de Saborde, Commander of the French fleet, gave the signal, "Carry out order B."

Instantly the fleet began to commit suicide. First the Strasbourg, 26,000 tons, blew itself up. Roar followed roar over the harbor; vessel after vessel exploded. Those not immediately wrecking themselves were raked by gunfire from other vessels.

"In the glare of the explosions and searchlights the Germans saw the French masters, at rigid attention on their bridges, saluting the Tricolor as they went down." (*Time,* December 7, 1942, p. 29) By ten o'clock in the morning it was over. The ships were practically all sunk (with the exception of four submarines that escaped); the ammunition stores and coastal fortifications were blown up; and the sailors were captives of the Germans.

[1] Published through the courtesy of Mr. Vandercook. Text furnished by the authority of the National Broadcasting Company.
[2] For biographical note see Appendix.

The French thus contributed immensely to the successful United Nations campaign in the Mediterranean. If the fleet had fallen to the Germans, the whole balance of military power in the Mediterranean might have swung toward Hitler.

As Vandercook put it, "France's humiliation . . . has ended. . . . France, tied to the wheel of the conqueror's chariot for more than two bitter years, now can lift her head again and face any people of any nation, eye to eye."

What happened today in France, will, I think, live as long as there are human minds left to remember, as one of the bravest and, surely, as the most gallant deed in modern history.

Toulon, where the French fleet lay and waited so long for its hour of destiny—is a quiet town. The shutters of its neat, grey-white little buildings are often drawn during the long and drowsy hours of the Mediterranean afternoon. The port, and the people of the port, turn their backs on the main highway by which fashionable travellers drive to those more famous resort centers, farther on to the east, along the Riviera coast. And Toulon does not regret their passage. On the water-front, the sleepy promenade is hard and grassless earth, spaced by those plane trees which are the signature of France. But the old sailors on pension, who sit on the benches that look to the sea, and the young children in their blue pinafores and black aprons who play near them—in the shadow of a big blue and white sign which says "Be Good to Animals," have the sun of the azure coast for company—and they ask for little more. Inland, in the valleys between the nearby hills, are the fields of narcissus and of roses which supply the perfume makers of the town of Grasse. Beyond, somehow apart from Toulon itself, is the great naval port; a vast clanging basin of moles, and reaching cranes, and of great gray warships, which were the pride of France. But they too, and the strong Breton sailors with the red pompoms on their blue caps, were a part of that peaceful place, which, until today, had never known its hour of glory.

Two years ago, the foolish said, France died. With her motherland's defeat, Toulon grew shabbier, and desperately hungry. And the great ships, in that strange stillness of a nation's tragedy, never stirred. The ignorant might have fancied that they, too, were dead, and the spirits of the men aboard them. But France, where they hate to march, and where they hate all German marching men, was living. Her courage, burnished bright by shame, was glowing, under the ashes of defeat, more brightly, we know now, than it ever had before.

Today, Hitler, that futile fool, who thinks that you can conquer men's and nation's spirits with an iron bludgeon, ordered that Toulon be taken. He had lied again, for he had sworn Toulon and the fleet would be inviolate. The thundering Nazi columns poured into the Toulon streets without warning, just before dawn this morning. They, too, had made the brute mistake of fancying that France, and the French, were dead. Studiously, their masters had starved the bodies and pressed with all their German surgeons' skill on the minds of those men of Toulon, for two long years, to mold them into their own robot obedience. And then those invaders met such a scene of fierce courage, and of resurgent life, as they never dreamed could be.

The fleet was ready to go down, like the sun, in splendor. Explosives, stored in the ships' holds, were touched off—even as the German boarding parties climbed to the steel decks. French officers stood calm and smiling, as their ships blew up around them. By ten o'clock, the great naval harbor was filled with sunken, burning ships—and France had beaten Germany. There were sixty or more of those ships. They were of all kinds, from great battleships to slender submarines. Axis patrols outside the port had prevented their escape. But if ships, or men, or nations have souls, they have joined us now, risen from the bravest funeral pyre in Europe's history. With that glorious gesture, seemingly ended the last pretence that there was a coward government of France, in Vichy. That collaborationist group has had few friends. And those few, one may be quite sure, today sank finally into the mud which bore them—as those Toulon ships went down.

The first accounts of the Toulon affair came exultantly over the Vichy radio. Abruptly that radio went dead. The great story was repeated. Then the Vichy radio went silent again, and has not been heard since. Perhaps the Gestapo is in charge. Certainly, few French voices will be found now to mouth the Germans' orders into any microphone.

The bewildered Nazis, so superbly tricked by a kind of spirit they have never understood, now have, they say, Toulon, in their possession. The shell, they may hold. Though they have admitted that the task of winning full control of the port took many hours. But the substance, and the fleet, are gone. Arsenals, munition dumps, and fuel tanks were all blown up. Toulon's very considerable harbor fortifications, the Vichy announcement said, were all destroyed. The French were ready. And let no one say again that the French, unlike others, have a singular respect for property.

That fleet—it is a minor aspect—of which they were so proud, cost them, a far poorer people than we are, far more than a quarter of a billion dollars. Yet they tossed it into the scales of our common victory like a condemned man's airy flip of a cigarette. In the town itself, the furious, muddled Nazis are piling prisoners into their waiting lorries, which had come on that fool's errand, and blank-faced German troopers stand guard over their proud prisoners.

The effect of this day's work on France, and on the whole progress of the war, is incalculable. France, though she has never died, has been reborn. It takes small imagination to picture the excitement, the tears, the pride tonight of that whole great people. France's humiliation, and I do not think I exaggerate a particle, has ended. France, tied to the wheel of the conqueror's chariot for more than two bitter years, now can lift her head again and look any people of any nation, eye to eye. What, they may ask now, have you done, that was any braver, that was any better, than what we did today? What single victory has yours or Britain's navy ever won that cost the enemy sixty ships at once? It is true, it was a strange victory. But the circumstances were shaped, the French would say, not by ourselves, but by fate. And now we, the men of France, have fashioned that fate to our own, and to your uses.

LIDICE [3]

WENDELL L. WILLKIE [4]

Mr. Wendell L. Willkie gave this talk on Sunday, July 12, 1942, at the ceremonies in Stern Park Gardens, Illinois, a suburb of Chicago, during which that city was renamed Lidice, Illinois, in honor of Lidice, Czechoslovakia.

The facts concerning the martyrdom of Lidice are fully brought out in the talk itself. Mr. Willkie, with characteristic vigor, dramatizes the tragedy, makes it all the more terrible by his contrast with the "black smoke of steel factories" in view of his audience, and expounds, through the medium of his emotional, imaginative recital, his philosophy of the cause for which he and America are fighting.[5]

Ten months after this moving Willkie oration was delivered, Senator Scott Lucas, of Illinois, in his address in honor of President Beneš,[6] at the Chicago Stadium on May 23, 1943, also discussed the significance of Lidice:

"Our meeting today is within a short distance from a little American community which out of respect and sympathy has named itself Lidice. The peace, the quiet, the civilized progress which this suburb of a great city enjoys are reminiscent of the peaceful quiet and the civilized living which the little town in Czechoslovakia enjoyed until that hateful, fateful day when a crazed beast in human form led his murderous hangmen through its streets and left nothing but ashes, despair and death. But the suburb is symbolic of the new Lidice that must and shall grow in Czechoslovakia as a symbol to all the world that the aberrations of a master race, destructive as they may be, are not and cannot be permitted to be lasting influences in our world.

"It is almost two years since Lidice, long just another community of homes and people, center of everyday happiness and sorrows of men and women and children, became immortal. A shocked world beheld men, once possessors of a proud culture, but now enslaved and mesmerized by a lust for power and the delusion of a mission, burn and destroy this simple dignified hamlet. Then proudly these despoilers of mankind boasted of their dastardly accomplishment. Lidice, they proclaimed, is wiped from the face of the earth.

---

[3] By permission of Mr. Willkie. Text furnished through the courtesy of the author.
[4] For autobiographical note see Appendix.
[5] For further comment on Mr. Willkie's speaking during this period see p. 105.
[6] See p. 56.

"But that was just another indication of their treacherous and false thinking. Lidice is now greater than it ever was before. Lidice is a symbol of a goal. The sympathies and, more important, the energies of mankind are directed toward the successful culmination of the Herculean task of making certain that there shall never again be a repetition of that which occurred in the little Czechoslovakian village."

Fellow Citizens and all who love freedom everywhere:

Let me tell you a story. Ten miles west of Prague, in Czechoslovakia, there was a little village called Lidice, spelled L I D I C E. It was a mining village, a mile off the main highway, with some lovely old inns, a blacksmith or two, a shoemaker, a wheelwright, a tailor. The village had been there for over six hundred years.

Above the ninety roofs of the town rose the spire of St. Margaret's Church, built in 1736, the home of the faith of the community. This town was remote, peaceful, almost like a village in a fairy tale. But it was not a village in a fairy tale, for its people had tasted the bread and wine of freedom. In this village one of the main streets was named Wilson Street, after an American who had a vision and wanted to share it with the world. And the people of Lidice dreamed the same dream, saw the same vision.

But the Nazis came, and with them misery and hardship. The altar of St. Margaret's Church was no longer open to the people as it had been for over two hundred years. Men had to watch their words and in their actions they could no longer be free. But in their hearts, the hearts of the inn-keeper and the tailor and the farmer and the miner and the priest, was the stubborn independence of their fathers.

Not far from Lidice ran a winding road. On this road on May 27th, six weeks ago, at 10:30 in the morning, a motor car was passing carrying Hitler's governor of Czechoslovakia, Hangman Heydrich, for his cruelties the most hated man in all Europe. The car was held up by two unknown men. Bullets burrowed into the spine of Reinhard Heydrich. The two patriots disappeared, and one of them, it is said, is now safe in London.

I do not wish to speak of the reign of terror that thereupon swept over all Czechoslovakia. I wish to speak today only of Lidice, and I will give you only the facts. This is not my version of the facts. This is not a version of the facts issued by any of the United Nations as propaganda. These are the facts as officially attested by the German government. They are facts of which the Nazis are proud. They are facts they wish the world to know. They are facts they believe will frighten you and me, and turn our hearts and our knees to water, and make us cry "Truce!"

For Heydrich the Hangman died in agony, as he had caused thousands of innocent people to die. No proof from that day to this has ever been adduced to show that any of the inhabitants of Lidice had anything to do with the assassination. But the Nazis made their own proof. They were afraid not to, for Heydrich was one of their great men. "One of the best Nazis," Hitler called him, and that, no doubt, is true.

On June 10th an official German statement was issued, not for domestic consumption, but for the world to hear. I quote from it:

It is officially announced that in the course of the search for the murderers of General Heydrich, it has been ascertained that the population of the village of Lidice supported and assisted the perpetrators who came into question. . . . Because the inhabitants, by their support of the perpetrators have flagrantly violated the law, all men of the village have been shot. The women have been deported to a concentration camp and the children sent to appropriate centers of education. All buildings of the village were levelled to the ground and the name of the village was immediately abolished.

That is the official Nazi report.

They came in the night, men in boots and brown shirts, and they took from their homes the bewildered miners and farmers, the tailor and the priest, the boy of seventeen and the old man of seventy, more than two hundred in all, and they shot them, because they could think of no other way to avenge the death of Heydrich. Fifty-six women they took also and killed, and proudly listed their names. The rest of the women they drove into what they called concentration camps; and these women the world will never see again. They herded the pale, terror-stricken children into trucks and carried them off to correction schools where they would be taught that they must honor the murderers of their fathers and the brutalizers of their mothers. The ninety homes they burned to the ground, the church of St. Margaret they stamped into the earth. And the name of the little town of Lidice, through which ran the street called after a President of the United States, they rubbed out, they thought, from history.

Why did they do this deed, more terrible than anything that has happened since the Dark Ages, a deed not of passion, but of cold, premeditated, systematic murder and rapine? Why? They did it because they are afraid. They are afraid because the free spirit in men has refused to be conquered. Theirs is a system of force and terror and Lidice is the terrible symbol of that system.

But it is not the only one. Of the five hundred thousand men, women and children who have been shot in Europe by the Nazis, at least twenty-five thousand have perished in mass massacres. Poland, Norway, Belgium, Yugoslavia, all have their Lidices. But this one—a symbol of all—we have sworn to remember, if only because the Nazis themselves demand that we forget it. Once more, they have misjudged the human spirit.

Because a hangman was killed, Lidice lives. Because a hangman was killed, Wilson Street must once again be part of a little Bohemian town. Because the lanterns of Lidice have been blacked out, a flame has been lit which can never be extinguished. Each of the wounds of those two hundred men and fifty-six women is a mouth that cries out that other free men and free women must not suffer a like fate. Everywhere, but particularly in our own country, the wave of stubborn, stern resolve rises. Lidice lives. She lives again, thirty-five hundred miles from Wilson Street and St. Margaret's Church, in this little village in Illinois.

I look about me here, and I can see in the distance the black smoke of steel factories, swarming with American workers of all bloods and races. No contrast could be greater than the peaceful Lidice the Nazis thought they had destroyed, and this

Illinois country, alive with factories in which the arms of victory are being forged.   But I tell you that the two are related. For while such deeds as Lidice are done in another country, we cannot rest until we are sure that they will never be done in our own.

Let us here highly resolve that the memory of this little village of Bohemia, now resurrected by the people of a little village in Illinois, will fire us, now and until the battle is over, with the iron resolution that the madness of tyrants must perish from the earth, so that the earth may return to the people to whom it belongs, and be their village, their home, forever.

INSIDE GERMANY [7]

Louis P. Lochner [8]

Mr. Louis Lochner gave this address before the Institute of Public Affairs at the University of Virginia, Charlottesville, on July 10, 1942.

This foreign correspondent, after 1930 and until 1942, spent much time in Europe. With the start of the World War II, he had headquarters in Berlin and had opportunity for two years to report for the American press his observations of the war. Because he frequently gave vivid accounts of the might of the Nazi war machine, some readers suspected him of pro-Hitlerism. The speaker's account of his personal adventures and attitudes and of the Hitler military organization at the peak of its power makes interesting reading.

The speech is to be partly weighed in the light of subsequent facts. Was Lochner accurate in his analysis of weaknesses within the Reich because of transportation, manpower, materials? If so, how did the Fuehrer attempt to overcome such military handicaps?

Mr. Lochner is an enthusiastic speaker who projects well and convinces both by voice and by persuasive material.

He gives some account of his career in learning to speak:

"When I entered the University of Wisconsin in 1905, a student who, like myself, had attended West Division High School in Milwaukee, but who was now a senior at the U.W. while I was a mere freshman, came to call on me the first Friday after my matriculation. 'Come along to Philomathia Debating Society,' he said.

" 'Debating society?' I countered. 'Why, I'm too scared to say one coherent sentence before a crowd. I can't debate.'

" 'Stupid,' was my friend's rejoinder, 'that's precisely why I'm taking you along. You're to learn how to speak. You won't get far in life unless you can express your thoughts while on your feet.'

"I need hardly tell you that my first attempts were woeful. I stuttered and stammered and floundered. My friend was relentless. He saw to it that I was put on the program frequently.

"Well, I ended by being one of two class orators at the commencement of my class in 1909.

"Since then I have been on the platform a good deal. The most important thing I learned about being successful in public speaking is that one must constantly bring in the human touch. It is then that the audience pricks up its ears." [9]

[7] Text furnished through the courtesy of Mr. Lochner.
[8] For biographical note see Appendix.
[9] Letter to the editor of this volume, June 11, 1943.

The other day, in New York, I had the first opportunity since my arrival on the Drottningholm on June 1st to relax a bit. I say it was my first opportunity, for, ever since my arrival I had been dragged from one intelligence office to another, from one luncheon or dinner engagement to another, from one off-the-record talk to another, from one mass meeting to another, and had to write one article after another.

With my family I went to see that charming picture in which Sasha Guitry stars: "Les Champs Élysées." We were reminded of the five months during which we took the Bad Nauheim "cure," in that many a profitable hour had then been spent by us in improving upon our knowledge of French. You see, a hundred and thirty-eight of us Americans were cooped up there in the same hotel, and I don't know what we would have done to overcome boredom had not some wise person organized what we proudly called "Badheim University." We soon found that there was every sort of college talent in our midst, and soon the place was teeming with language classes—French, German, Spanish, Russian, Portuguese, Italian—and with classes in drama, phonetics, biology, history, philosophy, mathematics, and civics. Even I found a group of people willing to listen to a course on the American Constitution which I offered!

Hence Sasha Guitry's picture recalled our Bad Nauheim internment days with its sounds of the beautiful French language.

But in me the picture awakened another memory. It was that of standing two years ago in that same Champs Élysées and seeing the victorious Hitler forces marching past the Arc de Triomphe and on to the Avenue Foch. Then as even now the whole thing seemed incredible to me. Like all the rest of the world I had trusted implicitly in the efficacy of the Maginot Line. I was simply dazed to find myself in a Paris occupied by enemy troops, in a Paris now so dead that I counted only a dozen people on its busiest spot, the Place de la Concorde, in a Paris at the Tomb of the Unknown Soldier of which I saw heartrending scenes of women weeping, old men kneeling down in prayer, young boys and girls silently strewing flowers.

We had entered Paris on the same day that it capitulated, June 14, 1940, after witnessing scenes at the front that have been seared into my soul so that I shall never be able to forget them.

I refer especially to the endless stream of civilian human misery wandering aimlessly over the roads jammed with military, then refugees pathetically carrying with them sometimes the most useless of animals or things to which they were fondly attached—house pets such as scraggy little dogs, underfed cats, scared birds; heirlooms such as a wedding picture in a large frame with the glass already broken, or a seemingly worthless old table loaded onto a baby buggy filled to the top with clothing and bedding.

I shall never be able to forget the look of bewilderment and utter despair of these simple western European peasant people as they trudged along the road, furtively glancing at our cars that enveloped these unfortunates in a cloud of dust, holding on with their last ounce of strength to the lean cow or skinny horse that they were leading by a rope to they knew not exactly where.

I ask you, Ladies and Gentlemen, how would you feel if in that endless refugee stream you suddenly saw a hearse, drawn not by horses or propelled by motor, but slowly pulled by some ten or twelve perspiring, dust-bespattered men and women—why? because in that hearse, where otherwise the coffin is placed, there sat a dozen or so little Flemish kiddies who had been made homeless by war's ravages, and for whom the fond parents had no other means of locomotion than this community hearse?

Wouldn't it have wrenched your hearts to witness that sort of scene? We saw old grand-daddies evidently too lame and feeble to walk, moved along the dusty highways in baby buggies, while the tots to whom they belonged, just about old enough to walk short distances, stumbled along for a while, then were carried again for a distance by tired mothers or fathers. We saw motor cars jammed to capacity with household goods and infants, drawn by fathers, mothers, and grown-up brothers and sisters; drawn rather than driven because nobody in civilian life anywhere had any gasoline.

Add to this the stench of the battlefields themselves, where men and horses were rotting in the burning May and June sun; add the pitiful lowings of cows whose udders were bursting and paining them as they had not been milked for days; add the nerve-racking roar of the planes above you, the swish of passing bullets, the holocausts of fire wherever shelling did its devastating work, the debris of once beautiful buildings that were brushed aside like card houses by the advancing, ruthless armored cars—add all this and you can understand, perhaps, why my last three years on the other side seem like a nightmare.

Before reaching France we had been in unfortunate Holland. There for the first time our eyes had been opened to the thoroughness with which Hitler had prepared his war, and to the premeditation that gave the lie to all his asseverations of peaceful intentions.

Just get this, for instance: Holland, as you know, is dotted with canals over which there are bridges of every size and width. Now, as Division X moved into the country say on Road A, that division carried with it "ersatz" bridges for every canal that had to be crossed until the assigned objective was reached. Hence, if on reaching canal crossing Number 5, this bridge was found to have been blasted by the retreating Dutch, the "ersatz" bridge was quickly thrown over the gap and the army proceeded almost without loss of time. If Bridge No. 5 was intact, then the "ersatz" bridge was quickly sent to the rear, to be used elsewhere and also so as not to encumber the advancing army.

Also, we noted how on this Road A, let us say, only Mercedes cars were used, while on Road B, let us say, they were all Opels. In such detail had Hitler prepared his attack on Europe that only one set of repair parts, one type of tires, one corps of mechanics was used on this particular road—of course at a great saving of men and materials. Incidentally, this principle of using only one type of car on one road had struck me even during my first trip to the Polish front in September 1939.

That was one profound impression we gained. There was no doubt in our minds, Adolf Hitler wanted this war and prepared for it with all the cunning at his command.

But then, as we got into Belgium and France, there was another fundamental lesson we learned: Modern warfare depends, in a measure hitherto undreamed of, upon air power for its efficacy. I cannot emphasize too strongly my belief that the sad story of the Lowlands and of France is chiefly that of the superiority of Nazi air power at that stage of the war. Thank God that superiority is waning rapidly and has in fact already waned, due to our American effort. But two years ago the story was a different one.

Why, my friends, wherever we drove in the German military car to which we were assigned, we saw the German air force above us, while the United Nations just weren't there. We correspondents tried to warn our compatriots by giving a truthful picture of what we observed. We were called pro-Nazi. I say with all the conviction at my command that I never felt myself a truer patriot than when, realizing as a layman that there was something sadly lacking in the United Nations setup, I conveyed as much of the truth as I could under the terrific obstacles of censorship under which we were working.

Take it from me, Ladies and Gentlemen, if a fellow has, like myself, been born on Washington's birthday in Abraham Lincoln's home town of Springfield, Illinois, has been educated in the liberal University of Wisconsin, and is now privileged to speak at Thomas Jefferson's great University of Virginia, he just cannot be a pro-Nazi! To have had so lucky a combination of birthday and birthplace and educational facility and emotional outlet entails an obligation ever to remain true to American ideals.

This is what we observed as we swept on with Hitler's army: The Luftwaffe, the German air force, was everywhere. Standing on a high hill—or, if you please, a miniature mountain—near Ghent, in Belgium, we saw the German troops in action during their successful attempt to cross the river near by. Before the actual crossing was attempted, German artillery got into action to silence the Belgian and French artillery on the other side of the river.

At first the shots fell wide of their mark. Then we noticed how German planes began to hover over the area—unfortunately there were no English or French planes there to drive them off—and within only a few minutes the shots went exactly where they were intended, silencing one battery after another of the opposing forces. The German officers accompanying us said, and we had no reason to doubt their words, that the battle that raged below was conducted by wireless from the scouting planes overhead.

Meanwhile the horrible Stukas, as we learned afterward, were dropping their devastating bombs and, descending with ferocious screeches, were striking terror into the hearts of the reinforcements that were on their way to this battle scene.

More than that, these bombers were far down in the heart of France, bringing confusion and working havoc in the endless columns of French soldiers who were on their way to the northern front. They were blasting railway stations, destroying airports, interfering with marching columns. And the other side had nothing to combat this onslaught effectively!

Again to show you how complete had been Hitler's advance preparations, let me tell you that in bombing the roads along which the French and Belgian troops moved, the Stuka pilots by no means destroyed the roads themselves.

No, they would drop one bomb on this side of the road, the next on that side, and so on. The violence of the repercussion from an exploding bomb was such that men and horses and vehicles, yes even heavy armored cars, were hurled off the roads and telescoped into each other, while the road itself was left intact.

The purpose of this type of bombing was obvious: Hitler wanted the roads for his own blitz drive into the heart of France; that's why he destroyed advancing men and materials, but not the roads themselves!

If there is any one military impression which I have taken here with me as a layman, it is that of the necessity of combating Hitler with air power and more air power and still more air power.

During that trip—one of many for me, for I have been at all fronts that Hitler has erected—I also had many an occasion to observe what the civilian population of Europe suffers while the armies are on the march. At Cambrai, for instance, right across the Franco-Belgian border, we had had to live on dry bread, champagne, and a little canned blood sausage because the entire water supply of the city had been destroyed and all activity had come to a standstill. We even had to wash and clean our teeth in champagne, that being the only liquid available.

In Greece, where I went in May 1941, one more terrible impression became a memory which haunts me even today: that of the thousands upon thousands of Greek soldiers who were returning, in the shoddiest of clothing, often without shoes, in the burning May and June sun all the way from Albania, where they had bravely defeated the Italians, to southern Greece.

What had happened was this: Unlike his procedure elsewhere, Hitler had set his Greek prisoners free immediately. This looked like a humane gesture. In reality he was thereby relieving himself of the responsibility of feeding hundreds of thousands of prisoners in a country entirely dependent upon overseas wheat and other commodities.

So here were these poor devils, footing it over the barren mountain passes, over fields on which they gratefully plucked a blade of grass here and there, at night sleeping on the street of some local German commandery in Greece—at Larissa, for instance, I was witness to such a scene—in the hope that in the morning enough might be left over from the German field kitchen to give them a little helping. It was a pitiful sight which I shall never forget.

I returned then from my trip to Greece convinced in my own mind that the first European country really to starve would be Greece. Alas, I have been right—starvation and even cannibalism are the order of the day in that unfortunate country which gallantly fought off its invader Italy until Hitler's men simply overwhelmed it.

And there was another impression with which I returned: After having seen the unparalleled natural positions of the Metaxes Line, I often wondered how different the story might have been if on the United Nations side there had been proper air protection to work havoc among the German troops as they advanced over lonely mountain passes, and to keep the Greeks properly informed when Hitler tried one of his famous encircling movements which could be detected from the air only, and not from below on the land. Again I for one correspondent drew the inescapable lesson: Air power and more air power is the most precious auxiliary to insure the success of the armed forces.

But I must not linger too long over memories of my front experiences. What I imagine you may want to hear more is this: Who is this Hitler who has brought so much misery into the world?

I have seen and watched Adolf Hitler ever since 1930 when I encountered him for the first time. He is a rabble rouser if ever there was one. He came into power partly because he was all things unto all men. If he faced a workers' audience he told them about the times when he was down and out, and he had a way of drawing on their emotions that often astounded me. If he encountered a university crowd, his appeal to students and faculty was that they, as intellectuals, should study up on the Treaty of Versailles, realize its iniquities and then turn against the existing republican government for attempting to live up to its provisions. If he was with bankers and industrialists, he conjured up a picture of a Greater Germany, freed from all foreign shackles.

Thus he promised heaven and earth to everybody at a time when Germany was having hard sledding economically, and when men like the late Foreign Minister Stresemann and ex-Chancellor Bruening were given but little encouragement.

In fact, I do not hesitate to express as my deliberate judgment that the French ambassador in Berlin did everything to undermine the Bruening administration and put Adolf Hitler into power, simply because he thought Hitler was a fool and would be easier to handle than the wise and honest Dr. Bruening.

What the world didn't realize at the time and what the devoted adherents to democracy in Germany did not divine at the time was that Hitler was doing exactly what Goebbels cynically admitted after the Nazis had taken over power in 1933:

"We utilized the instrumentalities of democracy to put democracy out of business."

There you strike at the root of Nazism: deceit and treachery all along the line. The German people were promised liberty and the full dinner pail and received slavery and deprivation instead. The Austrians, the Sudeten Germans, the Czechs, the Memellanders, the Danzigers—and later all the conquered peoples of Europe—were promised a better world, a so-called New Order. But as soon as the Hitler regime had them in its clutches, the Fuehrer about-faced and made mere slaves out of them.

Having, as Goebbels put it, undone democracy after hoisting himself into power through its instrumentalities, Hitler began a campaign of psychologizing the nation into thinking he was a superman of a kind that the world hadn't seen before.

The result was that, until Hitler since his declaration of war upon the United States has made one psychological blunder after another, his followers began to think of him as a New Christ.

Day in, day out, Hitler was pictured by his followers as the perfect man. The children in the schools were taught, "What our Fuehrer does is always right."

May I take you for a moment to a typical Hitler mass meeting, such as I have had to report or at least attend time and again?

For hours before such a meeting begins, the faithful have been streaming to the scene of the demonstration. The different factories, the government offices, the party headquarters—all must furnish so many participants, and as everybody is catalogued from cradle to grave in Germany, and his attendance at a demonstration checked, there can never be any doubt but that the hall will be packed and that thousands will stand outside to listen to the loudspeakers.

Snappy marches put the crowd in a receptive mood. Gigantic posters or streamers in strategic parts of the hall hammer away at the slogan of the evening. It may be "We demand colonies," or "We want a New Europe under Adolf Hitler," or, "The Jew is our misfortune." It all depends upon the occasion.

After this has gone on for about an hour, you suddenly hear excited "heils" at the further end of the hall, and people crane their necks. The first group of sub-leaders has arrived —the local district fuehrer, the chief of police, the head of the local SA, and so on.

After another ten minutes or so, more "heils," more commotion. Now the top hierarchy of the rank of Goering or Goebbels or Himmler proceed suavely through the center aisle as the audience salutes with outstretched hands. Each of these satellites just laps up the moment during which he feels himself a little Hitler.

A near-climax comes when next the flags and standards of all the participating groups are solemnly brought in. These flags and standards with their carriers are arranged as an effective background to the speaker's rostrum.

Excitement has by this time reached fever heat, and the audience is ready for the climax—for the supreme experience of seeing the New Messiah in person. Long before he has reached the hall, the ecstatic, hysterical cries of the followers stationed outside for blocks away, reach our ears. The cries assume organ-like dimensions when finally, at the rear end, He, the Leader, the Fuehrer, the man who has power of life or death over eighty millions, appears.

A searchlight plays upon his lone figure as he slowly wends his way through the hall, never looking right or left, but his right hand raised in salute, his left hand at the buckle of his belt. There is never a smile—this is a religious rite, this procession of the modern Messiah incarnate.

Can you wonder that a people who is thus psychologized after a while forgets by what means this man came into power, how he stole right and left from the Jews, how he had those who disagreed with him put into vile concentration camps, how he set aside all law and made himself the sole law giver, law executor, and law interpreter?

And yet there were and are brave men in Germany who opposed him. Their numbers are growing daily. And every once in a while someone leaves his enchanted circle because he simply cannot stomach Hitlerian godliness any longer.   Harvard-bred Putzi Hanfstaengl, who at one time had to play the piano for Hitler much as King Saul had a harpist play to him when the evil spirit overcame him, was one of the first from the inti-mate circle to skip out.   Rudolf Hess much later took a plane for England as all anti-Nazis in Germany shook with laughter. For here was a man who as nobody else was an exponent of Hitler party philosophy.   The Berliner has a way of responding when you tell him something that totally surprises him, "Gee, I'm going crazy."   After the Hess episode he changed his re-joinder to, "Gee, I'm going crazy—I'll take a plane for Eng-land."

May I offer you just an example or two of exceptionally brave conduct by German opponents of Hitler:

You all recall the name of Dr. Martin Niemoeller, the head, front and shoulders of the oppositional Protestant move-ment, who has been rotting in a concentration camp now for more than five years, but whose spirit is still unbroken.   It was my privilege to hear him make one of the most dramatic speeches to which I have ever listened.

Please remember the circumstances surrounding this episode. Niemoeller was accused of teaching subversive doctrines from his pulpit.   This was a silly charge to prefer against a man who had won fame during the First World War as a submarine commander.

"Twice in my life," Niemoeller said, "I have refused obe-dience.   The first time came at the end of the war, in 1918, when the captain in charge of our U-boat unit ordered me to take my little submarine and sink it at Scapa Flow.   'Captain,' I said, 'I cannot do that; I refuse obedience.'   I was discharged.

"Today the Reichsbishop advised me that I had been re-moved from my post; that I may no longer preach.   'Herr Reichsbishop,' I said, 'I refuse obedience.   The Bible says one must obey God more than man.   I have a mandate from God, as an ordained minister of the Gospel, to preach.   I shall con-tinue to preach!' "

The seed planted by Niemoeller has been sprouting ever since, and brave clergymen, now greatly heartened by what the Lutheran bishops and pastors of Norway have done in opposing Quisling, are continuing the fight.

But let me speak also of that wonderful Catholic bishop upon whom has fallen the mantle of the doughty, fearless, but now very aged and infirm Cardinal Faulhaber—I mean Bishop von Galen of Muenster in Westphalia.

Galen had become so outspoken in his denunciation of Nazism as a doctrine opposed to Christianity that the Gestapo came to arrest him. Now, Muenster is one of the most Catholic cities in Westphalia. The news that the bishop was to be arrested spread like wildfire, and soon thousands were milling around on the big square before the bishop's palace.

When the Gestapo informed the bishop that he was under arrest, he asked that he be excused for a moment while he changed clothes. The Gestapo, unaware of his intentions, acquiesced. To their dismay, however, Galen emerged from his room a few minutes later, dressed in the full regalia of an officiating bishop, with robe, mitre, and high bishop's headgear.

"That won't do," the officials said. "We cannot take you to jail that way."

"All that I have said and done," Galen replied with dignity, "I have done as a prince of the church. Hence I shall leave this building in your custody in my official robes, and only in those robes."

The Gestapo was so flabbergasted that it desisted from arresting the clergyman, and the episode ended by the bishop's stepping out on the balcony and bestowing the apostolic blessing upon the thousands outside.

All these men who oppose Hitler must, of course, work most carefully. The Gestapo is ubiquitous. It and the strict regime of censorship which Dr. Goebbels' so-called ministry of propaganda and public enlightenment exercises make it exceedingly difficult for the opposition to organize.

We on our part ought to do all possible to help this submerged opposition by intelligent radio broadcasts from here, the radio being one of the few means left for contacting the German world.

A further proof that an opposition is at work in Germany may be found in what I am about to reveal to you. Among the documents which in the course of time I have smuggled through to this country are the secret instructions, covering a period of at least half a year, issued to the German press.

Every editor who received these instructions was put under oath not to reveal them. And yet there were German men of the pen who were so shocked at the lies that Goebbels expected them to tell, at the censorship which the regime imposed upon them, at the interference with freedom of thought and expression which this meant, that at risk of life and limb they nevertheless communicated these instructions to me, hoping that by knowing what the Goebbels machine was doing, I might outwit it and give a true picture of conditions in Germany.

I have picked at random the instructions of May 29, 1941, because they refer to our President's declaration of a state of emergency. The proclamation, you will recall, was read in the presence of the Latin American diplomatic corps.

Here are the instructions:

Continue to harp on the Roosevelt speech. Point out that the only new thing in it was the proclamation of a state of emergency. This means that Roosevelt is meddling with the American people's lives in a dictatorial way. Though claiming to fight dictatorship he shows himself no longer to be a democrat.

To emphasize that South America is being threatened by us, Roosevelt conceived the idea of inviting the South American diplomats to hear his address. They know, however, that it is really the U.S.A. which threatens South America. To them we must make clear that we are protecting them against the U.S.A.

As to the claim that Germany invaded the Balkans, we shall in due time throw light, by the publication of documents, upon the role played by Colonel Donovan.

One Berlin paper was permitted for special reasons to report the American President's speech on the first page and with a double column head. This does NOT mean that other papers may do so.

Minor matters:

Don't report the rationing of eggs.

Point out that the U.S.A. can't produce enough steel, and that only 22% of the production is available for war purposes.

It is forbidden to refer to the *Daily Mirror* charge that German spies prepared the Crete action.

The Kaiser is ill. This fact may not, however, be published. Even in the "death notices" column nothing may be published on this subject without special permission.

I have a whole stack of these secret instructions. When one reads them one is appalled at what the German people have been told about us and about other peace-loving, law-abiding nations. Unfortunately the average German hears nothing except what is said over the government-owned radio and the government-controlled press.

Hence, however you and I may sympathize with the brave souls in Germany who dare oppose Hitler tyranny, don't for one moment deceive yourselves into thinking that American war effort is unnecessary, that Hitler will fall of his own weight, that the anti-Nazis are going to upset the German state without your having to do anything about it. Fact is that the Gestapo in Germany is so well organized and is so omnipresent that a good long time will elapse before the "anti" elements can do anything decisive.

Why, as we were leaving Berlin, the Gestapo was moving whole families out of houses at strategic street intersections and filling them with dyed-in-the-wool, honest-to-god-Nazi families—why? Because in the first floor front room of each of these houses the Gestapo was planting machine guns in order to kill off mercilessly anybody who dared start any overt act against the regime. What chance, then, does the opposition in Germany have so long as Hitler remains undefeated?

No, my friends, we must be unrelenting in our effort to inflict a smashing blow upon the Hitler regime. He's a "tough customer," I assure you. But from what I have seen and experienced, he is by no means invulnerable.

For one thing, Hitler is losing his psychic sense for divining the sentiments of the German people. The Hitler who foolishly declared war upon the American people, who pleaded for winter furs and woolens after having previously boasted that "General Winter" would be his ally in Russia, and who ended the worst winter that Germany experienced in centuries by telling the Germans that another winter of war lies ahead—that Hitler is no longer the spell-binder, the hypnotist of the earlier days in which I have known him.

Secondly, Hitler is confronted with a number of serious bottlenecks. One of his worst bottlenecks is transportation. He is beginning to pay dearly for his egotism in neglecting the railways and favoring the Adolf Hitler super-highways which are to carry his fame to the four corners of the globe. Let our bombers, now stationed on the British Isles, strike at German railway centers, engines, and moving freight trains, and Hitler will have been hit at one of his most vulnerable points.

A second bottleneck is manpower. The German people had been promised, when Hitler conquered Greece, that Macedonian tobacco would reach the Reich in untold quantities. Well, he hasn't the labor power to raise tobacco, and three to five cigarettes filled with everything but good tobacco are now the daily ration of the "victor."

He promised after the seizure of the Ukraine that wheat, another indispensable raw material, would come regularly from there. But in February, during our Bad Nauheim internment, we read German official press releases to the effect that nothing substantial may be expected from the Ukraine until 1943!

When Denmark was invaded, the talk in Germany, assiduously fostered by the Nazis, was that now Danish bacon and ham and eggs would be diverted from England and come to Germany. But since then the German people have had to be told that overseas fodder is lacking in Denmark, wherefore there must be wholesale slaughter of cattle and after that—nothing!

So Hitler has his third bottleneck besides that of transportation and manpower: the lack of raw materials wherewith to continue his fight. The frantic efforts to take the Kerch peninsula and then move eastward were predicated upon the crying necessity of his getting hold, if he can, of the Caucasian oil.

Not only does Hitler lack manpower to till the soil and take care of all the many other civilian needs of the population—a lack which he tries to compensate by the wholesale bringing to Germany of labor from the occupied, starving countries which he has subjugated—but he lacks manpower even for the gigantic war machine that is necessary to hold under the heel an area extending from northern Norway all the way to Irun on the Spanish frontier, and from the Atlantic coast all the way east into the far Russian steppes. Daily more and more people are being combed out of the industries at home and caught by the moloch war.

Before the present war started, about twenty-four million German men were engaged in gainful occupations.

Today, only about eleven millions are left in civilian life to work long hours. Over nine million women have been pressed into work to take the places of men at the front. They have been augmented by about one and a half million prisoners of war, by over two million foreign laborers, and, more recently, by several million children from ten years upward who have been sent out into the country to help bring in the harvest.

With their fathers, husbands, and sweethearts gone, the women at home have also been reduced to virtual slavery, and this, too, at a time when food is scarce, when everything, literally everything is rationed—and how!—and when the long absence of fats is severely undermining public health.

We who were at Bad Nauheim didn't really awaken to the food situation till we came to Lisbon, so gradual had the deterioration in Germany been. Severe rationing set in from the first day of the war, but the proportions it attained by the time we left in May were appalling.

Bread has become so vile that we at Bad Nauheim invariably took the center out of our rolls since they reminded us too much of putty. And one member of our group with an artistic bent of mind even modelled a statue out of this putty-like bread and let it dry and harden.

Twice a week we had nothing for lunch except a plate of soup with a diminutive piece of meat in it. A sirloin steak such as I have been eating here since my arrival was easily two weeks' meat ration. On two other days there was no meat at all—only stale-tasting vegetables, stale because they lacked condiments and fats. Solely on three days was a very thin slice of meat served. We were lucky if twice a month we received either two oranges or one orange and one apple. Yet we were given 150 per cent rations as compared with the ordinary German rations! We wondered, How can this German nation hold out indefinitely when such a shortage of food obtains?

I repeat, Hitler is slipping. Some day the crash is bound to come. But it will not come unless our nation joins in an all-out effort; unless every man, woman and child gets behind the crusade against Hitlerism with the greatest effort the world has known.

That's why I tried to give you an unvarnished picture of the situation; that's why I tried to tell you what a powerful machine Hitler's war machine is.

But because I have infinite faith in our ability and earnestness as a nation, and because I realize, more fully perhaps than any of you, for you have not lived under the Hitler system, that the Nazis must go, I close with this assurance of my unshakeable conviction:

Hitler CAN be beaten, Hitler MUST be beaten, Hitler WILL be beaten!

THOSE INCREDIBLE RUSSIANS [10]

FRAZIER HUNT [11]

Mr. Frazier Hunt gave this news broadcast over the Columbia Broadcasting System on Saturday, February 13, 1943, from 6:00 to 6:15 P.M., E.W.T.

The broadcast was a fitting tribute to the Russians, who at that time had destroyed the Nazi army at Stalingrad and had continued to envelop the retreating Hitler divisions in southern Russia.

Mr. Hunt has a large following of radio listeners. He has an excellent radio voice, a graphic style, and, with William L. Shirer and other foreign news commentators, speaks out of much experience.

About the only words that can fitly describe these Red allies of ours is the phrase, "those incredible Russians." And anyone who has had the opportunity to live with them and fight alongside them, will always use that word "incredible." I have known them for almost twenty-five years; in North Russia, immediately after the Armistice of the last war, I rode a thousand forty miles by sled through the white and silent vastness of this interminable northern land. And a year later, in the dead of winter in Siberia, I rode four hundred miles across country, and ate and slept and sang with brave boys fighting with few and inadequate weapons against Japanese intruders. And I have seen much of them during various visits to Russia proper.

A half hundred tales of courage and strange and exciting moments of life and death crowd forward this second to be told. It happens that from the very start of these adventures, I caught the hidden power, the vast reserves, the deep reservoirs of men and spirit and land. I wrote all this these many years ago.

I have always believed that Russia had the right to choose the social and political system she wished; and long ago I

---

[10] By permission of Mr. Hunt. Text furnished through the courtesy of Mr. Hunt and of the Columbia Broadcasting System.
[11] For biographical note see Appendix.

sensed the strong and alluring winds that blew out from the Kremlin to all the corners of the world—winds of unrest and revolt—to China, India, the Middle East, Europe, and to a small degree even to this country. And always I have known the power and capacity for stubborn resistance of the great Red armies; and, quite as important, the depth, and inner strength of the Russian millions, toward their new life and their old, Holy Russia. I saw with my own eyes Red Russia slowly turn from red dreams of world revolution, to demands that the Russian homeland be made impregnable against all assault, no matter by whom, or from what direction.

I understood why Russia fought Finland, three years ago— and even why she made her temporary marriage-of-convenience with Germany. It was in preparation for her duel to the death with Germany for the mastery of at least a great part of the Euro-Asiatic continent.

Russia took a terrific beating in the summer and fall of 1941. I thought then that she might lose Moscow, but that she would fight on. During that winter of 1941 and '42, I thrilled at what seemed the mighty Red victories. But realistic military friends pointed out to me, again and again, that the German armies had only withdrawn to prepared defense positions, and would attack in force when early summer came. Most of us would not accept that harsh viewpoint, but unfortunately it proved to be the correct one.

Then came the sledge-hammer drives of last summer and fall. In terms of cold military realism, it seemed that when the Germans had driven to the banks of the Volga, and to the heroic streets and cellars of Stalingrad, and driven deep into the Caucasus, it seemed then that Stalingrad was doomed, and the priceless oil of the Caucasus would be cut off from the Red armies, and that the last of European Russia's great food baskets would be lost.

To the everlasting glory of the Lord, cold military realism went down before the power of spirit and the grandeur of human dignity. "Whom the gods would destroy, they first make mad," and apparently the Nazi hordes were striking in anger and revenge. Even the mighty steel machines of the Nazis could only do so much. And when the mud and snows of late fall and winter bogged down this Nazi war machine, the flaming spirit, the men and women of Russia, dared bare their breasts and attack—and attack—and still attack.

The easy way was to ride high in your saddle alongside these victorious Russians; but military caution, and that largely unappreciated word, realism, advised a grave questioning of these vast and many Red victories. It was known, for instance, that many Germans in the once proud Axis armies of three hundred thirty thousand men that stood before Stalingrad had been drawn back, or flown out.

And to this day, when the Russian victories still mount and pile up to fantastic heights, there are some military students who still insist that the majority of the thousands of captured Axis soldiers are Rumanians, Italians, Croats or Hungarians, while most of the German divisions have been evacuated. That may or may not be correct.

But we do know that it is the Germans who now are trading space for time—vast spaces of Russian country for time to rebuild their war machines. It would seem clear that this is certainly a dark and gloomy winter for Germany—and for the man who conceived all this death and horror and brutality.

It may well be that German morale is suffering; but it will not be wise for us to be too optimistic of that desired goal. We must be prepared to face harsh and trying days in Tunisia and North Africa; and we must recognize that the Nazis may still have great machine power in their hands, and that the fair fields of Russia may once again be soaked in precious blood.

But we shall win, and our side shall lay out the peace, and mete out the just punishment. That is sure. And that is enough to sustain us, through good days and bad days. For we can stand both success and adversity—but we will stand them more nobly if we have Truth to help us keep our Faith.

THE HOME FRONT

THE WAR AGAINST INFLATION [1]

JAMES F. BYRNES [2]

Hon. James F. Byrnes, Director of Economic Stabilization, gave this talk over the Columbia Broadcasting System on February 9, 1943.

In October 1942, Judge Byrnes resigned as Associate Justice of the United States Supreme Court to accept the appointment as Director of Economic Stabilization. His new position aimed to "formulate and develop a comprehensive national economic policy relating to the control of civilian purchasing power, prices, rents, wages, salaries, profits, rationing, subsidies, and all related matters." In a word, he was to prevent inflation. He was given complete power to order any government administration to carry out the points of that policy.

The general outlines of our economic policy were fairly well drawn when he began his work. There were ceilings on prices and on rents (in defense areas). Wages were "stabilized," as were salaries and profits. There was general rationing, taxes had been increased sharply, and government bond purchases promoted.

In 1943, it was estimated that some $120,000,000,000 would be available in incomes. The people would put perhaps $25,000,000,000 into savings. Goods and services for purchase might represent $75,000,000,000. At least $20,000,000,000 would constitute a threat to further inflation.

Mr. Byrnes's job was to deal with that surplus amount of money. He prepared to have Congress set up a pay-as-you-go tax plan and to have compulsory savings. The new Congress threatened open revolt from Roosevelt's program to resist the upward spiral.

What were Byrnes's qualifications for the task? He had been a member of the lower house for fourteen years and had learned much as a member of the Appropriations Committee. He had been in the Senate for eleven years, where he had been an ardent supporter of Roosevelt policies and had been highly influential in getting them through Congress. He had a reputation for knowledge of human nature, for accomplishment, for persuasiveness in speaking, for practical judgment.

[1] *Congressional Record,* v. 89, no. 23, p. A 531-3, February 10, 1943 (daily edition), 78th Congress, first session.
[2] For biographical note see Appendix.

Soon after the Seventy-eighth Congress got under way, the farm bloc renewed its campaign to write into the farm parity formula the costs of farm labor. Prentiss Brown, O.P.A. administrator, had helped kill such a move in the preceding Congress.[3] The House Agricultural Committee approved a bill that would add $350,000,000,000 to food costs.

The agricultural clamor was matched by labor's demands for higher wages. Living costs had risen at least 4 per cent since May 1942, when the War Labor Board's Little Steel formula had gone into effect, a policy allowing for not more than a 15 per cent wage increase. Railroad employees, some 1,000,000 of them, were asking 30 per cent per hour increases. The United Auto Workers were also denouncing the formula and demanding a 30 per cent increase. Mr. John L. Lewis, of the United Mine Workers, announced that in March coal industry negotiations would begin. Two dollars a day increase for each of the 450,000 bituminous coal miners would be demanded.

In such an atmosphere did Mr. Byrnes deliver this speech. His argument is buttressed by close reasoning and by ample evidence. He grapples directly with the farm parity formula, with the problem of union wage increases, with increased taxes, with black markets, with increased working week, with the freezing of workers in industry, with gas rationing, and with corporate profits. These issues were foremost in the thinking and conversation of Americans in this period.

What effect did Mr. Byrnes's speech have? · It was, of course, part of the steady campaign against these inflationary movements. From February to July 1943, the situation with respect to inflation grew increasingly critical. The administrator tried (1) to appease the farmers with incentive payments or subsidies for greater production; (2) to veto any bill that destroyed the farm parity formula; (3) to stand fast on the Little Steel formula.

Early in April the President vetoed the Bankhead Bill, "a move by the Congressional farm bloc to boost farm prices."[4]

At this juncture, William Green of the A. F. of L., Philip Murray, of the C. I. O., and Alvanley Johnston, of the Brotherhood of Locomotive Engineers, apparently agreed to stop their pressure for higher wages and fight to reduce the high cost of living.

Early in May, Mr. Prentiss Brown promised (1) extension of price control to "every important commodity"; (2) the rolling back of prices which have got out of hand; (3) the establishment of maximum prices on all foods.

John L. Lewis, ignoring the War Labor Board, called his United Mine Workers on strike. President Roosevelt, on May 2, broadcast a request for the miners to return to work. They did so. When they

---

[3] For a notable speech in the Senate by Mr. Brown see *Congressional Record*, v. 88, no. 162, p. 7646-52, September 24, 1942 (daily edition).
[4] *Time*, vol. 41, no. 15, p. 9, April 12, 1943.

struck again, Congress passed the Smith-Connally strike-and-labor-control bill, aimed against Lewis. It outlawed strikes in government-operated war plants, forced a thirty-day cooling off period and secret ballot before any strike could be called in private plants, made strike incitement punishable by jail or fine, and imposed other restrictions on labor. Although the President vetoed the bill, Congress quickly overrode the veto.

Meantime, James Byrnes had been appointed as head of the Office of War Mobilization. He was still stoutly maintaining the battle against inflation.

I have little patience with those who tell us that American people are not ready to meet the requirements of total war. The day when it could be said that our people were only ankle-deep in the war is long past. The American people—in the armed forces, in the factories, on the farms, in the mines, everywhere—are eager to do their part to win a people's war and a people's peace. They await only the opportunity to work, to fight and when need be to die in freedom's cause.

There is considerable, and not wholly unwarranted, optimism about our present military situation, particularly compared with what it was up to a few months ago. There is danger, however, that we may not fully appreciate the terrible stresses and strains upon our accustomed habits of living that we must be prepared to undergo during the coming year.

Our optimism will be justified only by our ability and willingness to accept the burdens and deprivations which will be required of all of us to carry through our war plans for 1943.

Those plans call for a very substantial increase in our war production over last year's record-breaking goals. They require at the same time the enlistment of additional millions into our armed forces. They contemplate, within a measurable period of time, the invasion of Europe, one of the greatest military operations ever planned in history—a military campaign, which, no matter how successfully and brilliantly executed, will involve casualties such as this nation has never before endured. Supplies, in unprecedented volume, must flow constantly, and with consummate timing, over carefully guarded supply lines to the battle fronts. We must also pool our supplies with those of the experienced and well trained troops of Britain and our other allies who will form a part of the invading armies and gladly share the burden of fighting and dying. We must continue our support of our gallant Russian allies, who, having withstood two all-out onslaughts of the Nazi's total might, are now driving the Nazis whimpering back toward a disillusioned Germany. We must send more help to our Chinese allies, whose indomitable resistance constantly wears down the fighting strength of the Japanese military machine and holds for us the roads to Tokyo. We must also share our food with the peoples in free and liberated countries who are helping us to beat back our treacherous and still powerful enemies.

It will require the fullest mobilization of our manpower and our resources to carry out these war plans for 1943. It will require the wholehearted cooperation of agriculture, labor and industry to carry out these plans with the self-restraint and self-discipline necessary to avoid inflation and to preserve our system of free labor and free enterprise.

In the years before the war, we were struggling to improve the standard of living of the mass of our people. After the war is over, this struggle of man to better himself will continue. But we must face the fact that there is no way that we can hope to improve or even to sustain our customary standards of living during the coming war year. We shall be able to retain for our consumer needs at home only a fraction of our total production. Although we shall not have to endure the shame of poverty amid plenty that we did in 1932, we shall in fact have little more goods to use or consume at home than we did at the depth of the depression. We must all prepare to adopt for the duration a Spartan standard of living and to take patriotic pride in it. There is no way of giving any one group of our people a substantial additional part of the nation's goods or income without hurting all the rest of us.

Despite the rises in wages and prices which have thus far occurred, we have been able to maintain a fair balance between various producers and workers. There are inequities in the wages paid in every industry and in every factory. This has always been true. We cannot hope while fighting a total war to eliminate all the real or fancied inequalities of men. Our task is to see that the present balance does not change for the worse and that those on the lower rungs of the economic ladder are not ground down below the margin of subsistence.

In considering the ability of the wage earner to meet the increased cost of living, we cannot look simply at the basic hourly wage rates, even though such rates have risen far in excess of the increased cost of living. Men are working more than forty hours per week. For the hours over forty they are paid time and a half. The average weekly earnings of all factory workers (that is, the amount the worker takes home in his pay envelope) have increased more than 40 per cent since January, 1941, and more than 60 per cent since September, 1939.

Millions formerly unemployed, or on relief and W. P. A., now have full-time jobs. Millions more who formerly worked two or three days per week are now earning overtime pay. Other millions who formerly worked in low-paid occupations have been trained to become skilled mechanics at higher wages. Where a year ago one pay envelope came into the home on pay day, now two and sometimes three are received. The family requires no more shelter, little more food, and little more clothing, but the income of the family is far in excess of any increase in the cost of living to the family.

Taking into account the rise of living costs—which must and shall be halted—the actual weekly purchasing power of the average industrial worker is still 36 per cent more than it was in September, 1939.

In other words, the American industrial worker and his family today enjoy the highest purchasing power that has ever existed in this or any other country. If we preserve and protect this purchasing power it will constitute the basis of an unparalleled prosperity for American workers in the postwar period.

Rising prices will, on the other hand, destroy this purchasing power. A frantic race between rising wages and rising prices, far from helping labor, will only ruin and degrade the worker and his family, depriving them of all the gains they have so painfully built up over the years.

The position of the farmers is equally favorable. The relation of farm costs to farm income is the most favorable ever attained in our history. Between 1939 and 1942 total costs of farm production increased by 38 per cent; and farm production increased by 20 per cent. During the same period farm prices rose on the average by 71 per cent. Since 1939 unit farm prices have increased almost as much as five times unit farm costs. As a result of this extremely favorable relationship of costs to prices, the net farm income after all costs in 1942, stood at the highest level in our history, one billion dollars above the peak earned during the inflationary year 1919.

In a year of total war, we cannot iron out all the inequalities in the wage structure nor remove all the imperfections, real or fancied, in the farm parity formula. Certainly it would not be in the real interest of the farmers to introduce any change in this formula which would give him a temporary and illusory advantage during the war and which would, if applied year in and year out, actually reduce parity prices to the farmer.

The stabilization act of Oct. 2, 1942, contains the most significant and beneficial legislation enacted for the farmer since the Agricultural Adjustment Act. It proceeds on the principle recommended by the President in his message of Sept. 7, 1942, that there should be "a floor under prices of farm products, in order to maintain stability in the farm market for a reasonable future time" after the war. It provides a guaranty to the farmer of 85 to 90 per cent of parity prices on basic crops during the war and for at least two crop years after the first day of January following the formal declaration of the termination of the war. That is a real effort to protect the farmer against postwar deflation. But the effort will fail if we cannot prevent runaway inflation.

Our struggle against rising prices during this war has thus far been successful as compared with World War I. October, 1942, was the thirty-eighth month of the present war. In those thirty-eight months, wholesale prices have risen 33.3 per cent. In the same period during the last war wholesale prices rose 83.5 per cent. Between August, 1939, and October, 1942, the cost of living rose 20.7 per cent; in the comparable period of the last war the cost of living went up 32.2 per cent.

The situation today in many respects is potentially more dangerous than it was during the last war. In the last war we were obliged at the peak to devote only slightly more than a quarter of our output to war, while today we are already putting nearly a half of our output into our war effort.

We must not refuse to face the very real dangers in the present situation, and especially the threat of creeping inflation. Between May, 1942, when the general price ceilings were imposed, and Dec. 15, 1942, the cost of food rose 9.1 per cent, but because rents and other items did not increase so much, the cost of living rose only 3.8 per cent. With certain foods very scarce and the price of others very high, it is natural that the average housewife should feel that the cost of living has risen even higher than these figures would indicate. But it has risen, and this creeping inflation must not be allowed to continue and to nullify all the progress we have made.

Higher prices and higher wages will not bring us more food. They will not enable us to buy more canned goods or sugar, because these items are rationed. They will not enable us to buy automobiles or electric refrigerators, because these articles are not for sale. They will simply cause us to out-bid each other in grabbing for the food and goods available. They will increase our income, but the government will be forced to recapture the excess income in higher taxes. Higher prices will not help the merchant or farmer, but they will bring hardships and suffering to widows, to old folks with fixed incomes, to the schoolteachers, and to the unorganized workers in low-paid occupations. They will make unbearable the burden of the woman who has been allotted $50 a month upon which to live while her husband or her son has gone to the front to fight and possibly die for you and me.

We must not retreat in our fight to stabilize the cost of living. The act of Congress provided that prices, wages and salaries affecting the cost of living should be stabilized and except as otherwise provided in the act such stabilization should, so far as practicable, be on the basis of levels existing Sept. 15, 1942. We must hold that line.

We must adhere firmly to that program. There must be no further increases in wages beyond the Little Steel formula except in limited and special cases to correct patently gross inequities and to rectify plainly substandard wages. Today the National War Labor Board reaffirmed this policy in its decision in the meat packers' case. There must be no further price increases unless and to the limited extent required by law to meet clearly established cost increases which cannot generally be absorbed out of profits.

We must bring under effective control all food prices. We must break up the black markets. Some of the talk about black markets is exaggerated, but by no means all. Price Administrator Brown is making a determined effort to exterminate them. He needs money but even more he needs your help. The man who helped the bootlegger in prohibition days hurt only himself. The woman who today encourages a merchant to bootleg food is hurting her loved ones, her country and herself.

To ensure the effective and uniform administration of the policies which I have announced, I have requested the National War Labor Board to make no increase in wage rates which will change existing wage policies or which affects directly or indirectly an entire industry or substantial portion thereof without prior consultation with me. It is my purpose to exercise all the powers granted by law to prevent any further increase in the basic and essential cost of subsistence living. I am assured by all the agencies of government concerned that I shall have in this effort their wholehearted cooperation.

This policy of holding basic prices and basic wages firmly at their present levels does not preclude the limited use of price incentives or wage incentives to increase production. But such incentive payments must not be used as an excuse for a general increase in wages or prices. We cannot hand out incentives so freely that they only cancel each other and add to our inflationary gap.

In the labor field it has been customary to pay overtime for work in excess of the normal hours. Overtime payments have been an effective aid to increase production during the war. Paying more for the same work makes for inflation. Paying more for extra work does not.

To make more effective use of our manpower during the war period, the President has today signed an executive order establishing a minimum forty-eight-hour work week, without affecting the workers' existing right to overtime pay. Many war industries are already working forty-eight hours or more a week, but the order will compel other industries to go on a minimum forty-eight-hour week wherever feasible. In general, adoption of the forty-eight-hour week will enable us to get more work out of our limited labor supply. While overtime payments will add to the wage bill, the addition will be largely made up by the increased production secured. And we shall thereby release manpower for the armed forces, for war industry and for the farms.

Secretary Wickard has recently introduced incentive payments into our farm program as a means of securing increased farm production. Although the general relation of total farm costs to farm prices is extremely favorable, the farmer must incur unusually high costs in expanding the output of some crops beyond current peak level. To provide this additional output the farmer must shift from nonessential to essential war crops and must bring less fertile acreage into use. He must expand output in face of inadequate supplies of fertilizers, inadequate replacements of equipment and inadequate manpower. Incentive payments will enable us to increase production without increasing prices.

Some people have dubbed incentive payments subsidies, thinking thereby to condemn them. I disagree. To me they seem essentially sound economically. They will increase the production of basic foodstuffs just as they have been used to increase the production of copper and other critical materials. They cannot be said to be unfair to any one.

General and indiscriminate wage and price increases will not solve any of our real problems. They will not give us increased manpower. They will not give us increased production. They are advantageous to the groups that get them only so long as other groups can be kept from getting them. The apparent advantages obtained by the groups benefited will prove short-lived and illusory during the war and will bring retribution even on these groups when the war is over. Those who demand them are only demanding another depression.

No man hates regimentation more than I do. But I would be less than honest if I told you that the stresses and strains on our civilian economy could be met without a high degree of regimentation in our civilian as well as our military life. With the proper spirit and understanding among our people that regimentation may be largely self-regimentation. But whatever you call it, each one of us will have to take his place and play his part on our team.

When we are drafting men and youths into the armed forces at $600 a year, we cannot let other men and women work where they please, when they please, or allow them or persuade them to jump from one job or business to another because it pays more. No businessman, no farmer and no worker has a right to look upon this war as an opportunity for personal profit.

We must all serve, and I am sure that we want to serve where we are best fitted and most needed. Last week Mr. McNutt, the chairman of the Manpower Commission, took action to control the hiring of workers in critical labor-shortage areas. In the future, workers may be guided to employment where they are most urgently needed. In the future they must not leave essential employment, whether in the factory or on the farm, without good cause.

Last year many workers upon farms and in dairies went to industrial plants to get higher wages. They were splendid farm workers; they are indifferent mechanics. As we have urged men to volunteer for military service, we should urge these men to return to the farms where they are needed, even if the compensation is less. If they refuse to go, their draft deferments should be canceled. If some men can be drafted and sent abroad at $50 per month, every civilian must go where he can render the greatest service, even if it means less money.

Rationing can equalize some hardships, but it cannot blot out shortages. Nobody likes complicated rationing, but it is important for all of us to remember that the purpose of rationing is not to take goods away from us, but to see that the goods we have are equitably shared. If we evade the rationing rules, we are not playing a trick on some bureaucrat. We are taking something that belongs to our neighbor or something that our boys across the sea should have. Every man who buys on the black market is stealing from his fellowman.

We in the East are forbidden to drive for pleasure not because some bureaucrat at Washington enjoys our discomfort, but because the tank cars are needed to carry fuel oil to keep our homes above 60 degrees and to protect our children from pneumonia; and because our tankers are needed to carry high-octane gas to our boys who are bombing Berlin and Bizerte. Who but the slacker could begrudge this sacrifice?

As shortages grow, shopping for the average man and woman becomes more difficult. We do not find the things we customarily buy and we don't always know what else to buy. We are all working now to devise simplified and standardized utility articles so that while we may have less fashion and variety, we shall be able to get more readily the simple things we really need.

But in this field I do not think we should rely exclusively on government. Within the limits of wartime restrictions there is still room for manufacturers and processors to sense the need of the times and to take an active part in the development of utility articles which give the people what they need at the lowest possible price and in a form which makes the most effective use of critical foods and materials.

We cannot evade the hard and grim realities of the war. We can take pride and even pleasure in simple living—or we can grumble about our deprivations and make ourselves and those about us miserable. As fathers and brothers, wives and sisters of our fighting men let us show that we, too, have what it takes to win a total war for freedom.

But even if our manpower is used most effectively and our supplies husbanded most prudently, there still is inherent danger in a situation where our national consumer income is so abnormally large in relation to the goods available for consumption.

There is a $16,000,000,000 gap. We must tax ourselves to close that gap.

Inasmuch as the great volume of surplus consumer income is in the hands of the lower-middle-income groups, a part of the additional taxation which must fall heavily on this group should take the form of postwar credits or compulsory savings. Then there will be no feeling that from a long-term standpoint we are departing from the progressive principle of taxing in accordance with ability to pay. We must not shirk from high taxation during wartime. It is one of the most effective and most practical safeguards against inflation. If we can draft a mother's only son, we should not hesitate to draft her neighbor's surplus dollars.

Corporate profits, before taxes, have risen to unprecedented peaks. Apart from certain loopholes in the tax system, however, the great bulk of the excess profits is turned to the government through excess profit taxes. But in the struggle to achieve stable prices and stable costs, it would be desirable to keep costs and prices down rather than to let excess profits accumulate, even though most of them are ultimately recaptured by the government. Excess profits provoke inflationary wage demands. An excess profits tax is no excuse for maintaining exorbitant prices or for saddling excessive costs on the government or on consumers.

The casualties of war are many and cruel. The greatest and most irreparable loss is of course on the battlefield. But there are also casualties on the civilian front. Families are broken up, businesses are destroyed. When many people are bearing great sorrows bravely and silently, there must be no feeling that anybody is trying to profit from the war. When heavy taxes are being imposed on those scarcely above the margin of subsistence, there should not be even the basis for a suspicion that people in the higher income brackets are not bearing their full share of the burden of the war.

We are in total war. We are fighting for a common future. For that future we must all make common sacrifices. We must go through and come out of this war strong and confident. We want, and the world needs, a powerful and prosperous America

so that we may achieve an enduring peace. We do not want a
return to the deflation that followed the last war, when wheat
dropped from $2.16 to $1.03; when corn fell from $1.52 to
52 cents; when cotton declined from 35 cents to 15 cents and
hogs from $16.39 to $7.63; when a large part of our farm lands
was foreclosed; when wages fell and returning soldiers tramped
the streets hunting for work, when some men went into bankruptcy and some into suicides' graves.

This time we must hold the line against inflation and deflation. This time we must win the peace for the sake of ourselves and all humanity.

PRIVATE AGENCIES AND PUBLIC GOALS IN THE POSTWAR WORLD [5]

Lewis H. Brown [6]

Mr. Lewis H. Brown gave his address before the Washington members of the American Economic Association, in Washington, D.C., on January 5, 1943.

The speech represents the business leader's conclusions concerning the economic and political philosophy and pattern to be followed in our dealing with private enterprise. The issue was: To what extent shall government limit or control competitive enterprise in order to secure maximum benefits to all the people? Mr. Brown's answer is direct: Industry, to secure the maximum results in stimulating production and employment, and in maintaining or restoring the national economic health, needs maximum freedom.

The speech is well organized and logically arranged. It contains in outline the history of government in relation to American industry since 1933. The introduction, in Ciceronian fashion, first renders the audience attentive and well disposed toward the speaker. Second, this section defines terms clearly and limits the subject ("I refer . . . to the problem of providing a reasonable measure of employment for all citizens able and willing to work").

The main body of the discourse treats of (a) the need for dealing with the ups and downs of the business cycle, (b) the proper program for such control (stimulation of private enterprise), (c) the need to apply this philosophy of free, private enterprise in the postwar era, and (d) the application to his hearers, or visualization of this philosophy ("which is the best engine"). Finally the conclusion includes a plea for cooperation, a summary, and a dignified appeal ("We must rebuild America"). Mr. Brown is an effective speaker before business and professional groups.

At the State University of Iowa, as an undergraduate, he had his first experience in public speaking and debating in the Irving Institute, a college literary-debating society. In his freshman year he won the George W. Eagan prize in the freshman oratorical contest. He also had a course in extempore speaking under Professor Glenn Merry, head of the Speech Department and later president of the National Association of Teachers of Speech. "I consider this one of the most valuable

[5] By permission of Mr. Brown. Text supplied through the courtesy of the author.
[6] For biographical note see Appendix.

courses I took at the University," wrote Mr. Brown, "because it gave me a background that has been invaluable to me in subsequent years." [7]

It is with some temerity that I appear before the American Economic Association. Your members, whose deliberations are grounded in the quantitative data of economics, have presented papers giving with some detail economic blueprints for certain parts of the postwar economy. Your president asked for a layman's point of view on the utilization of private business agencies to achieve public goals in the postwar world.

In undertaking this assignment I want it distinctly understood I am appearing before this highly professional gathering *as* a layman, talking in a businessman's simple language. The economist must appraise long-term trends. The businessman's approach is usually limited to the short-term future. He must think in terms of budgets, operating schedules, of plans which usually cover only a year or two ahead; or, if a program covers several future years, it is usually a problem limited in scope, definite in objective and based on past experience from which can be derived concrete facts and trends that aid in forecasting futures. Thus, you see that, in discussing anything as indefinite in time as the postwar period, and as intangible as an assumption of what that far-off era is to be like, I must deal with wholly unfamiliar premises. Concerning the future there are as yet almost no known facts, and but little theory upon which to go.

At the outset, let me strongly emphasize one point. Presently one supreme task confronts us—there is one job to do. That job is to win the war! We must win—no matter what the cost or how great the necessary sacrifice. Every businessman will echo that sentiment. Fortunately since the First World War, we have learned a lot. As we approach the problem of consolidating an inevitable victory, we must strive to build a peace as nearly indestructible as may be devised by the genius of man.

To try to look ahead to the postwar future is, of course, desirable; but while we are in a deadly global war, fighting for our very survival as a nation, I have little patience, I confess, with those whose eyes are fixed solely on the postwar future;

[7] Letter to the editor of this volume, June 4, 1943.

who are intent only on drawing a pretty picture of what the world *ought* to be, while we do not yet know exactly how the *existing* world is to be saved.

I feel that I should at this point attempt to dispel two common misconceptions about businessmen. Many persons labor under the illusion that businessmen desire to "go back to the good old days of the nineteen twenties," and that they always want to maintain the *status quo*. Both assumptions are fallacies. Permit me to say, as one who became the head of a large corporation six months before the crash of 1929, that I have no desire to go back to the good old days of the twenties. Nor do I want to live over again the depression and experimentation era of the thirties. I will rejoice when we have behind us the first half of the forties—these days of a bureaucratically controlled economy made necessary by war. I look forward to the postwar future in the hope that we can profit by the mistakes of the twenties, and the errors of the thirties, and the lessons of war in organizing a better way of life for *all* of us here in America.

The businessman of today is not afraid of "change." Change is the essence of progress. It is the motive of modern research. We can be sure *tomorrow* will be *different* from *yesterday*. We must strive to make it better.

Industrial research is the actual process of *improving* on the present; always the goal is new and better things. Any business that, in times like these, attempts to stand still or look backward is a business doomed to extinction.

With these few preliminary statements, permit me to sketch with broad strokes the background for an answer to your question concerning the postwar future.

What do we mean by a postwar world? Everyone is entitled to his own definition based on his guess as to the duration of the war and the nature and circumstances of the reconversion process from war to peace. For my purposes here I shall assume the Axis nations will not all be defeated before 1945, and that in the United States the major reconversion from a war to a peace basis will take three years, up to the end of 1948. I will define the postwar period as the time after 1948.

Now what do we mean by public goals? The goal for which we are supposed to be fighting this war has been defined by the leaders of two of the United Nations in the Atlantic Charter as the Four Freedoms. Freedom of speech and freedom of religion are accepted almost like the air we breathe by the English-speaking nations. Probably to the rest of the world these are rights greatly desired but enjoyed only in part. Freedom from fear of aggression and violence by neighbors against personal property has been sought by men ever since civilization began. Progress has been tremendous, but painfully slow. We must, if possible, go forward, but we will again be disappointed if we permit wishful thinking to obscure sound judgment. If freedom from fear also means alleviation of fear of ill health and, in old age, fear of destitution, we doubtless can, by individual and collective action, move far toward this goal. Freedom from want, especially in countries blessed with productive land and an abundance of raw materials, is certainly attainable if we define our "wants" as necessities.

However, in my limited time I must confine the term "public goals" to a much more limited scope than the Four Freedoms. I will confine myself to an intermediate goal which, if attained, will supply the means for at least some of the Four Freedoms or, in any event, go far to supply health, home, happiness and hope to most of our citizens. I refer, of course, to the problem of providing a reasonable measure of employment for all citizens able and willing to work.

This question of employment has been the major problem of Europe since the dislocations of World War I, and of our country since the crash of 1929. The gravity of the crash that followed 1929 in this country should not be minimized. The great depression at its bottom left 12,000,000 to 16,000,000 entirely unemployed. Many additional millions worked part time for part pay. It wiped out thousands of banks and untold billions of savings. It reduced the majority of commercial farmers to near bankruptcy. In Liverpool, wheat was quoted in 1932 at the lowest recorded price since Queen Elizabeth. Short-term unamortized mortgages could not be paid. As a result real estate could not be sold at any price. In Chicago, building permits dropped to the lowest level since the Civil War. Building of home units throughout the nation dropped from 1,000,000 in 1925 to less than 50,000 in 1932. The great depression, conservatively figured, cost us, as a nation, $350,000,-000,000 in *non*-production.

You economists have each your own theories as to the cause of the boom of the nineteen twenties and the collapse of the early nineteen thirties. Irrespective of the causes, the fundamental fact is the world had not in a hundred years experienced a decline of the business cycle of such magnitude. There was no precedent in the new industrial world for government to supplement the economic machine or to intervene on any such scale as some now believe was required to restore economic balance.

The great mistake of the first years of that depression was twofold: (1) Failure to understand that the downward dip in the business cycle was a depression of unprecedented magnitude which could not be cured by "temporary" expedients; (2) Failure to understand how to get the economic machine functioning again after it got out of balance and stopped.

To the everlasting credit of the administration, vigorous action was applied to the problem. Some of the acts were inconsistent with others and showed little understanding of how the economic machine worked. Early measures were partly temporary expedients applied in the hope "of getting us through the coming winter"; nevertheless they were evidence of an earnest and vigorous endeavor to find and remove the cause.

Some of the steps were: Placing of a moratorium on foreclosures; the rescue work of the Reconstruction Finance Corporation and the Home Owners Loan Corporation; shortening hours to spread work; increasing wage rates; unemployment insurance and old age pensions; adoption of a public works and relief program; insurance of bank deposits; encouragement of building through insurance of marginal risks under the Federal Housing Administration. These were all encouraging steps in the right direction. In principle they had the support of businessmen even though the methods of applying the principles often partially nullified the good. Even though skeptical of some of the schemes, businessmen "went along" in an earnest effort to help bring about recovery. The cooperation between business and government was excellent and the results were definitely encouraging.

One act in particular shows the way government can properly utilize private business agencies to achieve public goals. Since I helped draft the original act, and mobilized the construction industry of the country to help get it passed by Congress, I have first hand knowledge of its origin.

When the Federal Housing Act was first under discussion in January 1934, there were many in government who proposed that the government lend money direct to home builders. They argued that the government could borrow at $2\frac{1}{4}$ per cent and should lend direct at that figure, paying out of taxes the cost of making the loans and for any losses. This was typical of an all too prevalent approach apparently activated by a philosophy that the government should do everything for everybody.

Some of the rest of us, representing the opposite viewpoint that the proper function of government was to help people to help themselves, contended that the banks, the insurance companies, the saving and loan associations, the realtors, the whole system of building contractors and material distributors, could do a better job than any new bureaucracy that could be set up and could do it at less cost. We argued for insurance of the marginal risk from a fund set up by a premium paid by the home builder and with a system of amortized mortgages covering a period of ten to fifteen years, to protect the home owner against mortgages coming due during depression times.

Under this act there have been loans amounting to $1,650,-000,000 made for Mobilization Title I, with a loss to the government of $40,000,000. Under Title II there have been close to a million loans to home builders totalling $4,200,000,000, with a loss to date of less than $143,000.

The organization administering the act has, in my opinion, been larger than necessary, but even so the cost has averaged less than $14,000,000 per year. The Federal Housing Act has been called the most successful of any innovation in the past ten years. In home financing it has revolutionized the mortgage banking system of this country. Here is an example of governmental stimulation of private enterprise as compared to competition with private enterprise.

In contrast to the F.H.A. we have experience of the Tugwell Towns; of the T.V.A.; of paying subsidies *not* to produce what could be consumed; of punitive taxation; publication and limitation of incomes; extermination measures of the S.E.C.; and such projects as the Florida Ship Canal and Passamaquoddy. It is not by such measures that we bring about cooperation and restoration of confidence, nor the full utilization of private agencies for achieving of public goals.

Favorable reference is made to the Reconstruction Finance Corporation, to the Home Owners Loan Corporation and to the Federal Housing Authority, not so much for the rescue work which they performed as for the *principles* which governed their operation. These principles differed fundamentally from those which were operative in programs to redistribute wealth, to give relief through unproductive work or to create needless governmental spending for spending's sake alone.

In the Federal Housing Authority, government and industry came closer, in my judgment, to real cooperation on sound constructive lines than was reached in any other field.

Here was a kind of planning which produced very tangible results; which stimulated the recuperative processes necessary to full recovery without arousing, at the same time, the fears of investors as to whether or not the free enterprise system would survive. Here was government aid functioning as an *accelerator* to human *initiative* and *resourcefulness*. This procedure relaxed restrictive brakes upon the national economy which were being applied through the *wrong kind* of governmental planning.

It was on this crucial point that, through the past decade, businessmen have differed with government economic theorists. It is here the difference was most manifest between the *political approach* and the *business approach* to the problem of recovery.

One philosophy involved the stimulation of confidence and cooperation on the part of *all* elements in the economy so they philosophy, by its very nature, stimulated suspicion and distrust and thus created *fears which paralyzed confidence.*

For example, while the government, with its right hand, was endeavoring to help the banks to help themselves through the R. F. C., at the very same time with its left hand it was competing with the banks through numerous lending agencies which had been established to deal with so-called "emergency" problems. Doubtless the motives of these government planners were sincere. Yet the net result was to create in the public mind distrust of possible unrevealed collectivist objectives for the future. That suspicion served to neutralize much of what the government was trying to do. Thus, the troublesome problem of unemployment, although eased, was never solved. As a result, every businessman, big and little, began to get the idea that government had taken on a job and a responsibility bigger than any government ought to assume or could carry without eventual financial disaster through excessive inflation or repudiation, or through conversion to some form of totalitarian government. This generated the fear that slowly, but inevitably, the private enterprise system was being secretly liquidated.

If we are to build soundly for the postwar future, it seems to me we must proceed according to the principle, learned at such great cost in the past decade, that no government should enter into direct competition with its citizens, and that the government of a representative democracy cannot do everything for everybody.

Bureaucratic planners' theory on this point reminds me of an incident that happened out in Iowa where I grew up. Every farmer had a milch cow. A natural rivalry existed among all the neighbors as to whose cow could produce the most milk. One farmer, thinking to outsmart the others, evolved an entirely new theory as to how his cow could be made to produce more. He figured out that if he could speed up her digestive processes, she would consume more food, and, therefore, give more milk. So he would go out three times a day with his dog and chase the cow around and around the pasture. Needless to say the cow soon went dry. The farmer with the novel idea failed to realize that nature had designed the cow to function along entirely different lines.

The free enterprise system has its natural way to function. It can produce jobs in abundance so long as it can have plenty of the right food and chew its cud of confidence without being chased all around the economic field by a lot of governmental experimenters with new, untried and unsound theories. You can't use a club to chase the business system around the pasture without drying up the whole productive process. You can't successfully approach the problem of obtaining greater cooperation between business and government, between business and labor, and between labor and agriculture on the basis of mutual hostility and truculence.

Perhaps it is too early for us to look at this chapter in our history from the sound and unemotional pinnacle of historical perspective and logic. Nevertheless we ought, at least, to try to distill out of these experiments with the lives and security of 130,000,000 people whatever we can of the virus or cause of our illness, so we may develop a preventive against the same mistakes in the postwar future.

The American way of life and our private enterprise system are predicated upon incentives which develop enterprise and stimulate people to work. To help others to help themselves has been, for a hundred and fifty years, the successful basic principle underlying the American way of life. Now a vast abyss is fixed between this sound, simple principle and the benevolent paternalism of a super-government which attempts to work on the reverse philosophy of trying to do everything for everybody.

As, in retrospect, we consider the turbulent thirties with their currents of cynicism on the one hand, and, on the other, a fervent faith in utopia, we can see the conflict which was under way between these two concepts. A large part of our people, mindful of the old traditions, were fighting desperately to maintain our heritage won through centuries of struggle—*political* freedom, *economic* freedom, and *religious* freedom. The new theorists scoffed at them for their "rugged individualism." For the scoffers had a philosophy—that the state was all important;

that the state could bring to pass the millennium. Expressed in another way, that basic conflict was between men who undertook risks to better the lot of man in return for rewards, under a system called "private enterprise," and those who believed government office holders without adequate experience had suddenly been endowed with a magical ability to operate a great complex economic society. These bureaucrats believed a little untried theory and plenty of compulsion would accomplish more than a lot of experience and plenty of hard work. These two fundamental concepts can be epitomized in two words: "opportunity" expresses the first; "security" the second. The first group strives for multiplication of wealth, and the second group for division of the wealth already created.

Now the pathological condition which lay at the root of this kind of thinking is not limited to America—it is world-wide in extent. Abroad it helped develop the Marxian doctrines of class consciousness, class warfare and open advocacy of destruction of individualism and the substitution of state ownership of all means of production. In this country, likewise, the movement took root, but in a somewhat different form.

Marxism sought to tear down; its premise was that a new economic order could be built only after an old one had been destroyed. American liberals in their thinking haven't been quite that ruthless. Instead the effort has been to *build a new order inside the old order,* so that, by throwing a switch, we could start off with a new economy and discard the old one. The label, "reform," was used, while the real purpose, in the opinion of many, was just as far reaching as Marxism itself. For a decade we have tinkered and experimented; we have tried "deficit financing" and one economic formula after another. But, despite the pulmotors and all the artificial stimulants, the national economy never seemed strong enough to stand on its own feet.

This period of economic experimentalism ended, at least temporarily, with Pearl Harbor. While the problems we face now are bigger and more serious than ever before, yet at least we have won a spirit of *national unity* and of cooperative effort which we did not have before. The specter of unemployment has been banished through the placing of billions of dollars worth of government orders for war materials in the sales hoppers of a relatively small number of large corporations. Temporarily those deep haunting fears which have had such a baleful influence over American political life have been quieted.

We have won, perhaps, nothing more than a breathing period. Let's hope it will be sufficient for us to rediagnose these past ills so that, while there is yet time, preventives can be developed against repeating, after this war, the mistakes which were so disastrous after the last one and in the great depression.

We have a choice of directions to follow. We have a choice of instruments to use. But we cannot possibly reconcile the principle of democracy, *which means cooperation,* with the principle of governmental omniscience under which everyone waits for an order before doing anything. That way lies loss of freedom, and dictatorship.

As an industrial engineer, I visualize for comparison the free enterprise system and the totalitarian system, by imagining each to be a machine, and each propelled by a different kind of engine.

There is the totalitarian machine driven by a powerful, heavy steam engine familiar to those of us who are industrial engineers. Its motive power is sweat converted to steam by the heat of compulsion. It is lubricated by fear. Usually its control emanates from the central plant. It is large, cumbersome and complicated and needs an unusually expert man at the controls. It has real power, and after it gets going, can deliver lots of energy. Its operation and efficiency are strictly limited by the training, experience and capacity of its engineer and his assistant.

The free enterprise machine is activated by the compact, easy-to-operate, flexible gasoline engine. Its fuel is human aspiration ignited by self-interest and it is lubricated by individual ambition and initiative. It possesses the power to do almost anything and goes wherever the people may guide it. The driver is the ordinary citizen who needs only a few rules to help him guide it so as not to endanger others. It needs no fettering central power plant. It needs no special tracks. It runs on the right-of-way of freedom available to all.

To win the war we have converted our governmental economic machine over from a gasoline engine to a steam engine. After the war, we want the limitless advantages of the private enterprise gasoline engine.

As an industrial engineer, I believe the private enterprise machine—streamlined—is the best from all standpoints to propel the American nation to new heights of spiritual, cultural and material progress. I would recommend it as the basis of our design for the postwar model of the American way. I believe the American people will prefer for peace the private enterprise machine controlled by the people.

As I read the pronouncements of many men in power today throughout the world about what *they* propose to do in the postwar world, I wonder if they have forgotten that someone else may be occupying the seats of the mighty, trying to direct the destiny of the world in that postwar era? I am convinced the American people themselves will decide what kind of a machine and engine they want when they write the closing paragraph on the last page of our history of World War II.

In that very fact lies the need for the American people to be thinking now and making up *their* minds as to what *they* want in the postwar world. The foundations of the postwar world are being laid right now—though not necessarily by the war leaders.

The future of America is being hammered out right now in the souls of our fighting men at the front; in the minds of the workers in the factories and on the farms, in the hearts of our American women, to be expressed in the acts of Congress over the next two or three years.

Out of the lesson of unity learned in war we must find some cooperative compromise to make the "general welfare" the joint responsibility of the people, the government, business, labor and agriculture. We shall have demonstrated that our representative republic is more efficient than any totalitarian state and in addition preserves freedom. We must find a way to distribute equitably the products of our economic machine without destroying the machine.

We must remove every obstacle that impedes private enterprise in doing its full job. Like Mark Twain's character, Tom Sawyer, who gave inducements to his playmates to whitewash the fence so that the more he got them to do, the less he had left to do himself, government must pursue the incentive plan with the people.

In the thirties, government tried the opposite way. The more government took over, the less of the burden private enterprise could carry. The more of the burden government tried to carry, the more the red tape tangled up, the more inefficiency developed, the more bureaucracy expanded and confusion grew.

Tom Sawyer was an organizer. He offered inducements to get others to do what he knew needed to be done. What they left undone was a burden he could carry.

When you ask how government and business can make the economic machine work better in the postwar world, I answer, by learning to cooperate—to be mutually helpful, to recognize the proper function of each in our social structure. To avoid dictatorship, we must encourage the private enterprise system to carry the load of providing employment to the utmost, so that government's load will be at a minimum.

But then some economists will say, "What about the portion private enterprise cannot do?" If the savings of the system are not reinvested promptly so as to provide work for all, should not government intervene in the economic system to stimulate and assure reasonable employment for all? In reply, I say that if, with every encouragement and inducement, private enterprise were not to provide reasonable employment for all, then the government, by means of guarantees to private enterprise and through its procurement staff, should place orders with private enterprise for sufficient public works and products to supplement and fill the gap left unfilled by private enterprise.

But even when the government intervenes, if it is not to thwart its own purpose, it must do so by means consistent with the basic design of the engine it has chosen to sustain the American standard of living. We should never again, as we did in the nineteen thirties, try to put totalitarian water in the freedom gasoline and expect the enterprise machine to work properly.

There is nothing to prevent the attainment of our goal except our own failure to find out and understand how our social-economic governmental machine works best.

In my opinion, we can make it work. We do not need to change over to an entirely new machine or resort to a very obsolete type. All we need do is to streamline and properly gear up the great American enterprise machine.

As I said in the beginning, businessmen build futures based on change. We shall not be satisfied in the postwar world of 1950 with the old enterprise gasoline engine model of 1925. We stand committed to a new model. But not merely *a* new model. We ask for changes in the American way consistent with the basic design of our engine, based on improvements tested on the proving ground of practical experience.

Moreover, we know there is more to the life of a nation than merely the political and economic machinery to provide reasonably full employment. Health, home, happiness and hope are our end objectives. Employment is only one means to these ends.

And so, we must reeducate every man, woman and child to a deep faith in our destiny. The American way is an ideal way of life citizens are willing to fight for—to die for if necessary. We must realize that working and sacrificing together in the common cause are just as necessary in peace as in war.

We must rebuild America. We must not destroy the system that has made America great. Instead, we must use incentives to stimulate private enterprise into channels beneficial to the good of all. Prosperity for America lies not in limiting opportunities for some, but in expanding opportunities for all. Honor and pride, properly appealed to, will put service in the common cause first, and the desire for profit second, as has been proven by this war. Cooperation, not conflict, must guide government, business, labor, and agriculture in their service to our people. From this new spirit and cooperation can come a new America that will be the Eldorado of the whole New World.

THE AMERICAN DEMOCRATIC TRADITION

TRUTHS THAT INSPIRED WASHINGTON [1]

Franklin Delano Roosevelt [2]

President Roosevelt delivered this brief address on the 211th anniversary of George Washington's birth date, February 22, 1943. The President spoke by radio from the White House to the Democrats at thirty dinners across the country, at which party members paid from $5 to $100 per plate to raise some $500,000 for party activities.

The speech was given at the request of Frank Walker, Postmaster General, and National Chairman of the Democratic Party.

The address is an interesting example of President Roosevelt's ability to present the demonstrative or commemorative address or oration. It has no pronounced partisan spirit. A similar type of speech the President gave on April 13, 1943, when he dedicated the Thomas Jefferson Memorial in the Tidal Basin at Washington.

The tribute to Washington is expressed with dignity of language; has organic structure that gives unity and progression to the thought; has an appropriate theme ("the truths which are the eternal heritage of our civilization"); incorporates significant illustrations out of Washington's experiences, illustrations the details of which the student of American history may well supply; and draws close parallels between the problems faced by the Commander in Chief of 1775-1783 and those of the Commander in Chief of 1941-1943. Hardly disguised is the President's denunciation of his critics and of the skeptics of 1943 who unwittingly aid Nazi propaganda. Significant here, and unusual in the President's addresses, are the Biblical references and the religious temper of the oration.

Today this nation, which George Washington helped so greatly to create, is fighting all over this earth in order to maintain for ourselves and for our children the freedom which George Washington helped so greatly to achieve. As we cele-

[1] Reprinted from *Congressional Record*, v. 89, no. 33, p. A835, February 25, 1943 (daily edition), 78th Congress, first session.
[2] For biographical note see Appendix.

brate his birthday, let us remember how he conducted himself in the midst of great adversities. We are inclined, because of the total sum of his accomplishments, to forget his days of trial.

Throughout the Revolution, Washington commanded an army whose very existence as an army was never a certainty from one week to another. Some of his soldiers, and even whole regiments, could not, or would not, move outside of the borders of their own states. Sometimes, at critical moments, they would decide to return to their individual homes to get the plowing done or the crops harvested. Large numbers of the people of the colonies were either against independence or at least unwilling to make great personal sacrifice toward its attainment.

And there were many in every colony who were willing to cooperate with Washington only if the cooperation was based on their own terms.

Some Americans during the War of the Revolution sneered at the very principles of the Declaration of Independence. It was impractical, they said—it was "idealistic"—to claim that "all men are created equal, that they are endowed by their Creator with certain inalienable rights."

The skeptics, the cynics of Washington's day, did not believe that ordinary men and women have the capacity for freedom and self-government. They said that liberty and equality were idle dreams that could not come true—just as today there are many Americans who sneer at the determination to attain freedom from want and freedom from fear on the ground that these are ideals which can never be realized. They say that it is ordained that we must always have poverty and that we must always have war.

You know they are like the people who carp at the Ten Commandments because some people are in the habit of breaking one or more of them.

We Americans of today know that there would have been no successful outcome of the Revolution even after eight long years—the Revolution that gave us liberty—had it not been for George Washington's faith and the fact that that faith overcame the bickerings and confusion and the doubts which the skeptics and cynics provoked.

When kind history books tell us of Benedict Arnold they omit dozens of other Americans who, beyond peradventure of a doubt, were also guilty of treason.

We know that it was Washington's simple, steadfast faith that kept him to the essential principles of first things first. His sturdy sense of proportion brought to him and his followers the ability to discount the smaller difficulties and concentrate on the larger objectives. And the objectives of the American Revolution were so large—so unlimited—that today they are among the primary objectives of the entire civilized world.

It was Washington's faith—and, with it, his hope and his charity—which was responsible for the stamina of Valley Forge—responsible for the prayer at Valley Forge.

The Americans of Washington's day were at war. We Americans of today are at war. The Americans of Washington's day faced defeat on many occasions. We faced, and still face, reverses and misfortunes.

In 1777 the victory over General Burgoyne's army at Saratoga led thousands of Americans to throw their hats in the air proclaiming that the war was practically won and that they could go back to their peacetime occupations—and shall I say, their peacetime "normalcies."

Today the great successes on the Russian front have led thousands of Americans to throw their hats in the air and proclaim that victory is just around the corner.

Others among us still believe in the age of miracles. They forget that there is no Joshua in our midst. We cannot count on great walls crumbling and falling down when the trumpets blow and the peoples shout.

It is not enough that we have faith and that we have hope. Washington himself was the exemplification of the other great need.

Would that all of us could live our lives and direct our thoughts and control our tongues as did the Father of Our Country in seeking day by day to follow those great verses:

Charity suffereth long, and is kind; charity envieth not; charity vaunteth not itself, is not puffed up.

Doth not behave itself unseemly, seeketh not her own, is not easily provoked, thinketh no evil:

Rejoiceth not in iniquity, but rejoiceth in the truth.

I think that most of us Americans seek to live up to those precepts. But there are some among us who have forgotten them. There are Americans whose words and writings are trumpeted by our enemies to persuade the disintegrating people of Germany and Italy and their captives that America is disunited—that America will be guilty of faithlessness in this war and will thus enable the Axis powers to control the earth.

It is perhaps fitting that on this day I should read a few more words spoken many years ago—words which helped to shape the character and the career of George Washington.

Blessed are the poor in spirit: for theirs is the kingdom of heaven.

Blessed are they that mourn: for they shall be comforted.

Blessed are the meek: for they shall inherit the earth.

Blessed are they which do hunger and thirst after righteousness: for they shall be filled.

Blessed are the merciful: for they shall obtain mercy.

Blessed are the pure in heart: for they shall see God.

Blessed are the peacemakers: for they shall be called the children of God.

Blessed are they which are persecuted for righteousness' sake: for theirs is the kingdom of heaven.

Blessed are ye, when men shall revile you, and persecute you, and shall say all manner of evil against you falsely, for my sake.

Rejoice, and be exceedingly glad: for great is your reward in heaven: for so persecuted they the prophets which were before you.

Those are the truths which are the eternal heritage of our civilization. I repeat them to give heart and comfort to all men and women everywhere who fight for freedom.

Those truths inspired Washington and the men and women of their thirteen colonies.

Today, through all the darkness that has descended upon our nation and our world, those truths are a guiding light to all.

We shall follow that light, as our forefathers did, to the fulfillment of our hopes for victory, for freedom and for peace.

CAN DEMOCRACY SURVIVE THE WAR? [3]

EDGAR EUGENE ROBINSON [4]

Dr. Edgar Eugene Robinson, Professor of American History at
Stanford University, gave this address before the Commonwealth Club
of California, on August 7, 1942.

The speaker here, as in his previous addresses, is a historian and
political scientist. He analyzes with unusual penetration the problem
of war and democracy. His illustrations are pertinent, his definitions
clear and plausible, his language original and efficient, his appeals to
his Commonwealth audience based at every point upon his analysis and
logical proof.

Dr. Robinson is alert and convincing as a speaker. He has been
in wide demand before educational and popular audiences. One of his
notable addresses was on "Faith and the University," delivered before
a Stanford University audience, on August 3, 1941, on the occasion of
that university's fiftieth anniversary.

The question is not new: "Can democracy survive?" America gave the answer long ago and has repeated it many times in
our history. This has been necessary, because democracy has
been denied—in theory and in practice—by some of the cleverest
minds that have darkened the earth. Defenders have been
needed every hour, every day, every year of our development
as a nation. At home and abroad scoffers have been legion,
and while many a battle for democracy has not been won,
there are those who do not observe that never has the *war*
for democracy been lost. There is a reason for this.

America is the product of the work of millions of men and
women, and democracy has been at once their dearest possession
and their ultimate objective. Much of their record has been
written in blood and tears. The deathless words of Jefferson
and of Lincoln and of Wilson have been proved over and
over again. Amid all the claims of recent converts and of
zealous defenders at home and abroad, we ought not to forget

[3] By permission of Dr. Robinson; of *The Commonwealth*; and of the Commonwealth Club of California. Text furnished through the courtesy of the speaker.
[4] For biographical note see Appendix.

that, from our birth as a nation, to countless millions all over
the world *America* has been thought of as synonymous with democracy.   If we are wise in our time, we ought to judge a
product—let us say, self-government, equality of peoples, justice
to all, tolerance of opinion, personal liberty, even democracy
itself—*not* by a prospectus, but by the record of the producer.
American democracy has been in the public view for a very
long time, and its practitioners are known to all mankind.

Consequently, if I were to modify the title of this address,
it would be to suggest, "Why American Democracy Should Point
the Way."   If we lose this war, there will be no democracy in
the world, and no necessity of discussing its future.   If we win
this war at the cost of our way of life, there will be no necessity
of discussing the survival of democracy.   It will have passed
from the face of the earth.   It follows that the *way* to win this
war will determine not only the nature of the peace, which con-
cerns so many of our public men, but the character of the democracy in the years to come.   It is the way our people *think*
and *feel* about what they are doing—it is how they *act* in this
war—that will determine what they can do in peace, and
whether the world *can* be made safe for democracy.   Only an
undying faith can save our people in the years that follow this
total war.   The world—which has suffered such impoverishment in the past five years as never before known by man—
will be no place in which new theories and untried practices
will have chance of success.   The one hope lies in our complete
realization that we long ago discovered an answer to the greatest
question that has ever been asked of man in his tragic days
on this earth.   That question is simple: How can men live together—the world around—in harmony, in dignity, and in
peace?   We have an answer that arises directly out of our history.   Only as our people realize that this war is now *their* war—
a continuation of the struggle that was evident at their birth
as a nation—will they remain true to their impressive record
and once more take an aggressive leadership abroad as well
as at home.

Would it not be well to survey our own contributions with
this record before us?   When it is suggested that Russia and

China will write the peace because they will have won the war, I do not find that in itself this will insure a continuance of American democracy. In terms of *our* democracy and the way it has been built, I see no democracy in China and I see no democracy in Russia. Nor in England, which I know as I do not know Russia and China, do I find the democracy which we would recognize as our own. Of course we are aiding these peoples and we will triumph together but when I say "yes" to the question asked, I mean democracy *here.*

Have we forgotten that the four freedoms which have been so much in discussion—freedom of conscience, freedom of thought, freedom from want, and freedom from fear—that these have been in our very lifeblood from the beginning? Have we forgotten that it is Europe that has ever been impoverished, and in successive bankruptcies? Have we forgotten that long-time poverty and low standards in the Orient have again and again impressed themselves upon us? It is in this rich land that the four freedoms have been won, and where in greatest measure they exist today. *Why is it so?*

Let me make clear just what I mean by this approach to what must seem to many of you an old story. "Can democracy survive?" like any other question as to the future cannot be answered with certainty. We have no means of certain forecasting. We ought to insist upon that. But we know that there are two questions we may ask which, if answered, will furnish a basis for faith and for action. One of these questions is always asked by historians—"What is the record?" The other question is asked by social scientists—"What is the present process?" It is not always easy and comfortable to listen to experts on either of these questions. Yet it is necessary, if we are to have a sound basis for any prophecy.

However, I surmise you do not wish to be told that the future of democracy is bright; that all is "true and beautiful" in our present state. You do not wish to be told—as we are hourly—how good we are, and how effective, and how wonderful! I assume that the much desired "good morale" to you does not mean that. You are anxious to know the truth. There are no easy answers in this search for the keys to the future.

Let me illustrate. If by going out of that door to certain death, any one of us or all of us could save our nation or preserve democracy, who of us would not do it, and do it gladly? But we do not *know* that by so doing we would produce the result. That is the ever present uncertainty of action. We cannot be sure, because we cannot know the result. Try as we may, inform ourselves as we can, prepare as we do, there is always the specter of possible failure. But it has always been so, and those who dared bravely have written the history of mankind.

It is not alone the historian who measures people by what they do and say; the people themselves see themselves in the mirror of their hopes and ideals. In self-respect the people must appear to reach their objectives, or at least to continue trying to do so. It is a rare man who openly flaunts his cynicism. It is a rare people who do not actively call upon their leaders for the best that is in them. Let a people admire a man of high ideals and constructive imagination and the man appears. Nations get what they deserve. One of the great appeals of our own nation is seen in the words of Gilbert Chesterton, speaking of a truly great man—a man who makes other men feel great. A truly great nation is one that makes other nations, however small, feel potentially great!

Before giving a direct answer to the question "Can democracy survive?" I would call your attention to three glaring misapprehensions. First, democracy is *not* anything and everything we happen to favor. Glib talk of democracy is highly dangerous. Democracy is often over sold; the product is depressed; abuse of the word makes for folly in action. We water the lifeblood of democracy. We poison the wells of truth. We offer hypocrisy to our enemies as a weapon of attack. The second misapprehension—we *cannot* dictate to the world—of course not—and be ourselves. To dictate to the world would be contrary to what we have always said of ourselves. You see, this misconception rests in the thought that democracy can be "handed around." This ignores essentials of the success of our historic democracy: constant thought on the part of great numbers of people; constant planning on the part of great numbers of people. We have to win this battle for democracy *every day*. A way of life is an eternal charge. When a people indulge in idle gossip, vain imagining and irresolute thinking, you may be sure that sloth and ignorance and selfishness and lack of vision have democracy on the run. And the third misapprehension (and to my mind the most important of the three)—it is assumed that quick action is desirable, as well as possible, and that it is a mistake to wait until an issue is clearcut, as we did in 1917 and again in 1941. I would remind you that waiting is inevitable in a democracy.

As a people we believed—as before in our history—that the righteousness of our conduct, the soundness of our thought on international relations, and the growth of what we called the civilization of the western world would make it possible for us to lead in a world of peace instead of a world of war. We were wrong. To be right, to be conscious of right, was not enough. But we moved as a democracy.

The three misconceptions as to the nature and availability and functioning of our democracy lead to a general view of the war which is basically false and alarmingly prevalent. This is not a war of nations—but a war of ideas. It is not strange that the United States is joined with twenty-seven other nations—including Russia and China and Great Britain—for they have come to *our* standard; we have not joined theirs. This conflict of ideas is *our* fight. We have been in revolt against dictatorship from the *beginning*. This is no new task—this defense of American democracy. As the American Secretary of State pointed out in his recent radio address, the four points in his program all rest in American action and thought in the past. For there is the record—even a tradition—on which we and others can build.

We meet in a tragic hour—made more tragic the moment you apply truth to the situation. Our critics, our quickies and our fears make us apprehensive. It is not easy to redirect the energies of our people. Eight months of defeat have marked the record of American participation. We are allied with nations who were (and are) losing the battles of this war. This has done much to speed up our own record. But it is not enough. As you have been told—in the press, on the radio, and in countless addresses—we can lose this war, and, if we are not the careful, thoughtful, creative people we claim to be, we can lose the peace that follows the war.

As I have said, *America's answer is to be found in our history.* It has been long in preparation. It is the basic fact in our existence. America in coming into being—in 1776—struck at tyranny and rule by force. Its existence through a century and a half has again and again challenged that tyranny. Throughout the nineteenth century we were comparatively free. But Europe in 1917 and Asia in 1942 pressed in upon us. It exists today—as it never existed so vividly before—the irrepressible conflict. The roots lie deep in the human mind. Racial hatred, the superiority complex, ruthless aggression, have engulfed the world. The so-called New Order in Europe and in Asia is, as Carl Becker has pointed out, neither new, nor is it order. It is old; we rejected it at our birth and .have denied it all through our history. That is why the answer we shall develop is, it seems to me, so clear, so definite, and—to countless millions of freedom-loving men throughout the world—so true. We must not fail them. This is our destiny. This conflict—we see it with increasing clarity—arises now out of divisions of the world into irreconcilable elements—not of nations but of ideas. Good faith versus ruthless might—continuous thought versus rigid doctrine—democracy versus the totalitarian state. We Americans know the difference between evil and good—and we do not call evil "good" even when it appears on our own soil and dons the raiment of patriotism. Ability to be fearless in thought is the direct product of our freedom.

But there are dangers at home that suggest we need to look even more closely at our record. Let us not be misled by every claimant to wear the mantel of democracy. I call your attention to free speech, its use and abuse. We have learned a great deal about both. In my opinion it is necessary at times to limit free speech in the interests of self-preservation. We cannot permit free speech to mean rigid indoctrination, fanatical speculation, crazy destruction. To warrant the right of free speech, a speaker should have ability to formulate a constructive program and to lead in its free discussion. Democracy has suffered in war and peace from incompetents and moral and intellectual idiots who use free speech not to lead and build, but to hold back and destroy. A nihilist has no place in a creative society.

The dangers I see in unthinking calls for democracy at home and abroad touching on race and business and government are that they overlook the fact that in America, equality of race, freedom of private enterprise, even the strength of the government have always been "in process," not definite and final. America has not been the impractical dream of utter and complete perfectibility. There are malcontents we ought to recognize as such. There is the man who insists on pointing out inequalities and incompleteness here at home (which exist of course), and suggests that we do something about it now and completely. There is the man who points out that in the past there have been men and organizations who have been mistaken in public questions and that therefore they ought to be discredited from any future participation. And then there are the men who pin unpopular symbols and throw foreign bitterness upon leaders with whom they happen to disagree. These are not honest practitioners of effective American democracy.

Liberty, equality and fraternity—how eagerly we respond! But let us remember, even at this dark hour, that liberty has slain its thousands—equality has beggared millions; and fraternity has enthroned the incompetent. None of these causes is acceptable or desirable in America unless tempered by intelligent discrimination. Each requires the work not of a *government that may free men,* but the work of *peoples who may teach men.* Liberty within the law, equality of opportunity, fraternity as coming from the heart—when any one of these is denied, the spirit is lost. Each must be a free gift.

Let us look more closely at the American way of life. You have had economic independence *and* security. Would you separate them? It allows for growth in accordance with ability. You have had social equality *and* independence. Would you separate them? It allows for variation in talent and ability and ambition. You have political freedom *and* responsibility. Would you separate them? Why neglect this? Why think of government as apart and away from our duty?

Let us now put a question bluntly, and give it a direct answer. *Why have we this democracy in America?* America of the nineteenth century was characterized by three conditioning factors. First, the whole nation experienced the frontier. Second, the whole nation realized isolation. Third, and often forgotten, the whole nation, in growth and expansion accepted and practiced capitalistic democracy. It was the mixture of these three that gave us the American freedom that seemed to promise so much for millions of men because it was not static. It has lived—this growing democracy—and all the hopeful of all the world through that century looked longingly to America, and millions came from Europe and from the Orient, and remember, they came to *live* here. The crowning achievement of all the struggles of men in what we call the modern years took form in the United States of America. We ought not to forget that.

At the end of the century and a half there came upon the world and upon us fundamental changes. In fact, they were long in coming, but finally they were realized. Our frontier was gone. Our isolation was gone. Our capitalistic democracy seemed to have reached a limit of productivity. Now what happened? Most of us refused to think through to the reality of a new physical basis, and the forces of darkness arose to say we had all been vain in our hope. We had been living in a fool's paradise. Mankind was doomed, said they, to live in the darkness of the dark ages. But what they did *not* see was that the inventions of our age, in widening frontiers, in destroying isolation, and in developing finance capitalism, had given us the greatest opportunity of all time. Power politics *denied* democracy everywhere; isolation *undermined* democracy everywhere; continued lack of responsibility and participation might lead to its destruction everywhere.

Consider now, not a map of the United States wherein we have lived for a century and a half—our great epic of expansion —but consider a map of the world. Upon this map, where the Axis Powers have made such gains, (1) we might again advance the frontier—the missionary, the merchant, the colonist; (2) we might help to develop hitherto untouched parts of the globe as we did our own vast expanses in time of isolation; and (3) we might give renewed scope to the capitalistic democracy of free men. If we did this task on a continent, which I would remind you is the size of all Europe, and did it under a representative government which insisted upon equality and tolerance and order and security, do you not think that with the awakened peoples of the earth we could do it again? The truth is we have forgotten the glory of our effort. We have even thought that as a people we were through—approaching a time of decline. Such a cycle is known in the history of nations. Every historian refers to it. But note here a difference, and, I think, a vital difference.

In the opening years of the twentieth century there was a shift in the political interest of our people, when there was a great expansion of economic interest in foreign lands. And there was a rebirth of a new nation, a young nation, new for the tasks of youth in a great world that lay beyond this continent. Looking out upon our continental extent and looking at our integrated nationalism, we were an old nation, but looking at the vision of such leaders as Theodore Roosevelt and Woodrow Wilson, who bade us look abroad, we were young. And we were. We had the qualities that the pioneer needed. We looked out upon a great task, as youth looks out. And for the world job we were young, and we dreamed for a while the dreams of youth.

I have lived much with young people during the past thirty years, and I think I know why they see a world to match their dreams. So did most of you—years ago. Sometimes it is well not to know so much, not to be so sure of failure, not to pause and hesitate and expect defeat. Sometimes there is soundness in a faith that expects to succeed!

In this room are men interested in politics—perhaps nine tenths of you—but not one tenth of you give your life to politics. Perhaps one in a hundred is actually in government. But all of you are concerned with economic democracy and its preservation, and most of you—or you would not belong to the Commonwealth Club—are interested in cooperation in democracy, that is, in social democracy. You know that under our system of procedure, democracy does work, but the political forms and practices are at once the least important *and* the most important. Gradually we have come to realize that, as far as our own development is concerned, we cannot depend upon our government to insure our democracy. In fact, dependence saps the lifeblood. We say glibly, "Men first and government second." Quite so, but we have as citizens a twofold task: First to insist that economic and social freedom come first; and second, to see to it that political democracy works, often in spite of the government.

Here, perhaps, is the greatest danger of all—our failure to realize that the conditions of the world, following this war, will not be conducive to democracy as we have known it here or elsewhere. At the close of this war, the nations of hope and the nations of despair will alike be defeated and impoverished beyond any computation. This world will have had a period of such harsh brutality as no memory of man will admit. This is the atmosphere in which we are told that democracy must flourish. How can it be expected?

If we may judge from our past, democracy flourishes not because government declares for freedom and opportunity, but democracy flourishes where there is soil and substance and food and work. Democratic protest, I admit, flourishes under tyranny and oppression. But democracy itself does not flourish under conditions of starvation and death imposed not by a few men in power, but imposed by the hard realities of an impoverished earth. Had we not had the richness of the American continent, there would have been no American democracy. Our democracy is rooted in economic wealth, opportunity, and free development.

I suspect that is a general rule. I do not believe that we realize that the conditions that follow this war are not the conditions that will produce a great flowering of the human spirit, that is, such as democracy. But do not misunderstand. As you well know, this nation and this democracy were built by men who had very little of the world's goods and who faced every privation and danger. But they built and lived in this fact: There was a great economic opportunity, and it was theirs. When some of them starved, they built no democracy. When some of them saw for a time no hope, they built no democracy. Economic strictures and rules produced not democracy, but revolt, sometimes rebellion.

Today in our land, as yet not impoverished, as yet not faced with continued and dismal failure, as yet where livelihood is possible, and millions look forward to more opportunity, there is not only work and play and freedom and liberty, but here is a functioning of the democracy that we know. The conditions are favorable. But my question at the beginning—What of the period after the war? It depends on the length of the war; it depends upon the depth to which we sink into the abyss For no political structure, however flexible in times of plenty, no social atmosphere, no matter how fluid in times of free growth, can possibly save us and our democratic way of life, unless with limited resources, a tremendous debt, a lower standard of living—we are still able to provide food and clothing and shelter to millions of our people.

No form of society other than the democratic form which I have been describing gives opportunity to direct economic conflicts into channels of order and arbitration and adjustment by the law of compromise. No form of society that provides for ruling power by birth or class or might, can be a society that provides for social growth and economic development, in a word, that has a future. Democracy is the only method that history brings to us of surviving social change without revolution.

You see, now, why the American way of life cannot disappear; why America cannot be defeated! And what is asked of America now *and* what are the answers?

(1) *Manpower.* But not only in terms of millions, but also in terms of individual capacity. We have it. Our experience as a frontier people put a premium on manpower and individual courage. Our own social structure demands it every day.

(2) *Machines.* Not only in terms of mass capacity but also in ingenuity, in inventiveness and in continuous growth, we look upon the miraculous expansion of industry in this country in the past fifty years. We were preparing, as we constructed, a new world for men. We did not know that we would use this great power for destruction. But we are doing so.

(3) *Self-government.* We have had it—and we developed a *colonial* system as we marched across the continent. No outlying frontier must remain a colony. It rises to man's estate and enters the Union of States on a basis of equality. That principle of conduct embodied in a great document—the Northwest Ordinance—made it possible to promise the Philippines self-government and have it mean just that. And look at the results!

(4) *Aid to the oppressed, the needy, the starving.* For more than a century we have built an effective program of private philanthropy. We beckoned the world, and the refugees came. We went abroad to feed the starving. Can you doubt that this history is remembered by those in dire need today? This weapon, that is, our record, our opponents do not possess. We can say—and be believed—"Follow us; this way lies your freedom."

(5) *Equality of treatment.* Closely related to a haven of refuge is America's early insistence upon the declaration that the doors of opportunity should be open to all—regardless of race, creed and previous condition of misfortune.

(6) *Code of international conduct.* Result of our growth as a people. A continent made up of "diverse interests" and resulting in sections has found a means of *intersectional* conduct that furnished us a code of international conduct. The Atlantic Charter is not enough. *We need a declaration for the common people of all lands; all of the people who are going our way.*

Here are six answers—but with them are two more that rise out of these and may transcend all other factors in America's will to win. These are:

(1) Our tremendous reservoir of informed personnel in technical, professional and governmental fields. This may provide the leadership we need.

(2) Our vast electorate of informed citizens, who may prove that the education of the people is the final guarantee of the perpetuation of freedom.

But shall we return once more to the question: Can democracy survive?   •

Yes, *if* we assume our responsibilities and use our power to maintain order, security and freedom. Yes, *if* we maintain the three principles of our success—economic freedom, social cooperation, and political adaptation. Yes, *if* we can find expanding frontiers, insist upon flexibility in living standards, and maintain a constant vigilance in political experimentation. Yes, *if* we restrain our perfectionists, curb our fundamentalists, and control the ignorant and the incompetent. Yes, *if* we maintain the fundamental directions of our own history, and in accordance with our own glorious tradition exert the will power of a vigorous, hopeful people.

In a word: Let us know our own history, not the shams and misinterpretations that parade about us. Let us know our democracy for what it has actually been. Let us know that if we win the war, we must win it as a democracy. Let us know that in winning, we are dedicated to feeding and policing the world.

In our own America we have achieved—never more so than in these days of intense national effort—a living unity. We are a *free* people. As Americans, we know that disagreements arise and conflict continues as long as man lives. A nation built of peoples from the ends of the earth knows that if unity is to be found in action, it must rest in freedom of thought. Our democracy, in war and in peace, must remain our democracy. That is the lesson of our history and our gift to the world.

Do you ask for a declaration of faith? A democratic people—conscious of the eternal values of their own history, dedicated to the advancement of all mankind, resolved to build a structure within which men can live in security and dignity and peace—*will survive.*

EDUCATION AND THE WAR

THE UNIVERSITY IN WAR AND PEACE [1]
Robert M. Hutchins [2]

This address was given at a University of Chicago Trustee-Faculty dinner at the South Shore Country Club, on January 13, 1943.

Since coming to Chicago, Mr. Hutchins continually startled the educational world with his writings and speeches, in which he denounced much of the current practices of higher education. He stressed with young vigor the necessity of education for understanding as contrasted with education for mere knowledge. He argued for education through the reading of great books in philosophy, literature, social sciences. He claimed that such education through reading of the ideas of our "great tradition" did not imply the neglect of study in laboratory science. His goal, he insisted, was to prepare the student for intelligent citizenship.

In the light of this philosophy, he helped set up the "Chicago Plan" with its program of junior college study in each of the areas of physical science, social science, and humanities, and the upper college concentration in one of these fields; its emphasis upon general examinations and educational results rather than merely upon required classroom attendance and the accumulation of credits. He proposed that education be adjusted to a 6-4-4 program—six years in the elementary school, four years in the junior high, and four years in the senior high and lower college. He announced that the bachelor's degree would be given "about the end of the sophomore year." President Hutchins has furnished as stimulating educational leadership as has any other college president since 1930. His uniqueness has been found in his program more than in his philosophy.

The present address is probably as original and provocative as any given by this speaker. Here are clear analysis of the problem, the personal, semi-autobiographical mood throughout, the latent or overt humor, the directness suggestive of a parliamentary speaker reporting his stewardship and frankly stating his own limitations and failures. Not the least of Mr. Hutchins' skills has been his decisive and mature delivery. He is completely at home with audiences and knows how to influence them.

[1] Reprinted by permission of President Hutchins. Text furnished through the courtesy of Mr. Hutchins. The address was printed in *American Association of University Professors Bulletin*, 29, no. 1:22-33, February, 1943.
[2] For biographical note see Appendix.

On December 31 I completed twenty years in university administration. This reflection causes me some pangs. Lord Northington said in 1765, when the gout caught up with him, "If I had known that these legs of mine were to carry a lord chancellor, I would have taken better care of them when I was a lad." If I had known that this head of mine was to be used by a university president, I would have tried to get some education when I was at Yale. One of my predecessors often talked about education as a substitute for experience. I have substituted experience for education. Still, twenty years is twenty years. The range of data I have examined over so long a period, illuminated by the earnest tutoring you have given me, entitles me to certain conclusions about universities in general and this one in particular. The greatest of Greek sages used to say that the opinions of the aged deserved respectful attention. They might not know very much; but, after all, they had been through a lot.

From this gray eminence on which I have placed myself I wish first of all to set at rest any fears you may have about the future of this University. On the basis of the accomplishment of the group assembled here tonight I have no difficulty in predicting that the University will last as long as the war. No organization of any kind anywhere has done a more rapid, complete, and effective job of converting itself into a war industry than the University of Chicago. The adaptability the faculty has shown, the sacrifices they have made, the inconveniences, even hardships, to which they have willingly submitted have made the University an essential part of the American military machine. No plans can now be made for war research or the special training of military personnel which do not include the University of Chicago.

Many of the uncertainties which have surrounded the government's plans for the use of universities and their students have now been removed. We see that government grants will stimulate scientific research to an extent undreamed of before the war. On the other hand, we know that we shall lose almost all our able-bodied male students above the age of eighteen and a half. We know that most of the male students we shall have will be in uniform, subject to military discipline. But even as regards education there are some bright spots. Nothing quite as bad as the S.A.T.C. is in the offing, and nothing anywhere near as bad as the course in war aims, the principal educational affliction of 1918. The draft age has at last been fixed at the right point. Volunteering may ultimately be prohibited, even including the wicked exception which has hitherto permitted the enlistment of seventeen-year-old boys in the navy. The Army Enlisted Reserve is to be liquidated; and the principle has been established that young men go to college in wartime because the country needs to have them go and not because they have the money to pay for it. The government will fill every square foot of space the University owns, and more besides, with soldiers, sailors, and men and women in training for war industries. We are likely to have more students on the Quadrangles by the end of this year than we had before the war.

At the same time we may be proud that the University of Chicago has in operation the only program through which liberal education can be preserved in the United States. The last four years of the 8-4-4 plan, the four years that were nominally given to liberal education, have now disappeared. The alternative proposed by many colleges, and resisted by all high schools, is the 8-3-1 plan, which substitutes one year of college for one year of high school, on the unquestionably valid theory that one year of liberal education is better than none. But only at the University of Chicago and at those institutions which follow its example is it possible for a boy to acquire the basic elements of a liberal education before he is called to the colors. We achieve this result by the simple device of operating our college, the last four years of the 6-4-4 plan, the year round.

I hope I do not need to add in this company that no program of liberal education, whether it ends at eighteen or twenty-two, can produce a man who will never have to learn anything more. A liberal education should communicate the leading facts, principles, and ideas which an educated man should possess, together with the intellectual techniques needed to acquire, understand, and apply more facts, principles, and ideas. This, and only this, the College of the University of Chicago pretends to do. Education is a life-long process. We are not so deluded as to suppose that educational institutions, by any age, can do what only a full life of study, reflection, and experience can accomplish.

The University's role for the remainder of the war is now fairly clear. It will have to do all the war research it can handle. It will have to take on all the soldiers and sailors it can accommodate. Insofar as it is allowed freedom of choice it should not do anything it does not know how to do or anything it does not believe in simply to fill its buildings and occupy its time. It ought to have enough on its hands if it limits itself to things it believes in and knows how to do. In education, as distinguished from research on the one hand and training on the other, it must concentrate on the College. The College is the University's real educational chance, and perhaps the only one it will have.

These activities will absorb the attention of most of the members of the faculty. Yet many others will not be engaged in war research or training and will not be teaching in the College. What is the function of such professors, appointed to divisions and schools from which the students have vanished? Here we have the real test of whether we have meant what we have said all these years. We have said that this was a research institution. Our great complaint has been that we have had so many students, or at least so many courses, that we could not get on with our research. Cynical presidents on other campuses have suspected that this complaint in their institutions masked an unwillingness or even an incapacity to do the research which the professor hinted the administration was keeping him from doing by loading him up with teaching. I wish to say now, in the most unequivocal terms, that the present administration of this University will support research worthy of the University of Chicago whether the member of the faculty who is doing it has any students or not. The only question that will be asked is the one that has been asked in peacetime, whether the research, to say nothing of the professor, is good.

It is impossible to sit down for lunch at the Quadrangle Club without being conscious of reverberations to the effect that it is very hard to work at education and research in wartime. It certainly is. But I believe that anybody who is good enough to be a member of this faculty is too good to be expended in Washington or the army. I do not deny that there are many special cases—the cases of men with peculiar qualifications for specific positions which only they can fill. Such men we must surrender for the duration. But that restlessness which occasionally afflicts us all, that feeling that we are not doing anything very important and that we ought to be able seamen, corporals, or clerks in the capital must, I am afraid, be traced to the low esteem in which our civilization has held the life of the mind, an esteem so low that even those who have committed themselves to that life must sometimes wonder whether they have not made a mistake. A university is a place where people think. Thinking is difficult at any time, and especially amid the distractions of war. But can we actually believe that thinking is not important to winning a war? If a member of this faculty is offered a post in the public service in which he can think to better purpose than he can here, he should accept it. If, as is far more likely, he has some chance to think here and none in the public service, he should stay here and try to think harder than ever. It is his patriotic duty to resist as long as he can the superficial attractiveness of what is called "doing something about the war" and to throw himself with grim determination into the essential task he was appointed to perform.

Subject to qualifications I shall mention in a moment, the future of the University is in your hands. Why has it received gifts of $148,000,000 since it was founded and $68,000,000 in the last thirteen years? Why are our reserves larger now, after ten years of deficit financing, than they were when we entered the depression? Why did we lose only nine hundred regular students last year, and why did the government send more than five thousand to take their places? Why have we a hundred and twenty-seven government contracts, with more coming in every month? Why do individuals and industries support the University in increasing numbers? Why am I confident that the University of Chicago will always be supported? The answer is that the name of the University of Chicago stands the world over for leadership in education and research. As long as the relative superiority of the University can be maintained, the University will be maintained.

So much for the future of the University during the war. We know the worst, and we know the University will be here when the war is over. It is unlikely that the draft age will be put below eighteen. It is impossible that war research and training can stop until the war does. But as a colored gentleman remarked on the Cottage Grove streetcar the other day, "It looks to me as if the duration would last longer than the war." The really serious new problems of the University will be those it will face the minute the armistice is signed. They will make the difficulties of the war period seem like the passing clouds of a summer day.

I have some doubts about the theory of accumulated demand now advanced by many economists. I have no question that after the war a great many people will want electric refrigerators, automobiles, radios, and typewriters. I am not equally sure that they will have the money to buy them. But I am positive that there is one accumulated demand that will be gratified, because the people who have it will have the power to insist that it be gratified, and that is the demand for the chance to get ahead. Entirely aside from the plans of the government to use the colleges and universities for selective demobilization, hundreds of thousands of young men and women are going to ask for and are going to get, either at their expense or that of the taxpayers, educational opportunities, or what they will confuse with such opportunities. The full impact of this returning flow will be felt here in those regions of the University from which the outgoing flow has most completely drained the students, which have been most disorganized by the war, and in which trained or even promising personnel will be most difficult to find.

Apart from the College of the University of Chicago education is being abandoned; the training of men for teaching positions outside the natural sciences is being extinguished. Where will the University find the teachers who will guide the returning hordes through the mazes of the disciplines which have lain neglected during the war? Where will it discover the investigators who will carry on the great tradition of research which began with its foundation? Merely to bring back the fifteen per cent of the faculty now on leave will not suffice. I regard a prediction of an increase of fifty per cent in the student body as extremely conservative.

What is much more serious, in the postwar era the University will be plunged into what Edith Wharton called the thick of thin things, and they will be very thin things indeed. Since the government is establishing in the public mind the doctrine that technical training is the only education for war, the public mind will eventually conclude that technical training is the only education for peace. The University will be asked to do all kinds of little jobs getting people ready for little jobs or rehabilitating them for this or that method of earning a living.

The most terrifying aspect of these changes is the rapidity with which they are going to happen when they happen. To meet them the University is going to need all the intelligence and fortitude it can muster. It must therefore strengthen its faculty now. It should do so especially in those areas in which there are likely to be few students for the duration. It will have no time to look around for a satisfactory staff when peace arrives.

It is fortunate that the faculty and trustees have begun to consider the clarification of the University's organization. As they consider the organization of the University they may be unable to think of a better one than it has at present; but I cannot bring myself to so low an opinion of their imaginative powers. On the face of it, the organization of this University, like that of every other, is a weird hybrid of business and political procedures, with some academic accidents thrown in for good measure. The president can do great harm, but not much good. In defiance of the first principle of administration he is held accountable for measures with which he had nothing to do. The trustees can contribute to obtaining a worthy administration only when a new president is elected. The faculty nominally controls educational policy, but cannot prevent the president from thwarting them through his power over money, over administration, and over relations with the public. And what is most important of all, the faculty has no way of making itself heard when a president ought to be removed. No matter what dreadful changes the passing years have wrought in his figure, disposition, character, or intellect, he goes on and on, entangling the affairs of the University and misrepresenting it to the country.

For twenty years I have been gravitating toward a view which I stated in the presence of many of you at a regional meeting of the Association of University Professors some three years ago. There I set forth the substance of the proposals which were reported to the Senate last week. My view is that a university must make up its mind either that it is *sui generis,* not subject to the simple truths which experience teaches us about organizations in general, or that it is an institution which does conform to those truths as modified by its peculiar needs and constitution. The first course would mean that it would have no president and no administration. The second would mean that it would recognize that responsibility and authority are correlative terms. It would also recognize that a university is not a business or political organization, but a community of scholars. The collective voice of that community should be registered at every step in its progress and should have a persuasive, and under certain circumstances, a decisive influence on the choice or continuance of its leadership. Either conclusion is simple, clear, and defensible. The present organization is involved, bewildering, and indefensible. It is not a system through which the University can hope to deal with the tremen-

dous issues which confront it now and the still more awful decisions which await it.

After twenty years I know as well as anybody that paper
schemes of organization solve no problems.   A perfect organization would not make the University any better.   It would
simply give it a chance to be better.   So the reorganization of
1930 could easily have come to nothing.   Because the faculty
wanted to make it work, it did work.   It brought us through
the depression, and it led to some significant developments in
American education.   If you do not want the University to get
better, it will certainly get worse, even with the best organization
in the world.   One of the things which has prevented it from
becoming as great as you want it to be is its organization.   If
it could escape from the confines of a narrow and antiquated
administrative structure, it could press forward to the realization
of its unlimited possibilities.

It may be that more can be done here than merely to give
a university a good organization.   It may be that the faculty
and trustees can make a contribution to the practice of democracy.   Certainly every university is a very low-tension democracy
today.   I should hope that this one might become a very high-
tension democracy, in which the administration, if it had one,
would be immediately responsive and immediately responsible
to the community of scholars which, legal technicalities apart,
is the University.   If this University could discover how to
operate a large and complex institution as a high-tension democracy, democratic and yet efficient, its example might be useful
far beyond the boundaries of the academic world.

Let us look at the educational situation once again and see
what is actually going on in the world.   When we say that the
future of the University is secure, what do we mean?   We
mean that there will always be here something called the University of Chicago, engaged in some kind of investigation and
some type of training.   We mean, in short, that the University
is financially secure.   But I have never worried about money.
I have worried about wasting it, but not about having it; for
it has seemed to me obvious that if any university would survive the financial vicissitudes of our times the University of

Chicago would do so. The natural preoccupation we have had with the financial consequences of the war has blinded us to consequences far more serious.

We now see that the large universities will emerge from the war at least as prosperous as they went in. They are working for the government at cost, but a nonprofit corporation that recovers its costs is doing very well indeed. The real danger that these universities run is intellectual bankruptcy. If they are intellectually bankrupt, the country will be so too; for it can hope for little aid from the smaller institutions. They may find themselves financially as well as intellectually extinct.

The symbol of what is going on in high schools is the High School Victory Corps, the mere announcement of which led the principal of the high school at Sandy Spring, Maryland, to tear up his curriculum and set his pupils to drilling, exercising, apple picking, rolling bandages, looking after working mothers' children, doing janitor work, and learning how to fly. I am prepared to believe that the curriculum at Sandy Spring was not very good. But I ask you to think what this country will be like and what higher education will be like if all the high school pupils in it devote the next four years to drilling, exercising, apple picking, bandage rolling, looking after working mothers' children, doing janitor work, and learning how to fly.

According to the plans of the army and navy some ten per cent of the male population of the ages of eighteen and nineteen are to be sent to college to learn enough mathematics and physics to study technology and enough reading and writing to understand commands. The rest of them, unless they have attended the College of the University of Chicago, will have only such education as the Victory Corps leaves in the high schools. With deference to the educational wisdom of the army and navy, I do not believe that technically trained robots will be effective fighting men in time of war. I am certain that they will be a full-grown menace to their fellow citizens in time of peace.

The colleges and universities have entered a new phase of their history, the phase of education by contract. Institutions are supported to solve problems selected by the government and to train men and women chosen by the government, in fields

and by methods prescribed by the government, using a staff assembled in terms of requirements laid down by the government.
The institutions cannot look at the projects too closely or in-
quire into their fitness to carry them on.   If they did, they
might not get the contracts.   All the questions with which colleges and universities have concerned themselves, who should
teach what to whom and how, the questions of the methods of
instruction, the qualifications of students and teachers, and the
ends and ideals of education, these questions can no longer be
decided by communities of scholars.

What, for example, do we want from the Humanities
nowadays?   Not philosophy, history, literature, or the arts.
We want intensive language instruction.   We want high school
graduates taught Malay, Eskimo, or Pidgin English in six weeks
so that when they are sent into occupied territories as military
police the execution of their orders will not be delayed by the
necessity of looking for an interpreter.   Do you want teachers
of Malay, Eskimo, or Pidgin English?   A six weeks' intensive
course will turn a professor of Greek or French literature into
an instructor adequate to the purposes of the military police.
If you can't find convertible professors of this type you may get
teachers from high schools or from business or you may drain
off the faculties of other institutions.

So attractive are these possibilities to some universities that
we hear reports that after the war they will abolish their present
organization into groups of departments, based on the traditional
intellectual disciplines, and reorganize on a regional basis, with
the geographic divisions of space instead of the intellectual activities of man marking the various lines of emphasis within
the university.

I see no reason to suppose that education by contract will
end with the war.   On the contrary, a government which has
once discovered that universities can be used to solve immediate
problems, or to pretend to solve them, is likely to intensify the
practice as its problems grow more serious.   The political and
industrial necessities of the postwar period may result in such
an expansion of education by contract that we shall have two
kinds of state universities in this country, those supported by

the forty-eight jurisdictions through grants of public money for general purposes and those supported by the national government through grants for special research or training.

Violent changes are going on in the composition of faculties, in the selection of students, in the content of courses of study, and in the structure of universities. They are not planned. They have no ulterior purpose. I speak in no critical or even hortatory spirit. I merely remind you of things you know already so that our own problems may be seen in the perspective of the larger question of education as a whole, and the still larger issue of the outlook for civilization. It may be that these developments are transitory afflictions. It may be that they are necessary. Still one wonders why they have not taken place in England, where the constitution, activities, and staff of the universities have remained substantially unchanged by the war. One wonders how Charles Dollard of the Carnegie Corporation can report after a survey of the Canadian universities that Canada still assumes that trained minds are a natural resource and is still conscious of the fact that war presents problems which cannot be solved with a slide rule.

If we were to attempt to locate the blame for these tendencies we should have to trace it to the educational forces of this country, who now reap the whirlwind for sowing the wind of football, fraternities, and fun, and for presenting their institutions to their fellow citizens as dazzling supermarkets with every conceivable object of human desire spread before the bargain conscious buyer. This vision is uninspiring in the best of times and terrible to behold when the fate of the world is hanging in the balance.

Whether the University of Chicago can change the vision I do not know. I think it ought to try. I do know that complacency, indifference, and the desire to maintain the *status quo* can lead only to the destruction of those beacons which our forefathers erected to light the pathway to a better world.

On armistice day the world will not be pleasant to look upon, millions dead, crippled, and homeless in every part of the earth. Until there is an international conscience, there can be no international state. We cannot expect an international conscience to spring up in the next three or four years. Mankind seems doomed for at least another generation to the perpetual fight for safety, always skirting resort to violence as the means of self-preservation, and sometimes not succeeding. Until there can be some semblance of agreement upon the aims of human life and the ends of organized society, humanity must fumble on from catastrophe to catastrophe, learning little as it goes.

Where can our fellow men look except to institutions like this for light in a dark world? If civilization is the deliberate pursuit of a common ideal, how can we become civilized unless men of learning show us the ideal and teach us how to pursue it? The University of Chicago cannot shirk its responsibilities by leaving unexamined the program, the policies, the procedures, or the persons that seemed adequate to less critical times. It must free itself from any fetters that confine it and release the full force of its moral and intellectual power. Your future is in your hands. In your hands, too, is no small share of the hopes and aspirations of mankind.

THE PRESERVATION OF THE UNIVERSITY [3]

MONROE E. DEUTSCH [4]

This address was delivered at the commencement exercises of Stanford University, on Sunday, June 14, 1942. The speaker came before his audience with a long and distinguished record as a commemorative speaker; he fully vindicated his reputation as an energetic, analytical, and dignified orator. He expounded the problem facing the university faculties and students of the nation who, under the necessary adjustments of the war, were apparently abandoning much of the educative function for which higher institutions were established. Rich in his reference to history and to culture, definite in the application of the principles to be applied to his audience, the speaker provided an affirmative and inspiring answer to the question, "Why preserve the university?"

Implicit in this address, as in his book, *The Letter and the Spirit* —from which the quotations come—is Dr. Deutsch's political and educational philosophy—his faith in American idealism and institutions; his belief in tolerance; his belief that true democracy means spiritual freedom ("We have become Americans by baptism in the waters of that spirit"); his insistence upon freedom of press as correlative with freedom of religion, speech, and assembly; his belief in America's responsibility for an organized world; his faith in the humanities as necessary ("Till that day the humanities should realize that their fate is bound up with the defense of the human spirit and be willing to make that 'costly sacrifice upon the altar of freedom'"); his belief in the universality of great literature and learning; his sympathy for and understanding of the United Nations, including Russia and China; and his concept of the university as an institution generating democracy and loyalty to both state and nation ("a vista of loyalties ever expanding before our eyes"). In thought, mode of expression, and delivery, this speaker is one of America's important orators.

In a world shaken in well-nigh every part by the shock of war, it is pleasant to gather in academic ceremonial mid the cloisters of the university. It is not that we are unaware of what is going on about us; it is not that we are unmoved by the

[3] Rerinted from *The Letter and the Spirit*, by Monroe E. Deutsch. University of California Press. Berkeley and Los Angeles. 1943. p. 337-48. Reprinted by permission of the University of California Press and through the courtesy of Dr. Deutsch.
[4] For biographical note see Appendix.

issues of the struggle; it is not that we do not realize how much the outcome of the war means to all mankind—including these universities of ours.

But amid all the din and tragedy of war an occasion like this furnishes in a sense a moment of relief from the noise of the fray. It takes us as it were out of the threatening present into the time—that quiet time—when we were at peace. For a moment it turns our minds from the events that are about us.

And on such an occasion it is good to recall that universities—and the university as an institution—have existed some seven hundred years, have survived wars again and again, have survived dictatorships, have survived periods of distress, periods of civil war. Yes, through everything of ill that seven hundred years could heap upon it, the university lived, the beacon light of learning and scholarship, however much the storms assailed it.

And so assembled here, we feel that we are attached to something that is sure to outlast this war and whatever other dire perils may come. To Hitler the university says: "Long after you, petty upstart, are gone and the world has wiped away all the signs of the disaster you have wrought, I shall live and shall preach everything that you scorned and on which you sought to trample. I shall encourage freedom of research, freedom of speech; I shall see to it that your pseudo science is exposed. I shall reprint the great works you have burned and striven to destroy; they will be all the more sought by a world that has thrown off your shackles. I shall live, for truth is eternal."

Among Hitler's many crimes there are few greater than the use of the free spirit, Learning, as a lackey, a slave.

Amid the welter of war let us guard the university and the freedoms which it preserves and embodies. It is easy to say this in the abstract; but when a concrete case occurs, when public hysteria rises, and patriotism assumes the guise of a baleful monster, then stand up for the freedom of your university— yes, of all universities.

In this period of war, colleges, like other institutions, have undergone certain alterations—external changes, I trust they are. Because technically trained men and women are desperately needed, we are all seeking to complete the basic education of physicians, chemists, engineers, physicists, and the like as rapidly as possible. And this we must of course do. We must also offer courses fitting men and women to participate in many ways in our war effort. These must include practical courses and those that seek to teach what the issues of the war really are.

All this is proper and good. But there is great danger that we may look at all university education through glasses clouded by the mist of war. After all, universities will go on living long after the struggle is over, and men and women will be educated once more, we hope, without immediate thought of preparation for war.

So I wish to make a plea for the studies that have no direct relation to warfare: for letters, the social sciences, pure science, art, music, and philosophy. I admit that each of these can be shown to be of use at the present time. The musician can write a stirring song; the poet may rouse men as Tyrtaeus the Spartan did; the historian may help by showing the roots of the struggle; the economist may aid in finance and other problems. Yet, though this is true, these studies do not exist primarily for such a purpose.

And the university must not let the temporary situation turn young men and women completely away from the pursuits that are essential in a civilized society. Let a Hitler shape all education to the uses of war; but if we imitate him, then, however the war may end, he will have won, for we will have turned not only ploughshares but harps and paint brushes into swords.

Mankind will need religion and letters, song and sculpture, law and the social sciences long after the trumpet sounds that prayed-for armistice. Think what a barren world—a desert—we should have if all these disappeared from the face of the earth.

Let us not forget Archimedes, that great Greek mathematician. You will recall the story that at the time of the siege of Syracuse by the Romans, he was found drawing a mathematical figure on the sand, and when the enemy soldier came upon him, he was so absorbed that he cried out, "Don't disturb my circles." And we remember Archimedes far more than the conquest of Syracuse.

So we may say, "Don't disturb my music—or my law—or my painting." I do not need to argue for their importance in a civilized society. And yet under the pressure of war the individual may feel ashamed to say that he is studying literature or art or history.

We must in short take the long look—and not let the 1942 scene blind us to the fact that there will be a world after 1942 and 1943.

To be sure none of these fields will be worth pursuing, if the Swastika wins. But that, I am sure, is in our hearts unthinkable. Stupendous as the success of the two Axis partners has been, time is our ally, not theirs; see to it that *we* do not fail this mighty helper of ours.

What I have been emphasizing is that we should not let our ideas of education for the future be determined by the events of the moment—by the war in which we are engaged. And so I feel strongly that in the same way we should not try to reshape educational procedures on the basis of the mood of the present.

Of course education, like everything human, changes throughout the centuries; but the change should not be based on the impact of a machine gun or the presence of an airplane. And, in thinking of the education we hope to see established hereafter, we must not let our plans be determined by the war and what it brings with it. What we thought before it broke out may be more valid than what we of a sudden decide amid the smoke of artillery.

I recall that, while San Francisco was still burning in 1906, someone commented on the fact that all the theaters had been destroyed. Another answered: "What of it? Nobody will want to go to the theater again." But it wasn't long before theaters were improvised, for the desire for drama was not destroyed by the earthquake or the fire which the city suffered.

So, in seeking to remold the university, wait till the war is over. And in the meantime let us see that we win it—for, if we don't, the air of freedom will certainly not blow here or anywhere else.

We should also remember that time is longer than the years of a war, however many they may be. And while wars go on, men and women perform deeds that last long after the din of battle has ceased. While the fighting goes on, artists are at work, poets are writing, scientists are making discoveries, musicians are composing, historians are publishing the results of their research—and what they have left, prepared amid the din of war, the world holds as a treasure for all time.

Thus from 431 B.C. to 403 B.C. Athens and Sparta fought the Peloponnesian War. During the years of the struggle Euripides was writing his dramas. Almost all the comedies of Aristophanes fall within that period. Then it was that Thucydides wrote his great history. That was the time of Socrates' activity; Plato and Xenophon were disciples at the master's feet.

Let us place the names together—Euripides, Aristophanes, Thucydides, Socrates, Plato. They are indeed a great company. They lived during a period of war and battle; yet their notable activities lay not in combat but in the fields of tragedy and comedy, of history and philosophy.

Now I ask you whether they were wrong. Should they have abandoned their life work and devoted themselves constantly, if not to actual warfare, to something closely related to it? No, the work of the great men I have named was far more important than anything else they could possibly have done; it has indeed influenced succeeding generations and centuries.

Let us now take an illustration from our own land. We have a Hall of Fame at New York University. The names chosen for inclusion in it are selected by a distinguished group of jurors. While doubtless there would be some difference of opinion as to the relative greatness of one or another on the list, nevertheless it certainly does include those who are among our most famous Americans. There are seventy-three names in all. And of that number but seven at the most are soldiers and sailors, while there are sixteen authors, seven scientists, and six musicians, painters and sculptors. So we, like those in other lands, recognize the fact that while great military leaders are indispensable, the ultimate greatness of a country does not depend by any means on such men alone; it is the achievements of a people in literature, science, art, education and the sister fields that determine its place in the history of civilization.

We must therefore retain a proper perspective as to the value of the various studies and should not scuttle pure science, art and literature because they may not be very useful in fighting the war. And likewise within each particular field do not determine relative values in the light of temporary and, we trust, transient conditions. I have heard speakers urge the importance of studying the Orient far more than in the past, and in doing so they stress the need of knowing China and India. They are right; but Japan will, I fancy, exist after the war, and if we really desire a correct view of the Orient, we cannot overlook that country and its people. But—and this is a large *but*—after all, our civilization is derived from Europe, and we must not discard or minimize the study of the history, literature and art of the European lands which are not only the founts of our own history, literature and art, but the countries from which individually we are nearly all of us sprung.

So, too, when I hear men arguing that in our education we have overemphasized the study of things European and should diminish our attention to them, stressing rather our own history and culture, I say, "Surely let us know our own land and its history far, far better than we do—but at the same time let us not become isolationist in our education at the very moment that the gates of isolationism are being battered down by airplane and submarine."

Do not, in short, determine what our education is to be wholly in the light of the war and the immediate present. In this connection Francis Bacon gives us wise advice, "It is good also not to try experiments in states, except the necessity be urgent, or the utility evident; and well to beware that it be the reformation that draweth on the change, and not the desire of change that pretendeth the reformation."

What, then, is your obligation and mine? Obviously if our nation summons us to serve her in any capacity whatsoever, in order that a free world may continue, we shall gladly answer her call.

But if because of age or sex or for physical reasons you are allowed to continue your university work, I want you to feel no shame that you are doing so, nor seek to turn your studies into a pretense of war service. Certainly you will strive to aid your government in every way possible. The Stanford student body has given an outstanding example of national service to other institutions. But, if you are studying law, your primary obligation is to make yourself as proficient as you can. And if your field is history or literature, do it with confidence that these are no less important in the world which is to be. You must not think that the only literature that is of consequence is war literature, or the literature of the United Nations. Dante is as great and as worth studying, whether Italy fights with us or against us. And that Goethe was a German does not remove him from among the world's greatest writers. Literature and science and art and scholarship in all fields transcend national boundaries; neither time nor space circumscribes them.

And while scientists will, like others, stand ready to serve, it must not be felt that each and every one must turn from the research which is his lifework to carry on studies which pertain directly to the war. If anyone can help find a cure for cancer, should we not eagerly encourage him, war or no war?

Life will go on through the period of combat and into the time that follows. The struggle will be of the greatest significance in our lives and those of all mankind—but when it is over, the tasks of peace will call us.

Some years ago a Chinese bishop of the Catholic church visited our shores. At a luncheon here someone asked him what he thought of the Chinese students carrying on work in American universities while their country was fighting desperately against the Japanese invaders. He paused a moment and then replied, "If they are studying medicine or engineering, they should continue their work, for China will surely need both physicians and engineers." Then after an instant he went on, "No, China will need leaders in all fields. If they are doing good work in any subject, let them stay on."

There you have the long look. We, too, shall need leaders of all kinds. We shall need not only physicists, chemists, physicians, dentists and engineers but also teachers, scholars in all fields, lawyers, foresters, businessmen, philosophers, artists, musicians. And unless those who are not summoned to the immediate service of our nation devote themselves to their training, we may enter the postwar era a generation taught but one thing—war.

After all, if our universities were to give themselves wholly to activities pertaining to the war, they would really be war colleges, not universities.

In this mighty struggle many things are being defended—not least the university. Yes, you are in very truth defending Stanford University.

Your motto, "The Air of Freedom Blows," would under Nazi rule became (to use their own elegant words), "We spit on freedom." Your library would be ransacked and most of the books—especially those dealing with the foundation and spirit of our government—burned in the Quad. Your faculty would be thoroughly purged. A Goebbels or some American Quisling would take the chancellor's seat. Regimentation would replace liberty. Selection of students would be made on the basis of adherence to Nazi philosophy. Stanford University would exist only in name. Indeed its founders would feel that all for which they had sacrificed had been destroyed. As you will recall, in the Founding Grant, Governor Stanford said: "And its purposes, to promote the public welfare by exercising an influence in behalf of humanity and civilization, teaching the blessing of liberty regulated by law, and inculcating love and reverence for the great principles of government, as derived from the inalienable rights of man to life, liberty and the pursuit of happiness." All the aims of the founders would be destroyed if the adherents of total-itarianism were to conquer.

You are therefore fighting for all the elements of a free society, including the freedom of all universities, when you fight in the cause of your country. And if you have been touched by the spirit of the university, you will go with pride to defend American ideals.

You are making great sacrifices, but sacrifices which your country has a right to ask. And you would feel shame at seeking to avoid the elemental duty of a citizen. Never forget what it is for which we are fighting. And beside us stand the soldiers of the brave people of the British Commonwealth of Nations, the long-enduring Chinese, and the undaunted soldiers of the Union of Soviet Socialist Republics, and every citizen of France and Norway, Holland and Belgium, Czecho-slovakia and Greece and Poland, Jugoslavia and Denmark, who could slip out of the prison walls of his conquered country. The fight is for each of these lands, and we shall have the joy of helping to restore them to freedom.

We are at last called on to assume the place in the world of nations that our power and wealth and strength impose upon us. We cannot fail our comrades.

And so my plea is that we defend the freedoms, including the freedom of the university, from external aggression, and no less maintain the true university even amid the din of the machine guns.

We must preserve a free world for ourselves, for the peoples united to us, for the stricken nations who pray that the cruel heel of the oppressor may be removed from their necks, and for the generations that are to come after us. And in that free world we must guard one of the stoutest pillars that uphold it, the university.

VALEDICTORY SERVICE ADDRESS [5]

JAMES BRYANT CONANT [6]

President James Bryant Conant delivered this address on January 10, 1943, in the Memorial Church, erected in honor of the men of Harvard who had died for their country in the last war. The occasion was a Valedictory Service, "unique in the history of Harvard University." It was a service of farewell "for fifteen hundred undergraduates about to enter the armed forces of the United States in the Second World War."

The undergraduates included those who had fulfilled the requirements for the bachelor's degree but who would be gone before their degrees could be formally voted by the university authorities. Few, if any, could be present at the next commencement when the degrees would be officially conferred.

The service was also for the hundreds of undergraduates who were interrupting their college program to enter the armed services, and partly for the members of the university faculty, parents, and friends—"those left behind."

To accommodate the overflow audience, a meeting was arranged for the same time in Sanders Theatre, equipped to transmit to the audience the program in Memorial Church.

An academic procession preceded the service. Dean Willard L. Sperry conducted the service. His Excellency, Leverett Saltonstall, Governor of Massachusetts, "rising from among the congregation and, taking his place at the lectern," read the Old Testament lesson from Deuteronomy, Chapter VI.

President Conant struck at the heart of the problem underlying our national future: How shall we preserve a just balance between social needs and individual freedom?

The speaker's political and educational philosophy was admirably stated in his baccalaureate sermon for the Harvard seniors on June 7, 1942, "A Statement of Faith." In that address the speaker said, "For centuries Christians have quarreled as to the question: 'What is man that Thou art mindful of him?' and I am inclined to think they will continue to disagree on this subject for many generations more. But it is the assertion implied in this question, not the answer, that is basic to any faith. And it is this assertion that gives significance to the individual, that makes imperative human liberty, the very cause for which we fight." Implicit in the address at the Valedictory Service is this doctrine of the sermon of the preceding June.[7]

[5] By permission of President Conant. Text supplied through the courtesy of Dr. Conant.

[6] For biographical note see Appendix.

[7] For further comment on President Conant see *Representative American Speeches*: 1939-1940, p. 337.

Gentlemen of Harvard College: There is no need for me to emphasize the unusual nature of this morning's ceremony. Not in June but now in midwinter we mark the graduation of the senior class. More significant still, we mark also the departure of many members of Harvard College whose academic course is far from finished. To be sure, there is nothing unique in what is happening here in Cambridge. Throughout the nation our colleges empty so that our armies may grow in strength. Throughout the nation able-bodied young men of eighteen and nineteen years of age are being called to join the armed forces already fighting on many fronts and on many seas. For more than a year now every day has witnessed an increasing impact of the war on academic life. You have watched a college devoted to the arts of peace being transformed into an establishment primarily concerned with the needs of war. With your departure, the conversion will be complete.

Under such circumstances you will not expect me to speak as though I were addressing only the members of a graduating class. Rather, I am sure, you wish me to think of this occasion as one on which the University salutes all who are leaving Harvard to serve the nation.

This is for the country an hour of need; the call has gone forth and you respond. For the next few years your one goal will be to contribute your utmost to the winning of a complete and speedy victory. To hasten the day of peace we must prosecute the war with ever-increasing vigor. We are not, as Great Britain was in the fall of 1940, fighting with our backs against the wall, grimly holding on, merely refusing to admit the possibility of defeat yet not seeing or knowing how victory can be won. For us, today, the way through to the triumphant end now seems to be outlined. Yet no one believes it to be an easy road; and the question is—how long—how many years before the end? The kind of world in which you and your generation will spend your days depends in no small measure on the answer to this question. Every day the war continues prolongs the agony of civilization; every month adds to the chaos with which the postwar world must deal; every year increases the hazards which liberty must encounter when the war is won. Therefore, to insure victory in the shortest span of time, no sacrifice can be too great.

The hazards to liberty when the war is won—may I take a few moments to explore this subject further? For surely next in importance to achieving a speedy victory stands the later perpetuation of the ideal for which we fight. And, I take it, you and I would agree that fundamentally this war is concerned with human freedom. This being the case, it is of the first importance that we consider how we shall preserve freedom after the war is won. I say we are agreed as to the basic issue of the war. For there can be doubts only in the minds of those who either fail to understand the full implications of the totalitarian philosophy or secretly admire it. To all others the choice is clear. It has been well illustrated in the film, *This Mortal Storm*. There was depicted the choice between a society which respected individual freedom and the Nazi system which rapidly led to the degradation of the human soul, led not merely to brutality but to the corruption of all the dignity with which a free man is clothed. It is the task of the United Nations to see to it that such a system will not dominate the world. That requires a decisive victory. It requires an ever-increasing stream of supplies to our allies and an ever-increasing body of our own fighting men. It requires on your part courage, boldness, and a knowledge of the ways of war. Such requirements now stand before us.

But at some later day, as we struggle through the confusion of a postwar world, it will be your task as citizens of the United States to see to it that a totalitarian virus does not corrupt this nation. That will require clear thinking, indomitable patience, and an understanding of the ways of peace. The two assignments—of war and peace—are paradoxically the same and yet far different. As regards objectives, they are identical; as regards methods, miles apart. Indeed, the winning of the war could engender such conditions in our minds that we would be unable to preserve liberty when the time of peace had come. And it is this dilemma which must be considered carefully by every young American, particularly every soldier. For only by recognizing the dilemma may we hope to solve it.

Let me illustrate by quoting from the novel, *Darkness at Noon*. In a striking dialogue one of the characters sums up the fundamental choice of the twentieth century in these words:

There are only two conceptions of human ethics, and they are at opposite poles. One of them is Christian and humane, declares the individual to be sacrosanct, and asserts that the rules of arithmetic are not to be applied to human units. The other starts from the basic principle that a collective aim justifies all means, and not only allows, but demands, that the individual should in every way be subordinated and sacrificed to the community. . . .

At another point in the dialogue the same speaker, a supporter of the totalitarian view, inveighs against what he calls the "humanitarian fog—philosophy" in these words:

Consider a moment what this would lead to, if we were to take it literally; if we were to stick to the precept that the individual is sacrosanct, and that we must not treat human lives according to the rules of arithmetic. That would mean that a battalion commander may not sacrifice a patrolling party to save the regiment.

But his companion objects, "Your examples are all drawn from war—that is, from abnormal circumstances."

To which the totalitarian replies:

Since the invention of the steam engine the world has been permanently in an abnormal state; the wars and revolutions are just visible expressions of this state. . . . The principle that the end justifies the means is and remains the only rule of political ethics; anything else is just vague chatter and melts away between fingers. . . .

These few sentences strike through to the bedrock which underlies the shifting muddy ground for which liberals and conservatives alike contend. This issue between the two ethics is basic to all discussions of the future of this nation. When we fail to come to grips with it, we flounder in a sea of good intentions and pious hopes.

May I illustrate by raising the old question of why we in America should continue to believe that minorities have rights. Why is it important to safeguard these rights and render more secure the bulwarks which protect the·individual from the power of those who govern? Would it not be more realistic to discard the whole concept of rights as a bit of eighteenth century rationalism and say merely that minorities have such a temporary status as the majority cares to give? So argued an ardent advocate of democracy in a conversation with me not long ago; he then proceeded to conclude that the majority was justified in revoking minority rights whenever the welfare of the state demanded. This is one of those superficially attractive doctrines, the product of so-called realistic thinking, which have found much favor in recent years. It is only a step from this position to that which sanctions the destruction of a minority whenever the majority so decides; and in practice, since plebiscites on such issues are rarely held, this means the destruction of a group when those who hold the reins of government so decide. In such a form the proposition becomes less attractive.

One need hardly point out that this is no academic argument. Repeatedly throughout the course of modern history the cry, "the state is in danger," has served the ends of revolutionaries and reactionaries alike. But the times when internal enemies were thus disposed of were not times when men were free. Quite the contrary. They were days of oppression, tyranny, and fear.

To my mind there can be no escape from the conclusion that a free society in times of peace (notice the qualification) must tolerate even those minorities which by their principles and doctrines seem to jeopardize the cause of freedom. This may seem absurd to some. Yet to conclude otherwise is to forsake the only ethics on which a free society may hope to thrive. (I am talking, of course, about the political rights of a minority, about free speech and free assembly, not about conspiracies or assassinations looking towards armed revolt.)

It is a paradox, if you will, that a free society must protect within these limits those who oppose the fundamental premise on which this society is founded. Yet, to my mind, this paradox is a necessity which springs from the choice between the two conceptions of human ethics as opposite as the poles. It is a consequence of a belief in the sacrosanct nature of the individual and a rejection of the view which glorifies the collective aim. To argue that the rights of the individual are a purely utilitarian invention is to deprive the characteristic American ideal of its cutting edge. You can build a free nation on a Christian view of human destiny. You can destroy it by substituting another.

In the illustration I have used—the question of minority rights—I have emphasized the distinction between peace and war. For in time of war, a free nation may be forced to safeguard its existence by measures which contradict the basic principles of its being. So, too, with individuals; for those who fight, the rules of arithmetic must apply to human beings. Free men must fight a war in essentially the same pattern as soldiers of a regimented nation. Hitler's generals and our own must draw their military decisions from the same essential premises. The danger lies not in our methods of waging war, but in the possibility that at some later time people may argue from war to peace.

We need not worry lest five or six years hence people justify murder because in war one fights to kill. But we may well be disturbed by the prospect that some may argue (from right or left) that dangerous minorities should be suppressed. And, if passions run high, it is even possible that others will declare that the security of the nation calls for ruthless violence.

Let us freely admit that the battlefield is no place to question the doctrine that the end justifies the means. But let us insist, and insist with all our power, that this same doctrine must be repudiated by free men in days of peace.

Let me make it clear that this issue between the rights of individuals and a collective aim is not the issue of radical or reactionary as the forces are aligned today. Modern history has shown that liberty can be crushed by an avalanche either from the right or from the left.

Furthermore, I have been discussing the development of American society, not the structure of other nations. After the war we shall have to learn how to keep the peace by cooperation with other great countries which have very different cultural patterns and different histories from our own. But we shall not promote the cause of international understanding by confusing our own internal problems with the great debt we owe to China, to Great Britain, and to Russia for their magnificent fight against our common enemies. If we are to live in a world of peace we must accept great responsibilities beyond our borders. But we must also find a solution of problems presented to us by modern technology at home. These problems we must solve in our own way. The future of this nation must spring from its past—it must represent a continuing evolution of the American pattern.

As a nation of idealists, we have hitherto held strong views about "human rights." But we have been naturally suspicious when overexposed to any set of slogans. Particularly, we have been inclined to test the validity of proclaimed intentions by comparing them with actions. No battle cry which can be read in two opposite senses will rally this country. You cannot long promote the welfare of the American republic with Machiavellian tactics. Totalitarian states have no such troubles. Those who adopt as their guide the rules of arithmetic applied to individual lives need never worry about the virtue of consistency. Power politics has no conscience and need stand before no moral accuser. But those who believe that human life is sacred must come into court with clean hands. The most convincing proponents of liberty are those who clearly have no personal stake in a special application of the general doctrine. Some blatant examples to the contrary were in no small measure responsible for the cynicism of a few years past.

The American people have historically taken their stand on the side of Christian humane ethics. And though there have been black lapses in practice, we are still committed to this basic position. The abnormality of war, if recognized as an abnormality, does not invalidate our stand. Clearly, we cannot repudiate our historic view of what is right and wrong without wrecking the continuity of our national life. Indeed, such a conscious repudiation seems to me inconceivable. The danger lies in the possibility that we may fail to direct our attention to the real issue—fail because we have lived so long in a world of war where power alone has ruled.

But even on that score we need not be too fearful. However hard boiled the average American may be, he is unlikely to accept the idea of liquidating his political opponents without mercy. Whether he bases his philosophy consciously on religion or not, he believes that it is wrong to coerce and torture human beings (wrong, mind you, not inexpedient), wrong to have a government based on informers and intimidation. He feels it in his bones that men ought to be free. He looks forward, therefore, to having more human liberty on this continent, not less. To this end he may wish to make radical changes in the political and economic structure of America. Like Thomas Jefferson, when he abolished primogeniture, a citizen of this republic may today wish to swing an axe against the root of privilege. But he will do so only that a greater number may be free within large limits, free to carry responsibility as well as to enjoy the benefits of modern civilization. It is because we have come to realize the confusing complexities of modern industrial society that we expect drastic alteration. We realize that there can be little or no real chance for many individuals to make significant choices—the essence of freedom—if there is not first of all freedom from want and fear. Social security for us, however, is not an end in itself but a means toward freedom. It is thus, in the spirit of the American tradition, that the problems of our day must be conceived.

I have spoken of the difficulties of the days of peace, of the problems you will be facing at a later time, when as returning veterans you are called on to shape the future of this nation. The experience immediately ahead is far different —it will be cast in days of war, yet this experience in the army or the navy may if you so choose make you more able to fight for freedom in civilian life. Once it is clear in a man's mind that the demands of war are one thing and those of a free society in peace another, the virtues which are developed on the battlefield reinforce the natural talents. And this education may prove as valuable in the postwar world as years of study in academic halls. I do not have to tell you that our troubles will not be over when victory comes. You do not expect the millennium once the fighting ceases. You know how long and difficult may be the postwar years. In this period you will need courage, endurance, patience (above all, patience) to see it through; you will need an understanding of what it means to work in close cooperation with other men. The fortitude, loyalty and steadfastness that come from hardship and danger serve the erstwhile soldier well even in civilian clothes.

Formal education for the present you leave aside, but you will grow in wisdom nonetheless. New knowledge will come to you by virtue of the sacrifices that you will be asked to make. Having been ready to run all risks for freedom, you will comprehend it as those of us at home cannot. On some subsequent commencement day you will return with the understanding born of great events. On that occasion it will be said of you as of the returning Harvard soldiers of 1865:

> Today, our Reverend Mother welcomes back
> Her wisest scholars, those who understood. . . .
>
> Many loved Truth, and lavished life's best oil
> Amid the dust of books to find her. . . .
>
> But these, our brothers, fought for her.

Gentlemen, with anxious pride, Harvard awaits the day of your return.

RELIGION AND THE WAR

THIS NATION UNDER GOD [1]

RALPH W. SOCKMAN [2]

Dr. Ralph W. Sockman, preacher at the Christ Church (formerly Madison Avenue Methodist Church), New York City, gave this sermon over the National Broadcasting Company network on Sunday, April 18, 1943, at 10:00 A.M., E.W.T. It was the twenty-ninth in the series of the "National Radio Pulpit" for the season of 1942-1943.

Dr. Sockman, as a preacher and sermonizer, ranks high among living American clergymen. His radio sermons, of which the following is typical, are in general similar to those given before his face-to-face audiences, except for the obvious techniques necessary for radio adaptation.

What are the homiletic characteristics of this speaker? (1) He almost invariably chooses a text (not so, Harry Emerson Fosdick, John Haynes Holmes, or Fulton J. Sheen). (2) He usually illustrates his theme with a Biblical narrative. (3) He enriches his sermons with Biblical, especially New Testament, references and language. (4) In spite of his broad social and economic philosophy, he is chiefly personal, evangelical, inspirational. In this sense he has kinship with the typical Methodist preaching tradition in America. (5) His broader social and political themes are closely linked with those of religion. As a thinker and crusader against contemporary wrongs he is no Parkhurst or Beecher. (6) His sermons are always well constructed. They will bear study by young clergymen and other speakers who wish to achieve clearness, coherence and force through the disposition of ideas. (7) His introductions and conclusions serve the usual purposes of these homiletic divisions and are effectively constructed with an eye to maximum audience attention, interest, and response. (8) His illustrations are numerous and timely. Not only does he weave into his discourse the sayings and appropriate episodes from both Old and New Testaments, but he inserts as concrete illustrations material from the New York life and from the every day experiences of the millions over the land. He cites extensively literature (e.g., Keats, Lowell, Kingsley, Tennyson, Shakespeare), educational thinkers, conversations with people in his comings

---

[1] By permission of Dr. Sockman. Text furnished through the courtesy of Dr. Sockman and the Department of National Religious Radio, New York, N.Y.
[2] For biographical note see Appendix.

and goings, American history, and those recently prominent in the news (e.g., Judge Wiley Rutledge). (9) His language is oral, concrete, personal, sometimes vivid. (10) His delivery is highly effective before various types of audiences, those of the radio, Sunday morning church, and open-air community gatherings. He is careful in articulation, emphatic in tone and gesture, with plenty of vocal resonance, variety in pitch range and intensity, and with persuasiveness in tone and manner.

Dr. Sockman in his student days at Ohio Wesleyan University had the tutelage of one of America's highly successful teachers of speech, Robert I. Fulton. Sockman was a member of intercollegiate debate teams. Later, at Union Theological Seminary, he felt the impress of sound scholarship, liberal thinking, and excellent homiletic training under such teachers as Henry Sloane Coffin and Harry Emerson Fosdick.

On this Palm Sunday which commemorates the entry of Our Lord into his capital city of Jerusalem, I wish to think with you about the rule of Christ in our country of America. Centuries ago the Psalmist said, "Blessed is the nation whose God is the Lord." When he said that, the great Hebrew singer was thinking of his own people. But we are the heirs of Israel's God. It is the God of Abraham, Isaac, and Jacob as well as the God of Jesus whom we have in mind when we sing "Our fathers' God to Thee, author of liberty." Hence we are justified in taking the Psalmist's words to our own hearts and in saying as Americans, both in the states and in Canada, "Blessed is the nation whose God is the Lord."

But, now, what are the blessings which a nation derives from her belief in God—the God who is the Lord as portrayed in our Bible?

First of all, such a belief in God gives the blessing of a solid foundation on which to build. A nation, like an individual, if it is to be strong, must settle the seat of sovereignty. There must be some voice which has the last word. And what is the sovereign authority in our nation? It is not our President. It is not our Congress. It is not our Supreme Court. Our President is the commander in chief of our armed forces and in time of war is granted almost dictatorial powers. He salutes no uniformed officer, no foreign ruler. But there is one thing which the President of the United States does salute. And that is the

American flag, because the flag stands as the symbol of the sovereign will of the people. When the citizens of our nation express their will through a majority vote, such vote is called the sovereign voice of the people.

Yet this so-called sovereign people when it inaugurates a new president requires him to take an oath or affirmation, symbolizing that he holds his powers under the dominion of a Divine Authority. And when our Congress convenes to represent our people in the making of laws, its sessions are opened with prayer invoking the wisdom and counsel of a Divine Lawmaker. Moreover our Constitution explicitly sets aside certain areas of freedom, such as that of conscience, in which the citizen is responsible directly to God alone. Thus implicitly and explicitly our so-called sovereign people recognize the supreme sovereignty of God. This is a "government of the people, for the people, by the people," but as that same Gettysburg address puts it, this is a "nation under God."

And now I maintain that this belief in God gives the blessing of a solid foundation on which to build. Consider the Pilgrim fathers. When the little Mayflower lay off Plymouth Rock after its hazardous voyage, the Pilgrims went into the cabin and drew up the Mayflower Compact declaring that the trip had been undertaken "for the glory of God, the advancement of the Christian faith and the honor of King and country." Suppose that instead of such a fundamental religious faith, the Pilgrims had merely held the Nazi belief in a superior race destined to rule by force. With such a creed they might have driven out the Indians but they could not have created the Commonwealth of Massachusetts. With a philosophy of racial superiority and ruthless force, men can destroy existing cultures, but they cannot build and perpetuate lasting societies. No, judging from recent events in Russia I am not sure that the Nazis if they had landed at Plymouth Rock could have endured the first New England winter.

Or consider Thomas Jefferson whose two hundredth birthday we have just been celebrating. Jefferson may not have been very orthodox, but he was very sincere in his religious beliefs; and when he had struggled to keep his breath going that he might live to see the fiftieth anniversary of the Declaration of Independence, his daughter heard him murmur the prayer of Simeon in the temple at the presentation of Jesus, "Lord, now lettest Thou Thy servant depart in peace." Think how much it has meant to our nation that our formative state papers, like the Declaration of Independence and the Constitution, were written by men whose God is the Lord.

Or consider John Marshall, whom we call the father of our American constitutional law. His simple faith and human tenderness were manifest in his domestic life. He nursed his invalid wife through long years, and after she died on Christmas Day 1831, Marshall spent Sunday afternoons in his old chair reading aloud parts of the Sunday church service to his beloved Mary, absent in body but present to him in spirit. There is a spirit of the law as well as the letter of it, and John Marshall, the man who did so much to set the tone of legal interpretation, was a man of God.

Or think what it meant in those dark days of the war between the states that the leaders of both north and south were in the main men who humbly sought God's will. Recall the words which Lincoln wrote amid the shadows of September 1862 when the outcome was so uncertain: "The will of God prevails. In great contests each party claims to act in accordance with the will of God. Both may be, and one must be, wrong." The man who wrote thus was no bigot assuming blindly that God was on his side. Rather, he was one who humbly and patiently sought to learn God's will that he might be on God's side.

Yes, when I think of the times wherein America's institutions were cradled and tested, I maintain that the belief in God has given our nation a solid foundation on which to build.

Secondly, "blessed is the nation whose God is the Lord," because this belief gives not only a solid foundation on which to build but also high standards by which to build. The belief in the God and Father of our Lord Jesus Christ begets dignity and value in the individual. Every man is a child of God for whom Christ died. However unequal in ability, all men are equal before God and the government. When a person feels this intrinsic spiritual worth, he has a basic self-respect and that makes for a refined and healthy social life.

In our early American colonies, the physical conditions of living were crude. But, nevertheless, human life took on a dignity. Look at the simple pure lines of the old New England meeting houses. Recently in Boston and at Purdue University I had had occasion to study some of the lovely early Americans, and I have been impressed again with the noble culture wrought by those who first settled the American wilderness. Moreover life has had more value along the Hudson and the Mississippi than along the Ganges. That is a difference which perhaps we do not sufficiently recognize in appraising the political problems of India. Whatever may be our opinions regarding the British occupancy of India, we should realize that the development of self-government is a most difficult task in a land like India whose prevailing religious philosophy has minimized the worth of the individual's earthly existence. Democracy can only be grounded on a faith in the individual's worth, and that faith was given to us by the religion of our founding fathers.

Esther Forbes in her biography of Paul Revere points out that the "Sons of Liberty" whom Sam Adams organized prior to the American Revolution and who made Boston a pretty turbulent place with their Tea Party and other rather rough tactics were in type of organization not too different from the Storm Troopers of the Nazi regime in prewar Germany. But while similar in organization, they were utterly dissimilar in spirit. The Sons of Liberty in Boston were never brutal. They tarred and feathered three or four persons but they never wantonly took life. She also reminds us that when the American patriots were out at Bunker Hill fighting the British, many of them had left their wives and families in Boston. Yet General Gage, whose British troops occupied Boston, did not mistreat those families. And again when the British evacuated Boston and the colonial troops returned, they did not take revenge on the Tory sympathizers who remained under their regime. Why this humaneness of treatment on both sides? A friend of mine explained it to me recently by saying that both the British and American leaders were mainly members of the Masonic Order. I have not had occasion to verify that statement, but if it be true it only bears out our contention that the basic Christian beliefs tend to refine and humanize life, for the Order of Free Masons, like most of our other great fraternal orders, is based on Biblical precepts.

And now it behooves us to see that these high standards by which our nation was built shall be maintained during the present war period. To see every man as a child of God, however misguided he may be; to keep the refinements of personal decency, however disordered may become our conditions of living through restrictions and regimentation; to judge the worth of a man not by his rank and authority but by his character and motives, whether he be a general or a private; to preserve a humaneness of spirit amid the inevitable cruelties of war; to prosecute this war not in the spirit of hate but as a grim bit of police work to curb criminals and create a better world, such are some of the standards by which a nation should be guided whose God is the Lord.

Thirdly, "blessed is the nation whose God is the Lord," because that belief begets a brotherly spirit in which to build. Some may feel inclined to challenge this assertion by saying that religion has often divided men. Yes, history records its wars of religious persecution. And America has seen the dark dealings of Salem witchcraft days and the bigotry which drove Roger Williams from Massachusetts. And our so-called Christian nation should repent of its ungodly treatment of the Indians and the injustice still suffered by the Negro in the north as well as in the south.

Yet confessing all these sins of the past, I maintain that America's brand of religion has by and large achieved a pretty good record of brotherhood. And I venture to assert that religion now offers the brightest hope of fellowship both within and beyond our national borders. When Jesus was asked what is the great commandment in the law he answered, "Thou shalt love the Lord thy God with all thy heart and with all thy soul and with all thy mind." And then Jesus added, "The second is like unto it, Thou shalt love thy neighbor as thyself." It is no accident that they stand together. We cannot sincerely say we love God unless we love our brother, and we cannot keep loving our brother without the aid of our Heavenly Father.

Fellowship with our Heavenly Father generates brotherly love, somewhat on the same principle that the atmosphere of parental love begets affection between children in the family. The late Horace Dutton Taft in his autobiography quotes a letter written by his father a day of two after his own birth. In the letter the father tells how little Willie, i.e., the future president William Howard Taft, was displeased by the arrival of his baby brother, but was appeased by his mother who promised him that if the new brother did not prove satisfactory he would be sent to an orphan asylum. Mr. Horace Taft adds whimsically, "I was never sent to the orphan asylum." No, of course not. In a true home's atmosphere of affection children learn to love another.

Not by law can we force people to be brotherly. We may compel them to keep the peace, but laws and police will not produce the milk of human kindness without which life is hardly worth living. Nor can we make men brotherly by fear of some foreign foe. The necessity of defeating Germany and Japan may create a temporary truce between hostile interests within our own country, but unless we can cultivate mutual respect between economic classes and racial groups, America is headed for trouble after the foreign danger is removed. Nor can we expect to hold men and nations together by the motive of enlightened self-interest on the principle of balance of power. That method has been repeatedly tried after past wars and always with tragic results.

Nothing less than the power of God and the principle of Christ-like love can beget a brotherhood strong enough to withstand the strains which will follow this war. If we are to treat men as brothers, we must so sensitize our imaginations that we can see how life looks to men of other races and backgrounds and nations. And that is what religion does for us when we pray week after week and day after day to

God the Father of all mankind. Brotherhood must become the very atmosphere in which we live and think and pray. We must go the second mile in our good will in order to make it creative. We must follow Christ in learning to love the seemingly unlovable and to forgive the seemingly unforgiveable. As the nails pierced his palms on the cross, he prayed, "Father, forgive them for they know not what they do." In that spirit, and in nothing less than that, can we find the bonds of unity strong enough to bind our broken world together. For that reason, we say, "Blessed is the nation whose God is the Lord."

And along with these blessings of a solid foundation, high standards and brotherly spirit goes a fourth. And that is a firm faith for which to build. Because of her faith in God and man a truly Christian nation is a land of hope. Justice Wiley Rutledge, the newest addition to our Supreme Court, writing some eighteen months ago, pointed out that the first problem of a democracy is not that of law. Deeper than the need for law is the need for hope. People, he said, "need an ideal, a goal, a direction, which colors all their thought and feeling. . . If they have this, and believe it, or some of it, can be achieved, they can survive any temporary tyranny. The task is essentially religious." Yes, Justice Rutledge is right. As Paul said, "We are saved by hope." And no nation has better reason to know this than America. America has fulfilled the prophecy of Joel when he said, "Your old men shall dream dreams, your young men shall see visions." Our Washington in his struggles, like Moses in the wilderness, "endured as seeing Him who is invisible." Our fathers so believed in the future, so banked on the triumph of justice and brotherhood, that this country which they built has become the land of dreams for youth in all the oppressed nations of the earth. And what is sustaining those American lads now in the sand dunes of North Africa and the bitter cold of Iceland? It is the dream of a world where life shall be richer and freer and better, with opportunity for every person according to his ability.

We must not let our deeds destroy their dreams. Shall we not here again, on this Palm Sunday, "highly resolve that this nation under God shall have a new birth of freedom and that this government of the people, for the people, by the people shall not perish from the earth."

PRACTICAL RELIGION IN THE WORLD OF TOMORROW [3]

HENRY A. WALLACE [4]

This address was given by Vice President Wallace at a conference on "Christian Bases of World Order," at Delaware, Ohio, the seat of Ohio Wesleyan University. The conference was under the auspices of the Board of Missions and Church Extension of the Methodist Church. The speech, broadcast over the Blue Network at 11:30 A.M., E.W.T., Monday, March 8, 1943, was effectively adapted to his well-educated, religious audience.

Mr. Wallace treats the same theme discussed in his address of December 28, 1943—America's role in the peace to come. This later analysis of the problem, however, is much more searching, much more revealing of Mr. Wallace's political philosophy. Here he speaks as a typical American leader—in the best tradition of Jefferson, Webster, Emerson, Lincoln, Charles Sumner, Elihu Root, and Woodrow Wilson. The Vice President turns out to be a devout follower of the Christian tradition—and clothes with New Testament interpretations his ideas of the ends for which America fights, and its postwar political, educational, economic, and social programs.[5]

This address was included in the Senate debates on March 9, 1943, on request of Senator Elmer Thomas, of Oklahoma. Earlier during the day Senator A. H. Vandenberg, of Michigan, interrupted Senator Tom Connally, of Texas, to observe:

> I am very happy that the Senator has presented the record this morning in the fashion in which he has presented it. The able Vice President of the United States sounded a timely warning yesterday about the necessity for our future friendly relationship with Russia. He said, among other things, that in connection with future contacts it is very necessary that we do not "double-cross" Russia. At least on the face of the record up to date I am sure we can all agree—can we not—that we have not double-crossed Russia as yet?

Later Mr. Vandenberg continued:

> I should like again to comment along the line of my interrogatories to the able Senator from Texas [Mr. Connally] when he was speaking.

[3] *Congressional Record* v. 89, no. 41, p. 1759-61, March 9, 1943 (daily edition), 78th Congress, first session. By permission of Mr. Wallace.
[4] For biographical note see Appendix.
[5] Cf. *Representative American Speeches*: 1941-1942, p. 45-6.

While the statement of Ambassador Standley was amazing, I believe it was equally amazing for the distinguished Vice President of the United States yesterday to suggest that America is even capable of double-crossing Russia, or double-crossing anyone. I desire to make it perfectly clear that in my opinion American policy in connection with the war will never result in double-crossing anyone; and certainly the record up to date clearly indicates that on our part, at least, there has been no double-crossing of anyone.

I thank the distinguished Senator for his contribution. I agree with his conclusions. Of course, there can be no thought of America ever engaging in any double-crossing. . . .

Then Senator Burton Wheeler, of Montana, gained the floor to add:

I simply want to say that I agree with what the Senator from Michigan [Mr. Vandenberg] said about the astounding statement which was made by the Vice President, when he intimated that we might double-cross Russia. The American people will not double-cross Russia or any other country. Russia can be sure of that. I was equally astounded by the statement made by the distinguished Vice President when he said that today no one in this country will admit that he is an isolationist. I do not know what the Vice President meant by that, but if he meant that no one in this country will admit that, before we got into the war, he stood for trying to keep this country out of it, then he is sadly mistaken in that viewpoint, because I did everything I could do to try to keep this country out of war. . . .

These attacks upon Wallace's speech should be weighed in the light of the text itself and of the aim of the discourse.

There are three great philosophies in the world today. The first, based on the supremacy of might over right, says that war between nations is inevitable until such time as a single master race dominates the entire world and every one is assigned his daily task by an arrogant, self-appointed fuehrer.

The second, the Marxian philosophy, says that class warfare is inevitable until such time as the proletariat comes out on top, everywhere in the world, and can start building a society without classes.

The third, which we in this country know as the democratic Christian philosophy, denies that man was made for war, whether it be war between nations or war between classes, and asserts boldly that ultimate peace is inevitable, that all men are brothers, and that God is their father.

This democratic philosophy pervades not only the hearts and minds of those who live by the Christian religion, both Protestant and Catholic, but of those who draw their inspiration from Mohammedanism, Judaism, Hinduism, Confucianism and other faiths.

When we look beneath the outer forms we find that all these faiths, in one way or another, preach the doctrine of the dignity of each individual human soul, the doctrine that God intended man to be a good neighbor to his fellow man, and the doctrine of the essential unity of the entire world.

Those who think most about individualism preach freedom. Those who think most about unity, whether it be the unity of a nation or of the entire world, preach the sacred obligation of duty. There is a seeming conflict between freedom and duty, and it takes the spirit of democracy to resolve it.

Only through religion and education can the freedom-loving individual realize that his greatest private pleasure comes from serving the highest unity, the general welfare of all. This truth, the essence of democracy, must capture the hearts of men over the entire world if human civilization is not to be torn to pieces in a series of wars and revolutions far more terrible than anything that has yet been endured. Democracy is the hope of civilization.

To understand the significance of these three philosophies dominant in the world today, let us look at each one in turn. During the last eighty years the outstanding exponent of the sacredness and inevitability of war has been Prussia. By nature the common people of Prussia are simple and hardworking, and make excellent citizens except where they have become infected by the Prussian doctrine that might makes right.

The Prussian philosophy causes its adherents to practice many of the highest virtues, but these virtues are all ultimately placed at the disposal of supreme evil. Hitler, seizing the Prussian militaristic tradition as a powerful instrument in his hand and putting it to use with his own religious frenzy, has become the Anti-Christ of this generation, perhaps the most complete Anti-Christ who has ever lived.

It is not enough to bring about the downfall of Hitler. We must understand the origin and growth of the Prussian spirit, and do something to counteract that spirit, if we wish to bring permanent peace.

The Prussian attitude toward war and supremacy has strong roots. Whether it reaches back to the days of Caesar or whether it first took form under the guidance of the Teutonic knights in the Middle Ages, we are certain of this: By the time of Frederick the Great the Prussians consciously adopted the doctrine of total war and the total state as the chief end of man. Bismarck and Kaiser Wilhelm II modernized and made completely deceitful and ruthless that which Frederick the Great had founded.

Shortly after Kaiser Wilhelm II rose to power, a general before the First World War, one of the more tenderhearted of the German generals, said, addressing his troops, "Our civilization must build its temple on mountains of corpses, on oceans of tears, and the groans of innumerable dying men."

We know now, to our sorrow, that those were not just idle words. But God grant they will not be true much longer!

Bernhardi and Treitschke, through the printed page and through the classroom, preached the glory of war and the necessity of Germany picking a quarrel with England or France. Frederick the Great, Moltke and Bismarck were proclaimed as being superior to Goethe, Schiller, Bach and Beethoven.

Hegel laid broad and deep the philosophy of the totalitarian state. Other philosophers, and especially Nietzsche, seized on the Darwinian doctrines of natural selection and survival of the fittest to erect a seemingly scientific but false materialism to justify their ruthless acts.

In saying all of this, I do not mean to indicate that Prussia was the only wicked state in the world. England, France, Russia, Spain, and the United States, were not always perfect. But Prussia and Japan were the only countries which systematically devoted the highest virtues of their citizenry, generation after generation, to the glorification of the state and to the ruthlessness of war.

The ancestors of many of the people of German origin in the United States were members of the minority in Germany who dissented from the extremist tendencies toward militarism. Thousands of these dissenters migrated to this country in the twenty or thirty years after the failure of the revolution of 1848. Their children, grandchildren and great-grandchildren today are among our finest American citizens. They are patriotically doing their part in the present war for freedom, and we honor them for the spirit they have shown.

It is in the years since 1848 that the liberal culture of the old Germany has been so completely submerged by the worship of strength and power. In this period of less than a century, under Bismarck, Kaiser Wilhelm II, and Hitler, Germany has launched five aggressive wars.

The result has been that over the last thirty years the spirit of Prussianism has cost the lives of at least twenty million men, has crippled at least ten million others, and has caused the nations of the world to squander hundreds of billions of dollars on death, destruction and hate. How different things would have been if this money had been spent instead on peace, prosperity and understanding!

Germans by blood are neither better nor worse than Englishmen, Americans, Swedes, Poles or Russians. But the Prussian tradition of the last century, and especially the Nazi education of the last ten years, have created a psychic entity so monstrous and so dangerous to the entire world that it is absolutely vital to exercise some control over German education when the war comes to an end.

Prussian schoolmasters have been of greater importance to the German army than Prussian captains, and Prussian textbooks have had greater value than ammunition. It is the disciplined will to power and the worship of war as the method of power that have made the Germany army such a terrible instrument of force.

Just as Hitler took the Prussian military tradition and organized it into gangsterism, so he took the Prussian education system and streamlined it to marshal the millions of German boys and girls behind his evil conspiracy of world conquest.

Hitler's children have been trained to believe implicitly that the state is more important than the individual, and that the individual must be willing and ready to sacrifice himself for the German nation and for the Fuehrer.

Starting with the young mothers and fathers, married or unmarried, and taking the children through the day nurseries and a series of schools for different ages, Hitler has indoctrinated the German children with what he calls his "leadership principle," that among men as in nature there is an eternal struggle between the weak and the strong, and that the "decadent" democracies are destined to crumble before the superior might of the Nazi élite.

German boys have been systematically trained in brutality. German girls have been systematically trained to believe that their supreme duty is to be mothers, married or unmarried, of children dedicated to the service of the fatherland and the Fuehrer. Through the use of mystic ceremonies—pagan dances, bonfires, sun festivals on mountain tops and many other types of ritual—both boys and girls have been trained to look upon Hitler as divine and they pray to him as God.

The evil influence of this systematic degradation of millions of German boys and girls cannot be counteracted in a short time. Even Hitler's death will not end it, because many of Hitler's children, conditioned as they are, will believe that he is still their leader, in the spirit if not in the flesh. Hitler dead may be almost as dangerous as Hitler alive.

This, then, is the vastly difficult problem with which the United Nations will have to cope, if the victory which now is coming closer is to bring more than just a short breathing spell before another Prussian attack is launched upon the world.

It is not up to the United Nations to say just what the German schools of the future should teach, and we do not want to be guilty of a Hitler-like orgy of book burning. But it is vital to the peace of the world to make sure that neither Prussianism, Hitlerism nor any modification of them is taught.

There are many cultured German scholars with an excellent attitude toward the world who should be put to work on the job of rewriting the German textbooks in their own way. I believe these men would glorify peace and international honesty, reestablishment of the German culture of Beethoven, Schubert, Schiller and Goethe, and the gradual preparation of the German spirit for an appreciation of the fact that a bill of rights for the individual is as vital as a bill of duties toward the state.

Doubtless thousands of German boys will come home from the war bitterly disillusioned of Prussianism and Hitlerism. Thousands of both young and old will feel the same way. They will honestly want to help build up a new democratic Germany, and we, without yielding at all to the old warlike spirit of Prussia, should encourage them to try.

We shall need the help of all Germans who give convincing evidence that they do not subscribe to the "master race" myth and are genuinely opposed to the doctrine that might makes right. The reeducation we insist upon should not crush out any sincere desire to practice democracy and live at peace among the world family of nations.

It will not be necessary for Americans to teach in the German schools. The all-important thing is to see that the cult of war and international deceit is no longer preached as a virtue in the schools. We cannot countenance the soft, lazy forgetfulness which characterized England and France in their treatment of Germany in the thirties. The cost of such short-sighted appeasement is too great in men and money. We must not go down that mistaken, tragic road again.

All of my discussion thus far has been concerned with Prussianism. Now I want to talk about Marxianism. This philosophy in some ways is the child of Prussianism, because Marx, its high priest, was molded in his thinking by Hegel, the great philosopher of the Prussian state.

Marxianism has used the Cheka, just as Prussianism has used the Gestapo, but it has never preached international war as an instrument of national policy. It does not believe one race is superior to another. Many of the Marxian activities of the last ten years which people of the west have most condemned have been inspired by fear of Germany.

The Russian people, who are the chief believers in Marxianism, are fundamentally more religious than the Prussians. The great mass of the Russian people is still hungry for spiritual food. The Russians have a better opportunity to find that spiritual food than have the Prussians under their regime, which glorifies the violence of the old Teutonic gods.

This question of religious freedom in Russia has been getting attention from the Church of England and from the Roman Catholic Church in this country. In a recent issue of the magazine *Commonweal,* which surely cannot be said to have Marxian leanings, the managing editor discussed two books by exiled Russians on the status of religion in Russia.

Quoting from both books, one written under the auspices of the Church of England and the other by a professor at Fordham University, the editor came to the conclusion that the position of the Christian church in Russia has definitely improved.

The future well-being of the world depends upon the extent to which Marxianism, as it is being progressively modified in Russia, and democracy, as we are adapting it to twentieth century conditions, can live together in peace.

Old-line Marxianism has held that democracy is mere words, that it serves the cause of the common man with platitudes rather than with jobs, and that belief in it results in a weak governmental organization. And we who believe in democracy must admit that modern science, invention and technology have provided us with new bottles into many of which we have not yet poured the wine of the democratic spirit.

In some respects both the Prussians and the Russians have perceived the signs of the times better than we, and I hope that reactionary politicians will not quote this sentence out of its context in an effort to prove that I have come out for dictatorship.

The fact is that the Prussians have done an effective job of making their bureaucrats efficient in coordinating the social forces in the service of the state. The Russians have put great emphasis on serving and gaining the enthusiastic adherence of the common man.

It is my belief that democracy is the only true expression of Christianity, but if it is not to let Christianity down democracy must be tremendously more efficient than it has been in the service of the common man and in resistance to selfish pressure groups.

After this war is over the democratic capitalistic nations will need to prove that they are supremely interested in full employment and full utilization of natural resources. They will need to demonstrate that the consuming power of their people can be made to equal their productive power. The right to work at a regular job and for a decent wage is essential to the true dignity of man.

If the Western democracies furnish full employment and an expanding production, they need have no fear of a revival of old-line communistic propaganda from within.

If they do not furnish full employment, communistic propaganda of this kind is inevitable and there is nothing which the Russian government or our government or any other government can do to stop it. In the event of long-continued unemployment, the only question will be as to whether the Prussian or Marxian doctrine will take us over first.

I believe in the democratic doctrine, the religion based on the social message of the prophets, the heart insight of Christ, and the wisdom of the men who drew up the Constitution of the United States and adopted the Bill of Rights.

By tradition and by structure we believe that it is possible to reconcile the freedom and rights of the individual with the duties required of us by the general welfare. We believe in religious tolerance and the separation of church and state, but we need to light again the old spirit to meet the challenge of new facts.

We shall decide some time in 1943 or 1944 whether to plant the seeds for World War No. 3. That war will be certain if we allow Prussia to rearm either materially or psychologically. That war will be probable in case we double-cross Russia. That war will be probable if we fail to demonstrate that we can furnish full employment after this war comes to an end and Fascist interests, motivated largely by anti-Russian bias, get control of our government.

Unless the Western democracies and Russia come to a satisfactory understanding before the war ends, I very much fear that World War No. 3 will be inevitable. Without a close and trusting understanding between Russia and the United States there is grave probability of Russia and Germany sooner or later making common cause.

Of course, the ground for World War No. 3 can be laid by actions of the other powers, even though we in the United States follow the most constructive course. For example, such a war would be inevitable if Russia should again embrace the Trotskyist idea of fomenting world-wide revolution or if British interests should again be sympathetic to anti-Russian activity in Germany and other countries.

Another possible cause of World War No. 3 might rise out of our own willingness to repeat the mistakes we made after World War No. 1. When a creditor nation raises its tariffs and asks foreign nations to pay up and at the same time refuses to let them pay in goods, the result is irritation of a sort that sooner or later leads first to trade war and then to bloodshed.

The gospel of Christ was to feed the hungry, clothe the naked, comfort the sick and visit those who were in hard luck. He said that treating your neighbor decently was the way to show that you loved God.

The neighborhood in Christ's day was a few miles in diameter. Today the airplane has made the whole world a neighborhood. The good neighbor policy, whether at home or abroad, is a Christian policy. Those who preach isolationism and hate of other nations are preaching a modified form of Prussian nazism, and the only outcome of such preaching will be war.

If we want peace we must treat other nations in the spirit of democratic Christianity. We must make our religion practical. In our relations with China, for example, we must act in such a way as to enhance the material as well as the spiritual well-being of her people. So doing will not only be of spiritual advantage to ourselves, will not only do much to prevent war, but will give us more material prosperity than we can otherwise enjoy. And in saying this I do not preach the missionary spirit as a forerunner of a new imperialism.

Nearly half the people of the world live in Eastern Asia. Seven eighths of them do not know how to read and write, but many of them listen to the radio and they know that the world is on the move and they are determined to move with it.

We can at their request help them to move in knowledge toward a higher standard of living rather than in ignorance toward confusion and anarchy.

Throughout history every big nation has been given an opportunity to help itself by helping the world. If such an opportunity is seized with a broad and generous spirit, an infinitude of practical possibilities opens up.

Thousands of businessmen in the United States have seen this kind of thing happen on a smaller scale in their own businesses, as their broad and enlightened policies have increased their prosperity and given jobs to their neighbors.

Christianity is not star gazing or foolish idealism. Applied on a world-wide scale, it is intensely practical. Bread cast upon the waters does return. National friendships are remembered. Help to starving people is not soon forgotten.

We of the United States who now have the greatest opportunity that ever came to any people do not wish to impose on any other race, or to thrust our money or technical experts or ways of thought on those who do not desire them.

But we do believe that if we measure up to the responsibility which Providence has placed on our shoulders we shall be called on for help by many peoples who admire us. When we respond to this cry for help we shall be manifesting not only a Christian spirit but also obeying a fundamental law of life.

We of the Western democracies must demonstrate the practicality of our religion. We must extend a helping hand to China and India; we must be firm and just with Prussia; we must deal honestly and fairly with Russia and be tolerant and even helpful as she works out her economic problems in her own way; we must prove that we ourselves can give an example, in our American democratic way, of full employment and full production for the benefit of the common man.

By collaborating with the rest of the world to put productive resources fully to work, we shall raise our own standard of living and help to raise the standard of living of others. It is not that we shall be taking the bread out of the mouths of our own children to feed the children of others but that we shall cooperate with everyone to call forth the energies of everyone, to put God's earth more completely at the service of all mankind.

FAITH OF OUR FATHERS [6]

EDGAR DE WITT JONES [7]

Dr. Edgar De Witt Jones delivered this sermon in the Central Woodward Christian Church, of which he is the minister, at Detroit, Michigan, on February 25, 1943.

Dr. Jones in this sermon has a high degree of homiletic skill. The discourse structurally follows the historic sermon pattern, with a text, a well-defined introduction, development by a series of propositions, and a conclusion that effectively summarizes and applies the message. No unusual doctrinal theme or analysis is attempted. The sermon is instructional and inspirational rather than doctrinal. The theme of "Faith of Our Fathers" is amplified through the succession of historical illustrations. Each picture is drawn graphically, with just balance between the demands of historical accuracy and narrative intensity. The language is carefully selected to avoid, on one hand, the verbal exuberance characteristic of such ministers as Dwight Newall Hillis and, on the other, the comparatively realistic style of Harry Emerson Fosdick. The striking paraphrase at the end has been much quoted. In composition the sermon ranks high.

Dr. Jones, as a pulpit speaker, has drawn large audiences. His delivery has fire. In pitch range, rate, vocal variety, and resonance, and in speaking personality and variety he is unusually effective.

This pulpiteer has been a close student of speakers, including preachers. His volume, *Lords of Speech,* [8] gives the portraits of fifteen American orators, from Patrick Henry to Woodrow Wilson. His *American Preachers of Today* is an appraisal of thirty-two pulpit leaders. [9] In these volumes Dr. Jones reflects his own philosophy of speaking and sermonizing. He says,

> Carelessness on the part of those who speak in public—shoddy sentences, commonplace phrasings, inaccurate use of words—sins against good taste, and is an affront to the auditors. The mastery of an excellent style of private or public speech is achieved only by tireless study, much writing, the hardest kind of toil. Some years ago the writer served for two weeks as a juror in the Recorder's Court of his city. The speeches of the lawyers provided profitable

[6] By permission of the author and of the Christian Century Press. Text furnished through the courtesy of Dr. Jones.

[7] For biographical note see Appendix.

[8] Edgar De Witt Jones. *Lords of Speech.* Willett, Clarke, and Company. New York. 1937.

[9] Edgar De Witt Jones. *American Preachers of Today.* Bobbs-Merrill Company. Indianapolis. 1933.

study. For the most part they were dull, uninteresting, badly arranged, and the language was evidently extempore. Occasionally a lawyer would appear whose speech was markedly different—concise, logical, carefully prepared. Invariably when this occurred the courtroom came to life; the judge, who had been covertly reading a newspaper, raised his eyes from the sheet; the jury awakened as men out of sleep.

And what should be said of ministers of religion, men privileged to speak upon the most important themes of life, who come into the pulpit with poorly prepared sermons, platitudinous statements, sentences that no one could possibly parse? One thing that differentiates poor from good preaching is the bare mechanics of it—the choice of language, the use of illustrations, the preparation and the vocabulary. Good diction may not be the most important thing in preaching but certainly it is not the least important.

The golden age of the orator is gone, but the era of good public speaking is here to stay. The style and manner of oratory changes, yet true eloquence persists. There will always be a place for the public speaker who has something to say and says it effectively. The radio has put a premium on careful preparation, clear enunciation, brevity, and good diction, and it has been proved that the invisible speaker can convey his personality over the air. Yet at its best the radio speech can never quite equal the power of the spoken word when it is mediated through the physical presence of a powerful orator. [10]

The eleventh chapter of Hebrews enshrines the founding fathers of the Jewish and the Christian faith. John Henry Jowett called this chapter the Westminster Abbey of the Bible, wherein sleep the pioneers and pathfinders of religion in heroic days.

There is a moral grandeur about this chapter. One approaches it with awe. For all about are the spirits of just men made perfect. Ponder the epitaphs inscribed upon the monuments, "These all died in faith, not having received the promises, but having seen and greeted them from afar." The Greek word translated "greeted" in this sentence has the idea of a gesture. Thus one sees, as across a vast distance, some long-sought-for goal. He catches sight of it and salutes it, and then dies without having actually obtained the prize or reached the goal. This is life, and it is not only something—it is everything—to glimpse the shining goal, salute it with a shout, and

[10] Edgar De Witt Jones. *Lords of Speech.* Willett, Clarke and Company. New York. 1937. Foreword, p. viii-ix.

pass on. It is indeed true that we count ourselves not yet to have apprehended, but we press on.

It is December 21, 1620 (new calendar), and the voyaging Mayflower has dropped anchor in Plymouth harbor. For sixty-six days she had battled with the Atlantic, encountering storms and deadly calm, fighting disease and other perils. And now she lay just off the bleak New England shore. Captain Christopher Jones had brought her over.

The Mayflower had as passengers one hundred two persons, eighteen married couples, twenty-six women. A baby was born in mid-ocean, and another as the ship rested in the waters of Plymouth bay. One passenger died at sea. Youth was on board the Mayflower. William Bradford, who became the second governor of the colony, was thirty-one; Edwin Winslow was twenty-six; John Alden, twenty-one. There were a number of small children on board.

Aboard the Mayflower, the Compact was signed, beginning with the words, "In the name of God, Amen." "This event," says Bancroft, the historian, "was the birthday of constitutional liberty." It was religion that inspired the Mayflower's voyage; it was religion that sustained that heroic colony through the hardships and privations of those early and terrible years.

It was religion that prompted those adventurers who dared all for freedom to raise their voices in hymns of praise:

> Amidst the storm they sang,
>> And the stars heard and the sea,
> And the sounding aisles of the dim woods rang
>> To the anthem of the free.

It is July 1776, and the place is Philadelphia. Great events are in the making. The Continental Congress is meeting a mighty issue. The committee appointed to draft a Declaration of Independence selects a tall, rangy, auburn haired Virginian, Thomas Jefferson, to write the document. He secludes himself in a boarding house with a minimum of aids, and in less than a month produces a paper which to this day when ably read in public sends tingles down the spines of the hearers.

Congress debated Jefferson's composition for two days, made a few slight changes and passed the resolution. There were dramatic episodes in the picture. Caesar Rodney, ill, with one side of his face covered with a silk cloth to hide the disfigurement caused by a malignant disease, rode all night and day from Dover, Delaware, arriving in time to stride, booted and spurred, into the assembly and say, "I vote for independence."

John Hancock led off with his bold signature, saying that he wanted George III to be able to read it without putting on his specs. Charles Carroll, fearful that someone would mistake him for another who bore the same name, signed, "Charles Carroll of Carrollton." There was humor and mirth even in so grave a moment. Benjamin Franklin remarked, "We shall all have to hang together or we will all hang separately." Whereupon Elbridge Gerry of Block Island, who was slender of build, remarked to Benjamin Harrison of Virginia of ponderous bulk, in substance, "You'll have the advantage of me when the hanging begins. When they are through with you, I'll still be struggling in mid-air."

The old bellringer, who had been told to be on hand to start ringing as soon as word reached him that the Declaration had been adopted, was pessimistic. "They'll never do it. They'll never do it," he repeated again and again. Then suddenly a boy appeared, running and shouting: "Ring! Ring! Ring!" And the event was history.

It is the spring of 1787, and the place is again Philadelphia. The Constitutional Convention is in session, and by the last of May fifty-five men had arrived, the picked men of the states. Of the fifty-five, thirty-four were lawyers or had studied law; eight were merchants; six were farmers; three were physicians; and two had been ministers of the gospel; one was a printer; thirty-nine were graduates of universities. Their average age was forty-three and a fraction.

The president of the convention was George Washington. The sessions were held behind locked doors. No inquiring reporters or candid cameras were present. Liberals and conservatives were in the group. It seemed at first that they could not possibly agree as to what should go into this important instrument. There was much confusion and disputation. Far into the summer the controversy continued. There came a day when Benjamin Franklin arose and suggested that they send for a clergyman of the city to invoke divine guidance upon them, that they might find their way to a happy conclusion.

Alexander Hamilton opposed Franklin's proposition on the ground that such a procedure would alarm the public. He had no objection to the prayer's being offered; he made that clear. So Franklin's resolution failed, but it is believable that from the hearts of the men who composed that gathering went up fervid prayers for guidance that unity might come out of chaos; and so it did. In the spirit of "give and take," the framers finished their stupendous task. Gladstone said of the document that it was the most inspired instrument conceived by the mind of man at any given time.

Sixteen of the fifty-five men refused to sign the Constitution, though it was adopted by a majority vote. Among the notables who refused to sign was George Mason, author of the Bill of Rights. These men gave various reasons, as for instance, "too much power vested in the Supreme Court," and again, "too much power given the Federal Government to levy taxes." Yet these sixteen men were not looked upon as unpatriotic. They had their say, and it was respected. Patrick Henry, whose speeches had stirred the people like the tap of a drum, fought the ratification of the Constitution in Virginia, but it carried in the necessary number of states and became operative.

The Constitution is elastic. It has been amended twenty-one times and "unamended" once. Chief Justice Hughes said that the Constitution is what the Supreme Court says it is; and that august court, generally speaking, reflects the trend of the political thinking of the masses. The Bill of Rights was put into the Constitution by way of amendment, assuring free speech, free religion and a free press. Here the people are protected from their government; here the case for the people is vested in the people.

It is January 1830, and a momentous debate is in progress in the United States Senate. The doctrine of nullification is the issue. That doctrine was "the formal suspension by a state within its territorial jurisdiction of a law of the United States." Nullification was strongly held in South Carolina, with Robert Y. Hayne and John C. Calhoun as protagonists. Colonel Hayne, youthful, aristocratic, cultured and a polished orator, in his notable speech made a formidable attack against the federalism of New England. The speech created a sensation and the opposition turned to Webster to answer it.

There was fear on the part of some that he was not prepared to reply to so able a speech immediately, but when they consulted the Massachusetts senator he explained that he had been for twenty years preparing to answer just such an argument. How well he answered it, history has recorded.

When Webster spoke on important occasions, he always dressed the part, his favorite attire being a blue broadcloth claw-hammer coat with brass buttons worn over a buff waistcoat, topped off with a white or black stock. The Senate was crowded to the doors as he arose to make reply to Senator Hayne. In the speech that followed Webster used all of the arts of great public speaking. He argued, analyzed, arraigned, indicted, chided, letting his opulent imagination have free rein. As he approached the mournful and magnificent peroration, his Jovelike presence seemed to expand, rhetorical thunderbolts crashed above his audience, his deep voice shook with emotion as he declaimed:

When my eye shall be turned to behold for the last time the sun in heaven, may I not see him shining on the broken and dishonored fragments of a once glorious Union: on States dissevered, discordant, belligerent; on a land rent with civil feuds, or drenched, it may be, in fraternal blood! Let their last feeble and lingering glance rather behold the gorgeous ensign of the Republic, now known and honored throughout the earth, still full high advanced, its arms and trophies streaming in their original luster, not a stripe erased or polluted, nor a single star obscured, bearing for its motto no such miserable interrogatory as, "What is all this worth?" nor those other words of delusion and folly, "Liberty first and Union afterwards"; but everywhere, spread all over in characters of living light, blazing on all its ample folds, as they float over the sea and over the land, and in every wind under the whole heavens, that other sentiment, dear to every true American heart— Liberty and Union now and forever, one and inseparable!

The doctrine of nullification had been scotched but not killed. In April of the same year, 1830, the birthday of Thomas Jefferson was celebrated with a big dinner in Washington. It was a gala occasion and the leading politicians were present. President Jackson was to participate, and he was told of what was going on among the nullifiers. The information but served to stouten the purpose of Old Hickory to preserve the Union at all hazards. There was a long list of regular toasts, after which volunteer toasts were called for. President Andrew Jackson arose, straightened himself to his full height, fixed his gaze upon Calhoun, paused for a dramatic hush, and proposed the toast: "Our Federal Union: It must and shall be preserved."

The President lifted his glass, the banqueters rose to their feet to drink it standing. Claude G. Bowers, in his vivid narrative of this event, says: "It was something more than a toast—it was a Presidential proclamation." Calhoun arose with the rest, and one present described his tension: "His glass trembled in his hand and a little of the amber fluid trickled down the side. When all were seated, Calhoun, who had remained standing, slowly and hesitatingly proposed: 'The Union: next to our liberty, the most dear.'

"He paused for half a minute and proceeded to say: 'May we all remember that it can only be preserved by respecting the rights of the States, and by distributing equally the benefits and burdens of the Union.' "

It was all over. Nullification was dead and Old Hickory was the executioner.

It is February 11, 1861, and in Springfield, Illinois, Abraham Lincoln is about to leave for Washington. The skies were overcast with clouds, and a gentle rain was falling. About a thousand people, neighbors and friends, had gathered at the station to see their fellow townsman off on his hazardous journey. Just before the train left the station Mr. Lincoln came out upon the rear platform of the last car, lifted his hand, and in a voice choked with emotion, said:

My friends: No one not in my situation can appreciate my feeling of sadness at this parting. To this place, and the kindness of these people, I owe everything. Here I have lived for a quarter of a century and have passed from a young to an old man. Here my children have been born, and one is buried. I now leave, not knowing when, or whether ever I may return, with a task resting upon me greater than that which rested upon Washington. Without the assistance of that Divine Being who ever attended him, I cannot succeed. With that assistance I cannot fail. Trusting in Him, who can go with me, and remain with you, and be everywhere for good, let me confidently hope that all will yet be well. To His care commending you, as I hope in your prayers you will commend me, I bid you an affectionate farewell.

It is Appomattox, April 9, 1865, and General Robert E. Lee has surrendered the Army of Virginia to the victorious commander of the Armies of the North, General Ulysses S. Grant. It was a scene that artists love to put on canvas and has supplied a theme for many a novel, poem, oration. The men in blue with "flaunting flags and prancing nags" returned to their homes mighty conquerors; some to go into business and to amass fortunes; some to enter politics, to become governors and senators; and five, who bore the title of general, to achieve the presidency of the United States. They were victors and entitled to praise and preferment.

Victorious General Grant became President of the United States. The period following the war was marked by corruption in high places, but no scandal touched the President himself. Out of office, he became partner in a financial enterprise, was betrayed by his associate, lost all his holdings and was burdened with a huge indebtedness. Though suffering with a fatal malady, he set himself heroically to the task of writing his memoirs. It was as if with one hand he pushed back the grim specter of death and with the other completed the writings that were to lift the load of debt and free his family name from any breath of dishonor.

The men in uniforms of gray went back to devastated regions, war-scourged cities, impoverished estates. Many of their homes were in ashes; they had to begin all over again. On that ninth of April, through long lines of weeping men rode General Lee, grave of countenance but calm of spirit. His material possessions were gone; beloved Arlington had passed out of his hands. There came an offer of a home in England, where he might spend the rest of his days in comfort, ease and luxury. He declined it. He refused $25,000 a year, offered him by a life insurance company, saying, "I can receive no money that I have not earned," and became president of a small and struggling college at a salary of $1,500. He nourished no rancor, showed no bitterness, urged his former soldiers to support the Union. One day a mother put her little child in his arms and asked him to offer a prayer for her firstborn. General Lee bowed his head over the child, held him close, handed him back to his mother, saying, "Teach him to deny himself."

> Love and tears for the Blue,
> Tears and love for the Gray.

The faith of our fathers. What an enchanting theme! Thanksgiving Day with us has both a political and religious significance. It unites uniquely thoughts of God and of government. When the pioneers blazed paths through the wilderness where highways never ran, they built, along with their cabins, the schoolhouse and the church. Our fathers had faith in God and provided places where he might be worshiped, humble meetinghouses at the crossroads, little brown churches in the wildwoods. One of the noblest developments of our nation has been the public school. The founding fathers put a premium on education and rightly separated church and state, but not state and religion.

No finer statement of the essence of democracy has been framed than these two closing paragraphs of Hamilton Fish Armstrong's book entitled *We or They:*

To be liberal does not mean to understand all principles and to have none. The democratic principle is that the majority has the right to govern and that the minority has the right to criticize and oppose the majority. The liberty of the majority is limited by the right of the minority to dissent from the majority; in this right originate all the other rights of the citizen. But the right of the minority to dissent is limited by the right of the majority to rule, and by the majority's duty to restrain minorities which threaten to overthrow the majority by force and destroy all liberties. The majority has the moral right to exercise power, but it is the trustee of that right and must so exercise its power that a different majority may overrule it tomorrow, and another majority may overrule that one the day after. The majority of today shall not put chains on itself and on all future majorities any more than it shall make people of a particular color slaves. It shall not accept a dictator. Even the sovereign right of the people stops short of the right of suicide.

This is not a compromise between doctrines. It is a doctrine, the democratic doctrine, which proclaims the right of free competition between political parties composed of free individuals as the best method of assuring peaceful progress. It proceeds through trial and error. It is based on the assumption that no man is infallible and that there does not exist a political science. When one discards this doctrine one must accept the dictatorial doctrine, according to which there are infallible men whose commands are not to be opposed. Lenin was right, Mussolini and Hitler are right. Between the two doctrines there is no compromise. Our society or theirs. We or they.

The weaknesses of a democracy are the abuse of liberty, and inefficiency. The cure for the ailments of democracy is more democracy. Mr. Jefferson said that the people could be trusted to act wisely if only they are informed upon the issues at any given time. How to get that information to the people, how to present it uncolored by partisanship and undistorted by particular interests, is a vexatious problem in a democratic form of government. If there are heartaches in a democracy, there are also heartbeats of gratitude and of joy. The right of a majority to govern and the right of a minority to become a majority—these rights are fundamental in the American way of life.

In the year 1892 a ship of the Holland-American line entered New York harbor. It was laden with immigrants and as the ship passed the Statue of Liberty Enlightening the World, the passengers crowded the side of the ship next to the statue. Some of them laughed and sang. Others shed tears of joy as they looked out upon the land of promise. By the guard rail stood a little boy holding his father's hand. "Father," said the little boy, "do you know anybody in America?" The father said he didn't know a soul. "Do you have a job awaiting you?"

the little fellow queried. His father replied in the negative. The little fellow was not through with his interrogations. "How much money have you, father?" The answer was that he had about $450. The little boy was silent for a time and then he spoke again: "If you don't know anybody in America, and if you haven't a job, and have only $450, what are you going to do if you don't get a job and your money runs out?"

"My boy, this is America," the father explained. "It was in this country where a boy born in a one-room cabin with a dirt floor and lighted by a single window climbed to the greatest gift within the power of the American people to confer, the presidency. In a land where such a thing could happen, there must be room for a Dutch immigrant who has faith in God and is not afraid to work. There must be a place for us."

And there was. The little Dutch boy who asked those questions is now the Rev. Joseph R. Sizoo, formerly minister of the New York Avenue Presbyterian Church in Washington, D. C., and at present minister of the Church of St. Nicholas, Dutch Reformed, in New York city.

If we walk in the faith of our fathers, believing that God is and that He is the rewarder of them who seek Him, if we have faith in our democratic institutions and are willing to sacrifice for them, if we have faith in the necessity and dignity of toil, this nation will endure, and no enemy without can imperil us. It is the enemy within—sloth, corruption, sectionalism, intolerance and injustice—which alone can defeat us and make us a prey to the enemies without.

Faith of our fathers! What a theme! May I not appropriately and with reverence paraphrase the noble passage from the eleventh of Hebrews?

By faith the voyaging Mayflower embarked from Old England and found harbor off the bleak New England shores. By faith the Pilgrim Fathers set up a government on a new continent dedicated to God and inspired by a desire to do his will on earth as it is done in heaven.

By faith Thomas Jefferson was stirred to strike a blow for political independence and wrote the thrilling document that declared that all men are created equal and endowed with certain inalienable rights. By faith he said, "Love your neighbor as yourself and your country more than yourself."

By faith George Washington left his spacious mansion at Mount Vernon and espoused the cause of the tax-burdened colonists. By faith he forsook ease and comfort, choosing rather to suffer hardship with his men at Valley Forge than to enjoy the favor of the king. By faith he became President of the newly born Republic and endured as seeing him who is invisible.

By faith Alexander Hamilton established the financial credit of the nation. In the eloquent words of Daniel Webster, "He touched the corpse of public credit and it sprang into life. He smote the rock of national resources and abundant streams of revenue flowed." By faith James Madison gave richly of his scholarly mind to form the Federal Constitution. By faith Andrew Jackson fought the battle of the impoverished and underprivileged many against the privileged few.

By faith Abraham Lincoln bore the awful burden of four purgatorial years seeking to preserve the Federal Union. By faith he carried a dreadful war to its conclusion without hate in his heart, saying, "I have not only suffered for the South, I have suffered with the South."

By faith Woodrow Wilson in the dreadful heartbreak of a world war dreamed a dream of a warless world, in which the nations should be leagued together to keep the peace. By faith he glimpsed that promised land which, like Moses, he might not enter.

And what shall I more say? For time would fail me if I should tell of that unnumbered host, the unnamed and obscure citizens who bore unimagined burdens, sacrificed in silence and endured nobly, that a government of the people, for the people, and by the people might not perish from the earth.

JUDGMENT OF NATIONS [10]

FULTON J. SHEEN [11]

This sermon, the twelfth in a series of seventeen addresses on *"The Crisis of Christendom,"* was delivered in the Catholic Hour on March 21, 1943, by the Right Rev. Monsignor Fulton J. Sheen, of the Catholic University of America. The Catholic Hour was initiated in 1930 by the National Council of Catholic Men. Father Sheen was the first speaker on this program and continues to contribute sermons each year.

The Catholic Hour is heard each Sunday of the year through some one hundred stations. States the National Council of Catholic Men, "Consisting of an address mainly expository, by one or another of America's leading Catholic preachers, and of sacred music provided usually by a unit of the Paulist Choir, the Catholic Hour has distinguished itself as one of the most popular and extensive religious broadcasts in the world. A current average of 41,000 audience letters a month, about 20 per cent of which come from listeners of other faiths, gives some indication of its popularity and influence".

Father Sheen has established himself as one of the superior American preachers. He composes sermons that have unusual analytical penetration into major issues, personal and social, related to religious problems; and his voice and speaking personality continue to enlist the support of millions of listeners.

War is a judgment of God, not in the sense that God acts *outside* history as a catastrophic effect following the breaking of God's moral law. Such was the burden of last Sunday's broadcast.

Today we shall mention two instances of how forgetfulness of God brought on the ruin of nations, namely Jerusalem and Rome, and then show how two great Americans expressed the same vision of judgment in our national life.

First, the fall of Jerusalem. The Great Patriot who loved the Holy City as His own, stood on a hill opposite, and looking down upon it wept at the consequences which He knew would inevitably follow from a refusal to submit to the truth of which

---

[10] The text was furnished through the courtesy of the Right Rev. Msgr. Fulton J. Sheen.

[11] For biographical note see Appendix.

their consciences had already been convinced. "Jerusalem . . . how often would I have gathered together thy children, as the hen doth gather her chickens under her wings, and thou wouldst not?" (*Matthew* 23:37).

That is the heart of sin! "I would . . . thou wouldst not." Human will set up against Divine Will.

"I would have gathered. . . ." One man? A carpenter? No man can gather a civilization. Only the Son of God can gather a whole people.

And it came to pass as foretold. Vespasian, going to Rome to become Emperor, gave the order to his son Titus, on Easter day in the year 70, to lay waste Jerusalem. The temple was destroyed as the Saviour had said, not a stone left upon a stone. History was the stage on which Jerusalem worked out the full effects of its severance from the laws of God. The city had not known the time of its visitation. "Unless the Lord build the house, they labour in vain that build it." (*Psalm* 126:1).

The second example of how forgetfulness of God brought on the ruin of nations is the fall of Rome. During the winter of 57-58 A. D., St. Paul addressed a letter to the Romans, and on the very year of his death St. Peter likewise warned Rome of a judgment that awaited them because of their sins.

Years later, in the year 370, at the mouth of the Danube, of a great Visigoth family, was born Alaric. Alaric himself was probably a Christian, but Baptism had not destroyed in him a warlike lust. On three occasions he made visits to Rome, the third time being on the fourth of August, 410. With horses darting like hawks, and moving battering rams like mountains, he forced the Salarian gate, allowing his soldiers, who were the scum of Europe, to put the metropolis of the earth to sack and to humble the giant of the nations of the world.

The fall of that city was terrible. Not for eight hundred years, since the taking of Rome by the Gauls in 387 B. C., had the capital of the Empire been invaded and outraged by barbaric hordes. Her surprise then was greater than her terror, and her shame greater than her surprise.

At the close of that century, the Holy Father, Gregory the Great, standing at the tombs of the Apostles Peter and Paul, preached this sermon affirming the truth of the words of these Apostles already mentioned:

> Today, there is on every side death, on every side grief, on every side desolation, on every side we are smitten, on every side our cup is being filled with draughts of bitterness. . . . [On the other hand] those saints at whose tombs we are now standing lived in a world that was flourishing, yet they trampled upon its material prosperity with their spiritual contempt. In that world life was long, well-being was continuous, there was material wealth, there was a high birth rate, there was the tranquillity of lasting peace; and yet when that world was still so flourishing in itself, it had already withered in the hearts of those saints.

In other words, almost four centuries before Rome fell, Peter and Paul said that it would, because it had forgotten God. Now Gregory says that these men of the Church knew it would fall— and they saw it when no one else saw it; namely, when Rome was strong, and mistress of the world. In their eyes the city had written its own sentence of death with its own godless hands.

Now turn to our American history. We find here also a recognition of the divine judgment. When Thomas Jefferson wrote the Declaration of Independence he penned these lines: "All men are created equal." He made no exception, *"All men."* But Jefferson kept slaves! And he knew it! To his credit, it must be said that he introduced a law into the Virginia legislature in 1778, prohibiting the slave trade, though slavery continued in the state. Recognizing, however, the inconsistency and knowing that the blood of some men was in his own time being spilled by other men, because they denied equality, Jefferson expressed his fear in these words, "I tremble for my country, when I reflect that God is just and His justice does not sleep forever." It was a language almost identical to that which Peter used against Rome. And well might Jefferson be concerned, for any nation which spills blood, either its own or another's, will have its own poured forth in reparation. "He who takes the sword shall perish by the sword."

We know well when the injustice was righted and the judgment came. One man was great enough to see in the Civil War, a manifestation of the justice of God: Abraham Lincoln. These were his words:

It is the duty of nations as well as of men [he said] to own their dependence upon the overruling power of God. . . .

And inasmuch as we know that by His divine law nations, like individuals, are subjected to punishments and chastisements in this world, may we not justly fear that the awful calamity of civil war which now desolates our land may be but a punishment inflicted upon us for our presumptuous sins, to the needful end of our national reformation as a whole people? We have been recipients of the choicest bounties of heaven. We have been preserved these many years in peace and prosperity. We have grown in numbers, wealth, and power as no other nation has ever grown; but we have forgotten God. We have forgotten the gracious hand that preserved us in peace, and multiplied and enriched and strengthened us; and we have vainly imagined, in the deceitfulness of our hearts, that all these blessings were produced by some superior virtue and wisdom of our own. Intoxicated with unbroken success, we have become too self-sufficient to feel the necessity of redeeming and preserving grace, too proud to pray to the God that made us.

It behooves us, then, to humble ourselves before the offended Power to confess our national sins, and to pray for clemency and forgiveness.

Thus spoke Abraham Lincoln.

This is one of the greatest documents ever written by the pen of any American. To Jefferson goes the credit of writing our Declaration of Independence. To Lincoln goes the credit of writing our Declaration of Dependence. Jefferson declared we were independent from tyrants; Lincoln added, we are dependent on God. The ethical complement to our Bill of Rights, Lincoln told us, is our Bill of Duties.

If Lincoln could come back today, would he not remind us in the midst of this awful war that we are under the judgment of God, and that prayer and reparation for our national sins may well be the essential condition of victory?

Are we convinced of this truth? How little prayer there is for victory and peace; how little thanksgiving there is for victory.

To make some amendment, we ask every Sunday that the Jews, Protestants and Catholics spend an hour a day in meditation and prayer. Catholics should include daily Mass and Communion in this hour whenever possible. Armies alone cannot defeat the cohorts of Satan. We need God's help. Let us pray therefore for it. Anyone wishing a prayerbook written expressly for wartime may receive one free for the asking.

On the other hand, are we thankful to God when we do have victories? What public thanksgiving was there for the victory at Guadalcanal, the Coral Sea, the Bismarck Sea? To the great credit of General MacArthur it must be said that, after his recent victory in the Bismarck Sea, where he lost less men than the Japs lost ships, he wrote in his communique, "A merciful Providence has granted us a great victory."

And what did the journalists of the country do to that message? One of the most widely syndicated articles ridiculed MacArthur's thanksgiving to God. And when a Rickenbacker is saved at sea by prayers, and boys on the rafts are rescued through prayer, and both thank God for their safety, our newspapers write of the prayerfulness of these heroes in the same startled spirit, as if these brave men had been saved by goblins. One would get the impression that for anyone to pray in danger is as unusual as for anyone to recite the soliloquy of Hamlet, and that to be saved through prayer was as little to be expected as that Hamlet himself should come to their rescue. The whole tone of the press in these affairs is, "Imagine—Prayer!" As if no one prayed! And as if there were no God!

How, except by prayer, can we make effective in deed the words of the Atlantic Charter?

We are on record in the Atlantic Charter as guaranteeing the freedom and integrity of small nations, e.g., Poland and Lithuania. Now the Atlantic Charter is a kind of political counterpart to the Sermon on the Mount, for it is a defense of the weak and the poor. That is no compliment but a tremendous responsibility, because the Sermon on the Mount, prepared for His own Crucifixion; how little do those who isolate the Beatitudes from the Cross understand that one is entailed in the other. He knew that the weak could not be defended except by bearing the slings and arrows of the strong, and that to speak for the poor was to invite a cross from the rich.

How then shall our Atlantic Charter, which defends the integrity of small nations, become effective except by bearing the opprobrium of the strong? How shall we liberate the oppressed, except by being smitten with the sword of the oppressor? I tell you, the day we wrote that Atlantic Charter we wrote in ink something that can be fulfilled only in blood. The Atlantic Charter can come into being only as the Sermon on the Mount—by enduring a Golgotha for a few hours from the powerful Caesars of the earth who would swallow up the weak and infirm.

Lincoln saw that when he wrote his proclamation for freedom of the Negro—and we must see it, too, as we proclaim the freedom of the children and nations of the world.

And we will need God's help to overcome the temptation to compromise with the strong.

The word "God" was left out of the Atlantic Charter, but our President did not leave it out of his declaration of war, for he ended it with these words: "So help us God." And all Americans who are one with him in this war, trust that when the day of victory dawns, we will begin to talk of peace with the same words, "So help us God."

APPENDIX

BIOGRAPHICAL NOTES [1]

BENEŠ, EDUARD (1884-   ).   Educated at Prague, Paris, and Dijon Universities; organized national movement of Czechoslovakia with Masaryk; Foreign Minister, 1918-35; lecturer in sociology at Prague University, 1922-39; elected President of the Czechoslovakian Republic, in succession to Dr. Masaryk, 1935, resigned, 1938; visiting professor, University of Chicago, 1939; President of the Czechoslovakian Republic since 1940.

BROWN, LEWIS H. (1894-   ).   Born in Creston, Iowa; A. B., State University of Iowa, 1915; with Montgomery Ward and Company, 1919-27; president of Johns-Manville Company since 1929; trustee in Mutual Life Insurance Company; captain infantry, U.S. Army, 1917-19, A. E. F., France, 1918-19; received Vermilye medal, 1939, from Franklin Institute of Pennsylvania for "outstanding contribution in the field of industrial management."

BYRNES, JAMES F. (1880-   ).   Born in Charleston, South Carolina; admitted to bar, 1903; editor *Journal and Review,* Aiken, South Carolina, 1903-07; court reporter, 1900-08; solicitor, 2nd Circuit, South Carolina, 1908-10; member 62nd to 68th Congress, 1911-25; practiced law, Spartanburg, South Carolina, 1925-31; United States Senator, 1931-41; Associate Justice, U.S. Supreme Court, 1941-42; appointed head of the Office of War Mobilization, 1943.

CHIANG MEI-LING (SOONG) (MADAME CHIANG KAI-SHEK) (1898-   ).   Born in China; educated in Georgia and at Wellesley College; LL.D., Rutgers University; married Generalissimo Chiang Kai-shek, 1927; held various administrative po-

[1] The chief sources of these notes are *Who's Who in America, Current Biography, Religious Leaders in America, International Who's Who, Who's Who in American Education,* and the *Congressional Directory.*

sitions in China with such organizations as National Chinese Women's Association; accompanied husband on military expeditions; visited the United States 1942-43, and addressed many audiences in 1943; author of *China in Peace and War*, 1939; *China Shall Rise Again*, 1941.

CHURCHILL, WINSTON (1874-). Educated at Harrow and Sandhurst; entered the army, 1895; served with Spanish forces in Cuba, 1895; service in India, 1897-98; with Nile army, 1898; correspondent with *Morning Post*, South Africa, 1899-1900; in various battles of the Boer War, 1900; Member of Parliament, 1900-22; an officer in the British Army in France, 1916; First Lord of Admiralty, 1911-15; Minister of Munitions, 1917; various ministerial offices, 1918-22; Chancellor of the Exchequer, 1924-29; First Lord of Admiralty, 1939-40; Prime Minister, First Lord of the Treasury, and Minister of Defense since 1940; visited the United States in 1942 and in 1943; author of a long list of books, including *Marlborough*, (4 vols.), 1933; *Blood, Sweat, and Tears*, 1941; *The End of the Beginning*, 1943.

CONANT, JAMES BRYANT (1893-). Born in Dorchester, Massachusetts; A.B., Harvard, 1913, Ph.D., 1916; LL.D., University of Chicago, 1933, New York University, 1934; honorary degree, Bristol University (England), 1941; Sc.D., Cambridge University (England), 1941; D.C.L., Oxford University (England), 1936; instructor, assistant professor, professor of chemistry, Harvard, 1916-17, 1919-33; President of Harvard since 1933; Chairman, National Research Defense Committee, 1941-43; lieutenant, Sanitary Corps, U.S. Army, 1917; major, Chemical Warfare Service, 1918; member of Sigma Xi, Phi Beta Kappa, and many other learned societies; author of *The Chemistry of Organic Compounds*, 1933, and other books and articles.

DEUTSCH, MONROE EMANUEL (1879-). Born in San Francisco; A.B., University of California, 1902, A.M., 1903, Ph.D., 1911; LL.D., St. Mary's College, 1933, and various other colleges; instructor, assistant professor, professor of Greek and Latin, since 1907, University of California; dean of the College of Letters and Science, 1922-30, Vice President and Provost since 1931; officer in many philanthropic and learned societies; member, Phi Beta Kappa; author of *Our Legacy of Religious Freedom*, 1941; *The Letter and the Spirit*, 1943.

EDEN, (ROBERT) ANTHONY (1897-   ). Educated at Eton and Christ Church, Oxford; D.C.L., Oxford, Durham; LL.D., Cambridge; Conservative M P. for Warwick and Leamington since 1923; Under Secretary of State for Foreign Affairs in National Government, 1931-33; Lord Privy Seal, 1934-35; Secretary of State for Foreign Affairs, 1935-38; Secretary of State for Foreign Affairs since 1940; publications include *Places in the Sun*, 1926; *Foreign Affairs*, 1939.

FLEMING, DENNA FRANK (1893-   ). Born in Paris, Illinois; graduate of Eastern Illinois, State Normal School, 1912; A.B., University of Illinois, 1916, A.M., 1920, Ph.D., 1928; instructor in Illinois high schools, 1912-14, 1916-17, 1919-22; teacher at Monmouth College, 1922-27; teacher of political science at Vanderbilt University since 1928, and chairman of the department since 1940; radio commentator, Station WMS, Nashville, since 1939; with A.E.F. in First World War; Delta Sigma Rho; author of *The Treaty Veto of the American Senate*, 1930; *The United States and World Organization*, 1938, and other books.

GREW, JOSEPH CLARK (1880-   ). Born in Boston; educated at Groton (Mass.) School, 1892-98; A.B., Harvard, 1902; LL.D., George Washington University, 1926; assigned to Consulate General's office at Cairo, Egypt, 1904; in Embassy office, Mexico City, 1906-07, St. Petersburg, 1907-08, Berlin, 1908-11, Vienna, 1911-17; in Department of State, Washington, 1917; at Versailles, 1918-19; negotiated and signed treaty with Turkey, 1923; Under Secretary of State, 1924-27; Ambassador to Turkey, 1927-32; Ambassador to Japan, 1932-41; returned to United States, 1942; member of various learned societies; author of *Sport and Travel in the Far East*, 1910; *Report from Tokyo*, 1942, and of magazine articles.

HAYES, CARLTON J. H. (1882-   ). Born in Afton, New York; A. B., Columbia, 1904, A. M., 1905, Ph. D., 1909, Litt. D., 1929; LL. D., University of Notre Dame and other institutions; lecturer in history, 1907-10, assistant professor, 1910-15, associate professor, 1915-19, professor, 1919-35, Columbia University; U S. Army, World War I; major, O. R. C., 1928-33; member of numerous learned societies, including Phi Beta Kappa; Ambassador to Spain since 1942; author of *Political and Social History of Modern Europe*, 1916; *Essays on Nationalism*, 1926; *World History*, 1932; contributor to numerous magazines.

HUNT, FRAZIER (1885-   ). Born in Rock Island, Illinois; graduate of Michigan Military Academy, 1904; A.B., University of Illinois, 1908; newspaper work in Chicago, 1908-1910; editor paper, Alexis, Illinois, 1913-16; staff, New York *Sun*, 1916; in Europe, 1918, as correspondent for American Red Cross; war correspondent, Chicago *Tribune*, 1918-19; interviewed Lenin, Moscow, 1919; radio commentator; author of *This Bewildered World*, 1934, and numerous other books.

HUTCHINS, ROBERT MAYNARD (1899-   ). Born in Brooklyn, New York; A.B., Yale, 1921, honorary A.M., 1922, LL.B., 1925; LL.D., West Virginia University, Lafayette College, and other institutions; Dean, Yale Law School, 1928-29; President, University of Chicago since 1929; in ambulance service, U.S. Army, 1917-19; Italian Army, 1918-19; decorated Croce di Guerra (Italian), 1918; member of numerous honorary and learned societies, including Phi Beta Kappa, Order of the Coif; author of *The Higher Learning in America*, 1936, and numerous other books and magazine articles.

JONES, EDGAR DE WITT (1876-   ). Born in Hearne, Texas; attended University of Missouri, 1894-95; Transylvania, 1898-1900, D.D., 1934; numerous honorary degrees, including LL.D., Texas Christian, 1938; began ministry in Disciples of Christ Church in 1901; pastorates included those at Bloomington, Illinois, Cleveland, Ohio; at Central Woodward Church, Detroit, since 1927; member of staff, *Christian Century* since 1927; contributor to numerous magazines; president of International Convention of Disciples, 1917-19; member of Authors' League of America; author of numerous books, including *Preachers of Today*, 1933; *Lords of Speech*, 1937.

LOCHNER, LOUIS P. (1887-   ). Born in Springfield, Illinois; graduate of Wisconsin Conservatory of Music, 1905; A.B., University of Wisconsin, 1909; editor of Wisconsin Alumni Magazine, 1909-14; director Central West Department, American Peace Society, 1914-15; on Henry Ford Peace Mission to Europe, 1915-16; newspaper correspondent since 1919; chief of Berlin bureau Associated Press of America, 1928-41; interned in Germany and later exchanged and returned to America, 1942; author of numerous translations and other publications; winner of 1939 Pulitzer Prize for distinguished service as foreign correspondent.

LODGE, HENRY CABOT, JR. (1902-   ). Born in Nahant, Massachusetts; grandson of the late Senator Henry Cabot Lodge; A.B., Harvard, 1924; with Boston *Evening Transcript*, 1923; New York *Herald Tribune*, 1924; member of the Massachusetts General Court, 1933-36; elected to United States Senate from Massachusetts, 1936, for term ending 1943; on leave, major in U.S. Army Tank Corps, with British forces, 1942.

ROBINSON, EDGAR EUGENE (1887-   ). Born in Oconomowoc, Wisconsin; A.B., University of Wisconsin, 1908, A.M., 1910; instructor in history, Carleton College, 1910-11; assistant professor, associate professor, professor of history at Stanford University since 1911; assistant educational director, Northwestern district S.A.T.C., War Department, 1918; member of various learned societies including Delta Sigma Rho, Phi Beta Kappa; author of *American Democracy in Time of Crisis*, 1934, and other books, and various monographs and articles on American history.

ROOSEVELT, FRANKLIN DELANO (1882-   ). Born in Hyde Park, New York; A.B., Harvard, 1904; attended Columbia University Law School, 1904-07; honorary degrees from Rutgers, Yale, Notre Dame, and other institutions; began practicing law in New York, 1907; Assistant Secretary of the Navy, 1913-20; Governor of New York, 1929-33; President of the United States since 1933, elected to a third term, 1941; visited Casablanca and other places in North Africa, 1943; author of

Whither Bound, 1926; *Looking Forward,* 1933; *Political Papers,* 1938, and other books.

SCHUMAN, FREDERICK L. (1904-   ). Born in Chicago; A.B., University of Chicago, 1924, Ph.D., 1927; instructor in political science, University of Chicago, 1927-32; assistant professor, 1932-36; professor of political science, Williams College, since 1936; member of various honorary and learned societies, including Phi Beta Kappa; author of *The Nazi Dictatorship,* 1935; *Europe on the Eve,* 1939, and other volumes.

SHEEN, FULTON JOHN (1895-   ). Born in El Paso, Illinois; A.B., St. Viatore College, 1917, A.M., 1919; St. Paul Seminary, 1919; S.T.B. and J.C.B., Catholic University of America, 1920; Ph.D., Louvain University, 1923; D.D., Rome, 1924; honorary degrees from Marquette, Loyola, and other colleges and universities; member of faculty, Catholic University of America since 1926; author of *God and Intelligence,* 1925; *Divine Immanence,* 1931; *The Way of the Cross,* 1932; *The Eternal Galilean,* 1934; the *Mystical Body of Christ,* 1935, and other publications.

SOCKMAN, RALPH WASHINGTON (1889-   ). Born in Mount Vernon, Ohio; educated at Ohio Wesleyan University, A.B., 1911, D.D., 1923; Columbia University, A.M., 1913, Ph.D., 1917; Union Theological Seminary, graduate, 1916; numerous honorary degrees; minister Madison Avenue Methodist Church (now Christ Church), since 1917; preacher, National Radio Pulpit, since 1937; Lyman Beecher lecturer at Yale, 1941; trustee of a number of colleges and universities; member of Phi Beta Kappa, Delta Sigma Rho; author of *Live for Tomorrow,* 1939, and numerous other volumes on religion.

VANDERCOOK, JOHN W. (1902-   ). Born in London, England; graduate of St. Paul's School, Garden City, New York, 1919; student at Yale, actor, 1921-24; worked on *Columbus Citizen* and other papers until 1923; worked on Macfadden Publications, 1923-24; has been active in radio since 1940; author of *Black Majesty,* 1929; *The Fool's Parade,* 1930; *King Cane,* 1939; *Empress of the Dusk,* 1940; has made explorations in forest regions of Dutch Guiana, Liberia, and in Fiji, Papua, and Solomon Islands.

WALLACE, HENRY AGARD (1888-). Born in Adair County, Iowa; B.S., Iowa State College, 1910; honorary M.S. in agriculture, Iowa State College, 1920; editor of *Wallace's Farmer* since 1910; Secretary of Agriculture in Cabinet of President Roosevelt, 1937-1941; Vice President of the United States since 1941; visited Latin America, 1943; author of *America Must Choose*, 1934; *Statesmanship and Religion*, 1934; *Whose Constitution*, 1936; *Paths to Plenty*, 1938, and other books and articles on agricultural, political, and religious subjects.

WILLKIE, WENDELL LEWIS (1892-). Born in Elwood, Indiana; A.B., Indiana University, 1913, LL.B., 1916; practiced law in Indiana, 1916-19, in Ohio, 1919-20, in New York, 1920-32; President of Commonwealth and Southern Corporation, 1933-40; candidate for the Presidency of the United States on Republican ticket, 1940; although defeated, polled over 22,000,-000 votes; visited England, 1940, after the election; in 1941 and later, strongly supported Roosevelt's foreign policy; member of law firm, New York, N.Y., since 1941; encircled the world via airplane, 1943; author of *One World*, 1943, and of numerous articles.

INDEX

CUMULATIVE AUTHOR INDEX

An author index to the volumes of *Representative American Speeches,* for the years 1937-1938, 1938-1939, 1939-1940, 1940-1941, 1941-42 and 1942-43. The date following the title of each speech indicates the volume in which it appears.